JN125978

# PIONEER

American edition

pre-intermediate

H. Q. Mitchell – Marileni Malkogianni

student's book

mm
publications

# PIONEER PRE-INTERMEDIATE CONTENTS

| Reading | Listening | Speaking (Pronunciation/Intonation*) | Writing |
|---|---|---|---|
| • Quiz: *Then and now...* <br> • A magazine article: *All you need to know about sunglasses and sneakers* | • Four short dialogues <br> • A conversation about what gifts to buy for friends | • Pair work: Greeting, making plans and saying goodbye <br> • Pair work: Interviewing each other and reporting answers <br> • Pair/Group work: Talking about clothes <br> • Pair work: Talking about likes/dislikes <br><br> * The verb *used to* | • An online conversation <br> • A questionnaire <br> • A short text presenting yourself <br><br> **Developing skills:** <br> • Brainstorming and organizing ideas with the help of a mind map <br> • Linking words (and, but, so, because, or) |
| • A website: *Top tips for better photos of people* <br> • A magazine article: *Direct communication is dying out...* | • A conversation between two strangers <br> • Three monologues about instant messaging <br> • A conversation about a questionnaire: *Choose the right roommate* | • Pair work: Discussing experiences <br> • Pair work: Role play situations meeting people <br> • Group work: Conducting and taking part in a survey about communication habits <br> • Pair work: Talking about the right kind of roommate <br><br> * The reduced form of *did you* and *have you* | • A description of a person <br><br> **Developing skills:** <br> • Using intensifiers to emphasize adjectives <br> • Organizing your description with the help of a plan |
| • An article: *Neologisms!* <br> • A magazine article: *Be part of the art* | • Three teenagers playing a guessing game <br> • Three short dialogues about art <br> • A conversation between two friends | • Group work: Describing what food tastes and looks like <br> • Pair work: Role play situations at restaurants <br> • Pair work: Guess the word being described <br> • Class discussion about different forms of art <br> • Pair work: Giving news and responding to news <br><br> * Word stress: nouns ending in *-ion* and *-ation* | • An e-mail giving news <br><br> **Developing skills:** <br> • Organizing an e-mail with the help of a plan <br> • Set phrases for informal letters/e-mails |
| • A comic strip: *The blackout* <br> • A newspaper article: *Double Disaster in Japan* | • Four news bulletins <br> • A conversation between two friends about a missing person | • Class discussion about accidents and injuries <br> • Group work: Narrating a bad experience and responding by showing concern and/or criticism <br> • Pair/Group work: Speculating about newspaper headlines <br> • Group work: Narrating a story <br><br> * /tʃ/, /dʒ/ | • A paragraph describing a bad experience <br> • A story based on prompts <br><br> **Developing skills:** <br> • Using adverbs and adverbial phrases <br> • Organizing a story with the help of a plan |
| • A historical journal: *Robert O'Hara Burke* <br> • A magazine article: *Top tips for a comfortable trip* | • Five short announcements <br> • A radio show about packing <br> • A recorded message from a travel agency | • Pair work: Information gap activity about two explorers <br> • Group work: Role play situations related to traveling <br> • Pair work: Asking for and giving advice about a trip, and making suggestions <br> • Pair work: Discussing day trips and reaching a decision <br><br> * Consonant clusters | • A description of a place <br><br> **Developing skills:** <br> • Using topic sentences and forming well-organized paragraphs <br> • Organizing a description of a place with the help of a plan |
| • A magazine article: *Life on Earth a hundred years from now* <br> • An Internet advertisement: *Solar cap!* <br> • A magazine interview about Space Tourism | • A conversation about a quiz on carbon footprint <br> • A radio interview with an expert on Mars <br> • People giving their opinion about the Internet | • Pair work: Making predictions about the future <br> • Pair work: Role play situations <br> • Group work: Discussing things people will be able to do 100 years from now and comparing with other groups <br> • Group work: Discussing positive and negative aspects of the Internet and expressing opinion <br><br> * The contracted form of *will* | • Predictions about the future <br> • Making a list of things people will be able to do 100 years from now <br> • A paragraph expressing an opinion <br><br> **Developing skills:** <br> • Linking words/phrases to list or add points |

| | | Vocabulary | Grammar | Functions |
|---|---|---|---|---|
| **7** p.67 | Choices | • Conversational English<br>• Words/Phrases related to signs<br>• Word building: opposites with *un-*, *dis-* | • may, might, could<br>• Conditional Sentences Type 1<br>• if vs. when<br>• Comparisons | • Expressing possibility and certainty in the present and future<br>• Expressing preference<br>• Guessing the meaning of unknown words<br>• Understanding signs and messages<br>• Talking about conditions and their results<br>• Comparing and contrasting people and situations<br>• Talking about lifestyle changes and intentions<br>• Taking notes<br>• Inviting and accepting or refusing an invitation<br>• Making suggestions and arrangements |
| **8** p.77 | All the action | • Words/Phrases related to sports<br>• Conversational English<br>• Phrasal verbs<br>• Words/Phrases related to movies | • Exclamatory sentences<br>• Clauses of result<br>• have to, don't have to, must, mustn't, need to, don't need to, needn't<br>• Passive Voice (Present Simple – Past Simple) | • Expressing enthusiasm, surprise, admiration, disappointment, anger, annoyance, etc.<br>• Expressing result<br>• Guessing the meaning of unknown words<br>• Understanding information on flyers and signs<br>• Expressing obligation, lack of obligation, and prohibition<br>• Talking about movies and expressing opinion |

**Task 7 & 8:** Collaborating with a partner to reach a decision based on specific criteria **p.130**

| | | Vocabulary | Grammar | Functions |
|---|---|---|---|---|
| **9** p.87 | Career paths | • Occupations<br>• Academic subjects<br>• Conversational English<br>• Words easily confused<br>• Words/Phrases related to employment and qualifications | • So, neither, too, either<br>• Reflexive pronouns<br>• Present Perfect Progressive<br>• Present Perfect Simple vs. Present Perfect Progressive | • Talking about one's studies and one's job<br>• Expressing agreement and disagreement<br>• Distinguishing between words easily confused<br>• Linking the past with the present<br>• Talking about language learning experiences<br>• Guessing the meaning of unknown words<br>• Understanding information in job advertisements<br>• Describing one's qualifications |
| **10** p.97 | Facts and figures | • Words/Phrases related to banks and money<br>• Conversational English<br>• Words with more than one meaning<br>• Units of measurement | • too / enough<br>• Infinitives<br>• -ing form | • Carrying out money transactions<br>• Indicating degree and extent<br>• Giving and understanding different kinds of instructions<br>• Guessing the meaning of unknown words<br>• Expressing opinion and giving information |

**Task 9 & 10:** Understanding the key features of a résumé and creating one's own **p.131**

| | | Vocabulary | Grammar | Functions |
|---|---|---|---|---|
| **11** p.107 | Different cultures | • British English vocabulary<br>• Conversational English<br>• Words related to traveling<br>• Adjectives + prepositions<br>• Words/Phrases related to celebrations<br>• Prepositional phrases with *in* | • Indirect questions<br>• Conditional Sentences Type 2<br>• Wishes | • Asking for information informally and formally<br>• Asking for clarification and repetition<br>• Giving information<br>• Understanding differences between American and British English<br>• Talking about imaginary situations<br>• Making wishes and expressing regret<br>• Talking about celebrations/festivals/events<br>• Guessing the meaning of unknown words<br>• Distinguishing between formal and informal language |
| **12** p.117 | That's life | • Words/Phrases related to different medical situations<br>• Conversational English<br>• Phrasal verbs<br>• Idioms describing feelings<br>• "Strong" adjectives | • Negative questions<br>• Tag questions<br>• Reported Speech: Statements, Questions, Commands, Requests | • Expressing uncertainty and asking for confirmation<br>• Expressing emotions like surprise, anger and annoyance<br>• Guessing the meaning of unknown words<br>• Describing feelings<br>• Narrating events<br>• Reporting<br>• Asking for and giving advice<br>• Describing problems<br>• Taking time to think when talking |

**Task 11 & 12:** Preparing for and taking part in a debate **p.132**

| Reading | Listening | Speaking (Pronunciation/Intonation*) | Writing |
|---|---|---|---|
| • Signs and messages<br>• A magazine article: *What happened to Nicholas Baines?* | • A conversation about a night out<br>• Three short dialogues<br>• Three voicemail messages | • Pair work: Discussing and deciding which event to go to<br>• Pair work: Discussing posters and trying to persuade each other<br>• Class discussion about lifestyle changes<br>• Pair work: Inviting and accepting or refusing an invitation<br><br>* Sentence stress in Conditional Sentences Type 1 | • A few sentences about lifestyle changes you would like to make<br>• An e-mail based on prompts<br><br>**Developing skills:**<br>• Expanding on prompts |
| • A flyer and an Internet confirmation e-mail<br>• A magazine article: *Football Codes* | • Four people talking about a hockey game<br>• Four short dialogues about movies | • Pair work: Discussing events, showing enthusiasm and disappointment<br>• Group guessing game: Talking about rules at different places<br>• Pair work: A sports quiz<br>• Group work: Talking about a movie<br><br>* The schwa sound (ə) | • Describing the rules of a sport<br>• A movie review<br><br>**Developing skills:**<br>• Organizing a movie review with the help of a plan<br>• Set phrases used in movie reviews |
| • Eight cartoons about employment<br>• An Internet forum: *Tell us your language learning experiences* | • Three short dialogues related to employment<br>• A conversation about learning Mandarin<br>• A job interview | • Pair work: Talking about one's studies and/or job<br>• Group work: Expressing opinion on different issues and agreeing or disagreeing<br>• Pair work: Role play at work<br>• Pair work: A survey about learning English<br>• Pair work: Role play a job interview<br><br>* Pronunciation variants | • A paragraph about your experiences in learning English<br>• A cover letter<br><br>**Developing skills:**<br>• Distinguishing between formal and informal language |
| • Instructions and labels<br>• A magazine article: *Memory* | • Three short dialogues involving instructions<br>• A radio show with an expert giving tips about memory<br>• A radio announcement about an event<br>• A conversation about an event | • Pair work: Role play situations at a currency exchange office, at a store, at the bank and at an ATM<br>• Pair work: Asking for and giving instructions<br>• Pair work: Discussing ways to remember different kinds of information<br>• Group work: Talking about places you've been to and events you've attended<br><br>* The different /gh/ sounds | • A note with instructions<br>• An e-mail giving information and opinion<br><br>**Developing skills:**<br>• Replying to the sender's requests suitably |
| • A quiz: *What kind of traveler are you?*<br>• A magazine article: *Notting Hill Carnival* | • A conversation about working abroad<br>• Three short dialogues about celebrations<br>• A conversation at a travel agency | • Pair work: Information gap activity: Asking for and giving information<br>• Pair work: Speculating about unreal situations<br>• Pair/Group work: Talking about a celebration/festival/event<br>• Pair work: Role play: Simulating a conversation between a visitor and an information desk clerk<br><br>* Intonation of direct and indirect questions | • A short description of a celebration/festival/event<br>• A formal e-mail asking for information<br><br>**Developing skills:**<br>• Set phrases for a formal e-mail<br>• Linking words/phrases for listing points<br>• Organizing a formal e-mail with the help of a plan |
| • A magazine page: *Now that's embarrassing!*<br>• An extract from a novel: *Oliver Twist* | • Three people describing experiences<br>• A girl describing a problem to some friends<br>• People giving advice | • Pair work: Role play different medical situations<br>• Pair work: Giving an account of an experience<br>• Class discussion about books<br>• Pair work: Asking for and giving advice<br><br>* Intonation of tag questions | • A short account of an experience<br>• An e-mail asking for or giving advice<br><br>**Developing skills:**<br>• Set phrases to ask for or give advice<br>• Organizing an e-mail with the help of a plan |

*American and British English p. 151*      *Learning Tips p. 152*      *Listening Transcripts p. 154*
*Task Listening Transcripts p. 162*      *Word List p. 163*

# DON'T MISS...

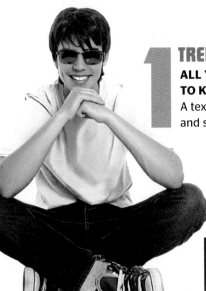

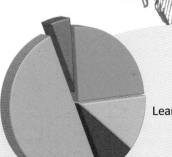

**DOUBLE DISASTER IN J...**

Yesterday, the fourth largest earthquake since records began hit the northeast coast of Japan. The 9.0 magnitude earthquake occurred at 2:46 p.m. local... caused serious damage... However, soon after the... hit the coast causing ev...

Eyewitnesses are sa... the tsunami were... Miyako City and t... inland in the Se... destroyed entir... flooded Sendai... tsunami warni... the Pacific co... have reporte... even broke o... the Sulzber... 8,100 miles...

Already... people have...

**news**

**social media**

**gadgets**

**entertainment**

**celebrities**

**style**

**sports**

**Discuss:**

- Look at the topics shown in the pictures. What is trending at the moment?

- Which is the most popular topic for discussion with you and your friends?

## In this module you will learn...

- to distinguish between permanent and temporary situations
- to make plans and future arrangements
- to talk about the present and past
- to distinguish between words easily confused
- to talk about past habits and events
- to describe clothes and talk about fashion
- to express likes/dislikes
- to use linking words (and, but, so, because, or)
- to make a mind map to come up with and organize ideas
- to write a short text presenting yourself

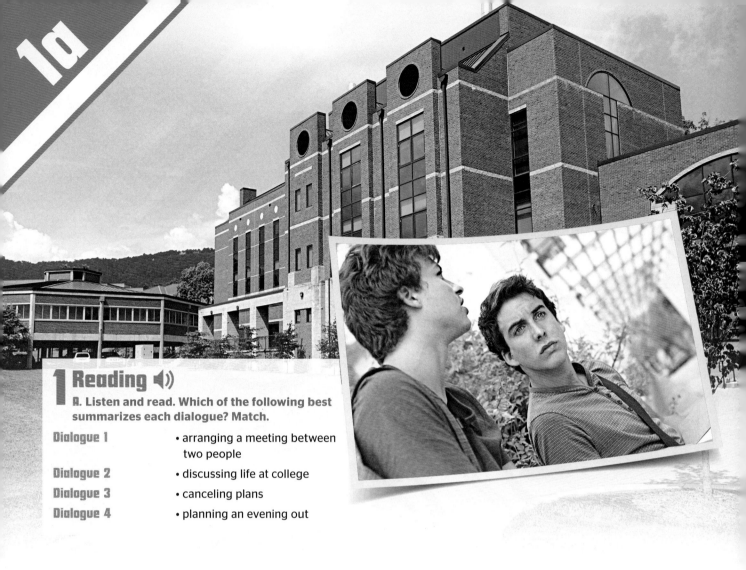

# 1 Reading 🔊

**A. Listen and read. Which of the following best summarizes each dialogue? Match.**

**Dialogue 1** • arranging a meeting between two people

**Dialogue 2** • discussing life at college

**Dialogue 3** • canceling plans

**Dialogue 4** • planning an evening out

---

**1. Gary** Hi, Sophie. How's it going?

**Sophie** Not too bad, thanks.

**Gary** So, what do you think of college so far?

**Sophie** It's great. I'm enjoying it.

**Gary** Me too. Most of my classes are in the mornings, so I have lots of spare time in the afternoons.

**Sophie** Lucky you! Anyway, see you later.

**2. Neal** Hey, do you want to catch a movie later?

**Toby** Sorry, I usually go to the gym on Thursdays. What about tomorrow?

**Neal** No, I'm taking Spanish this semester, and I have a class on Friday evening. I'm free on the weekend, though.

**Toby** OK, then. Let's say Saturday night.

**Neal** That would be great. How about watching that new sci-fi movie?

**Toby** Sure, why not? You know I love sci-fi movies.

**3. Anne** Hey, Lisa. What are you up to?

**Lisa** Nothing much. I'm waiting for my next class.

**Anne** Listen, my sister is coming to visit on the weekend.

**Lisa** Great. I really want to meet her.

**Anne** I know.

**Lisa** Does she often visit you?

**Anne** Not really, so this is a good chance for the two of you to meet.

**4. Paul** So, what time are you coming over to study tonight?

**Tom** Sorry, but I can't make it. I'm going to the game tonight.

**Paul** Wow! Those tickets are really hard to find.

**Tom** Yeah, well my sister won two tickets and she doesn't like baseball at all. So, I'm going with my dad. Maybe we can study together tomorrow night.

**Paul** Sure, no problem.

---

**B. Match the phrases 1-5 from the dialogues with their synonyms a-e.**

1. How's it going? ☐   **a.** What are you doing at the moment?

2. I'm free. ☐   **b.** That's a good idea.

3. Sure, why not? ☐   **c.** How are you?

4. What are you up to? ☐   **d.** I don't have any plans.

5. No problem. ☐   **e.** Don't worry about it.

# 2 Grammar Present Simple vs. Present Progressive, Stative verbs → p. 140

**A. Read the examples and match them with the phrases a-e.**

| Present Simple |
| --- |
| **1.** I **study** in the evenings. |
| **2.** My sister **doesn't live** here. She **lives** in London. |

| Present Progressive |
| --- |
| **3.** Sue **is waiting** for the bus at the moment. |
| **4.** I'm **taking** driving lessons this month. |
| **5.** Tomorrow we're **going** to the movies. |

**a.** right now ☐   **b.** in the future ☐   **c.** usually or repeatedly ☐   **d.** permanent situation ☐   **e.** this period of time ☐

**B. Read the examples and answer the question.**

Sally **wants** to go to the mall tomorrow.

She **likes** shopping.

*Want* and *like* are stative verbs. Which tense do we usually use with stative verbs, the Present Simple or the Present Progressive?

**C. Complete with the Present Simple or the Present Progressive of the verbs in parentheses.**

**1. A:** Where's Sandy? I know she **1** _____ (not work) this week.

 **B:** She **2** _____ (travel) around South America at the moment.

 **A:** Really? **3** _____ (she / travel) a lot?

 **B:** Yeah. She **4** _____ (love) it. She **5** _____ (usually / go) on vacation three times a year.

 **A:** How exciting!

**2. A:** What **6** _____ (you / do) there, Phil?

 **B:** I **7** _____ (look) for my car keys. I **8** _____ (need) them.

 **A:** You **9** _____ (sometimes / leave) them in the kitchen.

 **B:** They aren't there, or in my bag. I **10** _____ (not understand).

 **A:** Calm down.

 **B:** Oh, I **11** _____ (not want) to be late for my meeting and I **12** _____ (hate) taking the bus to work.

 **A:** Listen, I **13** _____ (leave) in ten minutes. **14** _____ (you / want) me to take you to work?

 **B:** Yes, please.

# 3 Speaking & Writing

**A. Talk in pairs. Greet your partner, make plans to go out tonight and say goodbye. Use some of the phrases in the boxes.**

Hi, how are you?
Hello, how's it going?
What's up?
What are you up to?
How are you doing?
How's everything?

Are you doing anything tonight?
What are you doing tonight?
Do you have any plans for tonight?
Any plans for tonight?
Do you want to...?
Let's go...
How about going...?
Why don't we go...?

Bye.
Goodbye.
See you later.
See you tomorrow.
Take care.

↓

Not bad.
Not too bad, thanks.
So-so.
Not much.
Nothing much.
I'm good, thanks.
I'm fine / very well. And you?

↓

I'm free. I don't have any plans.
Of course. I'd love to.
Sure, why not?
That would be great.
Sounds awesome!
How could I say no?

I'm afraid I'm busy.
I'm afraid I can't make it.
Sorry, I have other plans.
I'd like to come but...
Maybe some other time.

How's it going, John?

Not bad. And you?

Hey, let's go for coffee after class.

Great idea. How about...

**B. Work in pairs. Pretend you're having an online conversation with this person. Close your books and take turns to write on a piece of paper.**

# 1 Reading 🔊

**A. Discuss.**

- Which of the following do you associate with modern life?

| Internet | environmental issues | speed | gadgets | junk food | social media |

**B. Do the quiz and test your knowledge. Then listen and check your answers.**

# Quiz: Then and now...

**1** In the past not many people bought electric cars but now, because of environmental issues, they are becoming more and more popular. However, long journeys are difficult because you have to charge these cars regularly. Nowadays, U.S. car manufacturers produce over 30,000 electric cars every year. But when did the first electric cars appear on the roads?

**a. in the 1890s**     **b. in the 1920s**     **c. in the 1950s**

**2** These days it is common for large sports organizations to buy and sell players for millions. Sports stars are some of the richest people in the world. In 2009, Real Madrid spent €93.9 million on Cristiano Ronaldo and in 2011-12 he made €33 million. But how much did Aston Villa pay for Willie Groves back in 1893?

**a. £10**     **b. £100**     **c. £1000**

**3** Nowadays traveling by plane is easy, comfortable, safe and fast. A flight from London to New York City takes about 7 hours. At the beginning of the 20th century, in 1919, John Alcock and Arthur Brown made the first non-stop flight across the Atlantic. But how long did this first transatlantic flight take?

**a. 27 hours**     **b. 20 hours**     **c. 16 hours**

**4** Most people these days can't imagine their lives without a cell phone. The first cell phone was available in stores in 1983. It was huge, it weighed 2.2 pounds, you couldn't talk for long and it cost the incredible amount of $3,995! Today, there are about 6 billion cell phone users globally. But how many cell phone users were there 20 years ago?

**a. 15 million**     **b. 75 million**     **c. 154 million**

**C. Read again and write T for True, F for False or NM for Not Mentioned.**

1. Electric cars are perfect for long journeys. ☐

2. The U.S. produces more electric cars than any other country. ☐

3. Real Madrid is the richest soccer team in the world. ☐

4. Real Madrid paid €33 million to buy Cristiano Ronaldo. ☐

5. Alcock and Brown flew across the Atlantic without stopping. ☐

6. The first people to fly across the Atlantic were Americans. ☐

7. Before 1983, you couldn't buy a cell phone. ☐

8. Cell phones were very expensive when they were first available. ☐

> **TIP**
> Don't rely on your general knowledge to answer questions. Check your answers with the information given in the text.

# 2 Vocabulary

Complete the sentences with the words in the boxes.

popular    famous

1. Social media websites are very _____ with young people.

2. Dan is a talented actor but he isn't very _____.

common    usual    normal

3. John and Emily sat at their _____ table next to the window.

4. It is _____ for people traveling by plane to watch movies on their tablets.

5. After a long vacation, it's difficult to get back to _____ life.

think    imagine    wonder

6. I can't _____ my daughter driving a car.

7. I _____ what Sandra is making for dinner.

8. Do you _____ I should visit my aunt in the hospital?

pay    spend

9. How much do you usually _____ on clothes every month?

10. Let me _____ for lunch today.

# 3 Grammar Past Simple, Prepositions of time → p. 140

A. Read the examples and match them with the uses of the Past Simple.

1. I **walked** to work yesterday.

2. In the past, I **went** to work by bike.

a. a habitual or repeated action in the past ☐

b. an action that happened at a specific time in the past ☐

B. Complete with the Past Simple of the verbs in parentheses.

1. Last week Susan _____ (sell) her old computer and _____ (buy) a laptop. She _____ (want) to buy a digital camera too, but she _____ (not can). She _____ (not have) enough money.

2. Our first trip abroad _____ (be) two years ago. We _____ (go) to Canada. We _____ (travel) around and _____ (see) many beautiful places. We _____ (not want) to leave.

3. **A:** When _____ (you / get) your first job?

   **B:** Oh, that _____ (be) in 1999. I _____ (work) at a computer store.

   **A:** _____ (you / like) that job?

   **B:** Not very much. The job I have now is better.

For a list of irregular verbs, go to page 150.

C. Read the time expressions below. Which of them refer to the past only? What about the rest? Make sentences using the time expressions.

on the weekend    yesterday evening    in 2010    at 7 a.m.
3 weeks ago    in the 20th century    in the evening
during the night    after lunch    at the age of five
last Friday    on Thursday    in May

# 4 Listening 🔊

Listen to four short dialogues and answer the questions.

1. When did Jack last fly by plane?
   a. last year
   b. last month
   c. last week

2. How much did Linda pay for her bike?
   a. $500
   b. $600
   c. $900

3. What doesn't Kelly use?
   a. a tablet
   b. a cell phone
   c. a GPS device

4. What is true about traffic lights 100 years ago?
   a. There were no traffic lights.
   b. They had only two colored lights.
   c. The colors meant something different.

# 5 Writing & Speaking

A. Create a questionnaire for your partner. Use some of the ideas below.

- Where / go / school?
- When / graduate?
- Where / live / when / be / young?
- When / get / first car?
- ...

B. Interview your partner and note down his/her answers.

C. Report the answers to the rest of the class.

❝ *Maria went to Whiteoaks High School. She graduated in...* ❞

# 1 Reading 🔊

## A. Discuss.

- Do you prefer wearing formal or casual clothes?
- What do you usually wear when you go out?
- Do you like to follow trends?

**B. What do you think the words below mean? Listen, read and check your answers.**

sunnies    Inuits    plimsolls    All Stars

# ALL YOU NEED TO KNOW ABOUT...

## SUNGLASSES

Shades, dark glasses or even sunnies. Whatever you call them, when the sun comes out, they do too. But who were the first people to wear them? Well, in snowy places, the sun can be very bright, and from prehistoric times, ancient Inuits of the Arctic regions wore glasses made of bone with thin holes (slits) in them. These didn't let a lot of light in and protected their eyes. Today, sunglasses are usually plastic and come in all shapes and sizes. People wear them to protect their eyes from the sun's harmful rays while doing outdoor activities or sports, or just because they're in fashion. But many celebrities wear them indoors too, because they want to hide their identity.

*Inuit sunglasses*

## SNEAKERS

In 1830, the Liverpool Rubber Company developed the first athletic shoes with rubber soles. They called them "plimsolls" and people used to buy them for a variety of activities. In the early 20th century, shoe makers started designing sneakers, like the Converse All Stars, for specific sports. Basketball players used to wear these sneakers back then. In the 1950s, sneakers became a fashion statement and more and more young people wore them. During the 80s and 90s it was common for sports stars to have their own brand of sneakers, like Nike's Air Jordans. Today, there is a massive market for sneakers, with new designs coming out all the time, and prices reaching $200 or more.

## C. Read again and answer the questions.

1. Who wore the first sunglasses?
2. How did these sunglasses work?
3. Why do some people wear sunglasses indoors?
4. What was different about the first sneakers compared to older shoes?
5. What activity were Converse All Stars designed for?
6. When did people start wearing sneakers to be in fashion?

## D. Look at the highlighted words in the text and match them with their meanings.

1. bright
2. region
3. ray
4. hide
5. sole
6. variety
7. massive

a. keep something secret
b. very large
c. a thin line of light from the sun
d. a number of different kinds of things
e. part of the world / a country
f. the bottom part of a shoe
g. giving a strong light, shining

## E. Discuss.

- Do you wear sunglasses? If yes, when do you wear them?
- Do you like wearing sneakers? If yes, where do you wear them?

## 2 Vocabulary 🔊

**A.** Do you recognize the symbols below? What do they mean? Match.

**a.** cotton    **b.** wool    **c.** leather

**B.** Look at the pictures and complete the phrases with the materials in the box. Then listen and check your answers.

| rubber | silk | leather | polyester | denim | plastic | woolen |

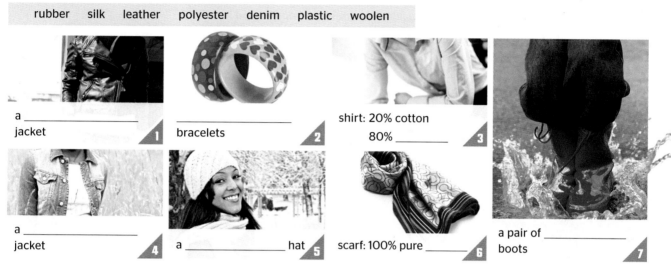

a _____ jacket **1**

_____ bracelets **2**

shirt: 20% cotton 80% _____ **3**

a _____ jacket **4**

a _____ hat **5**

scarf: 100% pure _____ **6**

a pair of _____ boots **7**

## 3 Grammar The verb *used to* → *p. 141*

**A.** Read the example below and choose the correct meaning a or b.

> My parents **used to read** newspapers.
> Now they read the news online.

**a.** My parents read newspapers in the past and still do so today.
**b.** My parents read newspapers in the past but they don't anymore.

| Affirmative | I/You/He/She/It/We/You/They used to read |
|---|---|
| Negative | I/You/He/She/It/We/You/They didn't use to read |
| Question | Did I/you/he/she/it/we/you/they use to read? |

**B.** Complete with the correct form of *used to* and the verbs in the box.

| ride | have | not go | call | exercise | not eat |

**1.** Ronald _____ for two hours every day, but now he doesn't.

**2.** _____ you _____ your bike to school when you were younger?

**3.** I _____ sushi but, after my trip to Japan, I love it.

**4.** People _____ me Budgie at my last job, and I hated it.

**5.** We _____ to the movies a lot, but now we go every weekend.

**6.** Roger and Lee _____ a car but they sold it.

## 4 Pronunciation 🔊

**A.** Listen and repeat. In which sentence is the phrase in bold pronounced / juːstə/?

I **used to** wear sneakers when I was young.
I didn't **use to** wear glasses.

**B.** Read the sentences below aloud. Then listen and check your pronunciation.

**1.** My brother used to hate watching the news.

**2.** We used to play tennis every weekend.

**3.** I didn't use to have a car.

**4.** Julie didn't use to eat vegetables.

**5.** Did you use to live in London?

## 5 Speaking

Discuss in pairs or small groups.

- What are your favorite clothes/ accessories at the moment?
- Where did you get them from?
- Are they in fashion? Are they casual or formal?
- Do you wear clothes that are out of fashion?
- What kind of clothes did you use to wear when you were younger?
- Why don't you wear them anymore?

## 1 Vocabulary 🔊

Listen and read. Which of the phrases in bold are used when you *like* something, which when you *dislike* something and which when you think something is just *OK*?

1. Neal **is crazy about** football. He plays every weekend.

2. I like most kinds of art, but for me modern art is **so-so**.

3. Rita **is really into** poetry, so I got her a book of poems for a gift.

4. **A:** Can we go to a different restaurant? I**'m not a big fan of** fast food.
   **B:** Really? I think **it's something else**!

5. Ernie **is interested in** old comic books and has a collection of over 1,000.

6. My friends **can't stand** sci-fi movies, so I usually go to the movies on my own.

7. My sister **finds** rainy weather **horrible**, but I **don't mind** it.

8. **A:** Why do you always buy that chocolate bar? **It's nothing special**.
   **B:** What are you talking about? **There's nothing I like more**!

## 2 Listening 🔊

Listen to Roger talking to his sister Vicky about gifts he wants to buy for some friends. Match the people with the gifts. There are two extra gifts you will not need to use.

Dan ☐

Tina ☐

Ollie ☐

Maya ☐

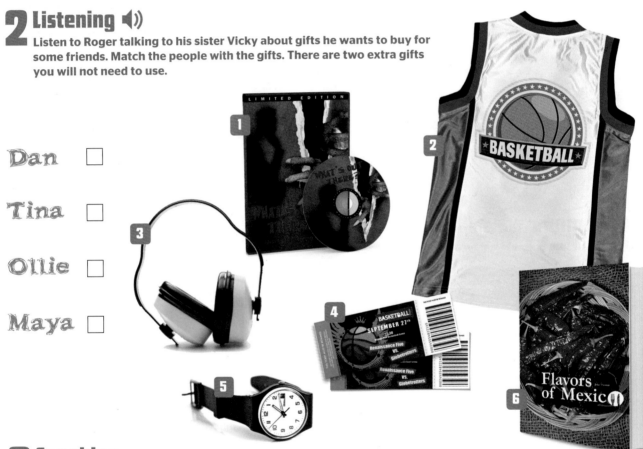

## 3 Speaking

Talk in pairs about the things you like and don't like. Use the ideas below and phrases from the vocabulary section.

sports

movies

video games

> *Do you like sports/movies/video games?*
>> *Yeah, I'm crazy about them.*
> *What... are you into?*
>> *I'm really into... at the moment. Last week I... and it was something else!*
> *How about...?*
>> *No way. I can't stand... at all. What about you?*
> *...*

# 4 Writing A short text presenting yourself

**A.** Read the blog below and answer the questions.

## Eddie Stewart's
### first blog!

Hi, I'm Eddie Stewart! First of all, let me say a few things about myself. I'm 24 years old and I'm majoring in Media and Communications.

### Sports
I'm crazy about soccer, like most people on the planet. I play twice a week with friends, but I'm also training because I'd like to join the college soccer team. In this blog, I'm planning on writing a lot about sports, especially about my favorite team, L.A. Galaxy!

### Movies
I'm also crazy about movies, and I try to see a new one every week. I particularly love sci-fi movies. I'm thinking of writing about really good (or bad) movies here in my blog, so make sure you read those reviews!

### Other interests
I'm interested in photography and I bought a new camera last month. I enjoy taking pictures of people in action so I often go to sporting events. In fact, yesterday I went to a game and took some nice pictures. You can see some of my photos <u>here</u>.

Hey, maybe I should become a sports commentator or a photographer. What do you think?

1. Who created this blog?
2. Why did he create it?
3. Who do you think is going to read it?

4. What words does the writer use to link his ideas?
5. What tenses does the writer use?

**B.** Look at the mind map below and try to complete it by brainstorming ideas about yourself. Try to write about interesting aspects of your life and don't worry if you have nothing to say about a particular category.

my job

my friends

sports

ME*

other interests

school life

dislikes

Remember that drawing a mind map helps you come up with ideas (individually or in groups) as well as organize them.

**C.** Look at the mind map again. Which 2-3 categories do you have more to say about and would be best for a blog about yourself? Expand on these ideas and write a few paragraphs presenting yourself.

## Vocabulary

**A. Circle the correct words.**

1. I'm going to a wedding on the weekend so I need to find something **casual / formal** to wear.

2. Tina isn't at home. I **wonder / imagine** where she is.

3. Mark always goes shopping at the mall, because he can find his favorite **brands / trends** there.

4. Jason wanted to buy a new laptop so he decided to do some research to see what was **available / incredible**.

5. It's **usual / normal** for parents to worry about their children.

6. Susan works for a shoe company. She **designs / develops** shoes.

7. Mr. Carson **created / canceled** the meeting and went home because he felt sick.

8. This store has a **review / variety** of boots. Let's check it out.

9. We're **planning / discussing** an evening out. Do you want to join us?

## Grammar

**B. Complete with the Present Simple or the Present Progressive of the verbs in parentheses.**

1. Helen and Joanna _____ (chat) on the Net with friends right now. They _____ (talk) about their college exams.

2. Tom _____ (not fly) to Boston next week. He _____ (drive). He _____ (hate) flying.

3. **A:** Excuse me, I _____ (look for) a gift for my sister. Can you help me?
   **B:** What _____ you _____ (think) of these bracelets?
   **A:** They _____ (seem) nice. How much _____ this bracelet _____ (cost)?
   **B:** Let me check.

4. Katie _____ (not wear) wool. She _____ (find) it uncomfortable.

5. My brother _____ (work) at an office downtown. However, this week he _____ (be) on a business trip and he _____ (travel) around South America.

**C. Complete with the Past Simple of the words in the box.**

| sell | find | let | not like | take | not work | buy |
|------|------|-----|----------|------|----------|-----|

1. I don't think Mrs. Bennett _____ her son go to the movies alone. You probably saw somebody else.

2. I _____ a new game console last week, but for some reason it _____ so I _____ it back to the store.

3. We _____ the book at all. We _____ it very boring.

4. **A:** Why _____ you _____ your car?
   **B:** Because now I go to work by bike.

**D. Complete with the correct form of *used to* and the verbs in parentheses.**

1. Laura _____ (not speak) French, but now she does.

2. I _____ (read) comic books all the time when I was younger, but now I don't.

3. **A:** _____ you _____ (live) in Newport?
   **B:** Yes, and I _____ (take) two buses to come to work. Now we live in this neighborhood and I can walk.

4. Mike _____ (not wear) sneakers, but now he wears them every day.

**E. Circle the correct words.**

1. My dad started working **at / in** the age of 16.

2. The company started having problems a year **ago / last**.

3. Ted finished studying **on / at** midnight.

4. We're going for coffee **after / until** work. Come with us.

5. In Spain many stores close for a few hours **at / in** the afternoon.

6. I heard a strange noise **at / during** the night. What was it?

## Communication

**F. Choose a or b.**

1. **A:** Hey, Jess. Are you doing anything tonight?
   **B:** _____
   a. Sure, why not?     b. I don't have any plans.

2. **A:** How about going bowling later?
   **B:** I'm afraid _____.
   a. I can't make it     b. it's nothing special

3. **A:** Hi, Terry. What are you up to?
   **B:** _____
   a. Nothing much.     b. Not too bad, thanks.

4. **A:** Do you like water sports?
   **B.** Yes, _____ them.
   a. I'm crazy about     b. I'm not interested in

5. **A:** Are you a fan of Chinese food?
   **B:** No way. _____
   a. I don't mind it     b. I can't stand it.

## Self-assessment

**Read the following and check the appropriate boxes. For the points you are unsure of, refer back to the relevant sections in the module.**

### NOW I CAN...

- distinguish between permanent and temporary situations ☐
- make plans and future arrangements ☐
- talk about the present and the past ☐
- talk about past habits and events ☐
- describe clothes and talk about fashion ☐
- express likes/dislikes ☐
- use linking words (and, but, so, because, or) ☐
- make a mind map ☐
- present myself ☐

shopping

**Discuss:**
● Look at the pictures. In which situation is it best to communicate face-to-face with the other person? Why?

learning a language

SORRY

apologizing

congratulating someone

IT'S A BABY BOY!

giving bad news

business meeting

## In this module you will learn...

● to talk about experiences you have had
● to use appropriate tenses to link the past with the present
● language to start, maintain and end a conversation
● to use time expressions related to the Present Perfect Simple
● to talk about different ways of communicating
● to describe the positive and negative qualities in people
● to emphasize adjectives
● to write a description of a person

# 1 Reading 🔊

**A. Discuss.**

- What do you take photos of?
- How good are you at taking photos?

**B. Look at the photos on the website. Do you think they're good photos? Why?/Why not? Listen, read and find out about them.**

**C. Read again and answer the questions.**

1. Where does the writer advise you to place your subject in a photo?
2. What does the writer advise you to say before taking a photo?
3. When do people feel embarrassed in front of a camera?
4. Why shouldn't you use flash?
5. Why is the early evening the best time for taking photos?
6. How can you fix red eyes in a photo?
7. Which tip did Ann follow?

**D. Find words/phrases in the text that mean the same as the following.**

1. to be different from and better than other similar things (tip 1).
2. to take a photograph (tip 1).
3. to put something somewhere (tip 1).
4. to sit or stand in a particular position (tip 3).
5. feeling nervous and uncomfortable, shy (tip 3).
6. to happen or develop in a way that you did not expect (comments).
7. to become better (comments).

**E. Discuss.**

- Do you follow any of the advice mentioned in the text? Does it work?
- What other tips can you share?

---

Have you ever wondered why other people's photos always seem more professional than yours? Well, here are some...

# Top tips for better photos of people

Do you want your photos to stand out? Then change your angle. Shoot people from high above, below or from an unusual angle or even from a different room. You always get interesting results. Also, don't always place your subject in the middle of the photo.

*continue reading*

Did you ask your subject to say "cheese" before you took the photo? Well, people are expecting this. Have you ever tried to surprise them by saying something completely different, like "chimpanzee"? They don't expect it, and you get a natural smile.

*continue reading*

Give people something to do. Photos are more natural when people are doing something. Otherwise they're just posing in front of the lens, feeling embarrassed.

*continue reading*

Light is very important. Try not to use flash because it makes a person's face look flat and ugly, like a passport photo. Natural light is the best and the best part of the day is probably the early evening when the light is warm and soft.

*continue reading*

Lastly, don't be afraid to use photo editing software to edit your photos. There are some very useful programs out there, and they're pretty simple. Have you ever seen a photo of a person with red eyes? Well, you can easily fix that.

*continue reading*

**Comments:**

I have taken lots of bad photos of people over the years. But yesterday I climbed a tree and took some photos of my friends and they turned out really cool. I'm improving! Thanks for the advice! I've uploaded them for you to see.

*Ann, Doncaster*

**UPLOAD YOUR PHOTOS HERE** ▶

## 2 Grammar Present Perfect Simple, Present Perfect Simple vs. Past Simple → *p. 141*

**A.** Read the example. Note the verbs in blue which are in the Present Perfect Simple and answer the questions.

> Jane **has sent** me a text message. She's organizing a DVD night.
> We've **watched** DVDs together many times before.

**1.** How do we form the Present Perfect Simple? Complete.

_____ or_____ + past participle

**2.** What kind of actions do we use the Present Perfect Simple for? Choose a or b.

   **a.** for actions happening now

   **b.** for actions that happened in the past and their results are obvious now and/or we don't mention when they happened

> For a list of irregular verbs, go to page 150.

**TIME EXPRESSIONS**

always, ever, never, before, once, twice, many times, so far, just, recently, lately, etc.

**B.** Read the examples. What's the difference between *I've uploaded* and *I uploaded*?

> **I've uploaded** lots of photos on my website.
> **I uploaded** a photo of me and my friends last night.

**C.** Read the examples. What's the difference between *has been, went* and *has gone*?

> Mike **has been** to Rome twice.
> He **went** to Rome in 2008 and in 2012.
> Mike **has gone** to Milan this week. He's coming back tomorrow.

**D.** Complete with the Present Perfect Simple or the Past Simple of the verbs in parentheses.

**A:** **1** _____ you _____ (ever / try) Kelly's strawberry cheesecake?

**B:** No, I **2** _____ (never / have) the chance, but I **3** _____ (have) some of her chocolate cake a few weeks ago.

**A:** **4** _____ you _____ (like) it?

**B:** No, I **5** _____ (not like) it very much. It **6** _____ (be) too sweet.

**A:** Well, Kelly **7** _____ (make) a cheesecake last night and it **8** _____ (be) awesome. I **9** _____ (always / want) to learn how to make cheesecake. Maybe she can show me.

**B:** Hey, where's Kelly now?

**A:** She's not here, but she's coming back in a while. She **10** _____ (go) to the supermarket to buy some things. She wants to make another cheesecake.

## 3 Pronunciation 🔊

**A.** Listen and repeat. What do you notice about the pronunciation of *did you* and *have you*?

Did you go shopping yesterday?

Have you ever been abroad?

**B.** Read the questions below aloud. Then listen and check your pronunciation.

**1.** Did you like the movie last night?

**2.** What did you do yesterday?

**3.** Have you tried Chinese food before?

**4.** Have you ever visited Paris?

**5.** When did you see Polly?

**6.** Have you taken any photos in the dark?

## 4 Speaking

Talk in pairs. Have you ever done any of the following? Discuss the details.

**take a bad photo?**
- Where / be / you?
- What time of day / be / it?
- What / take photo / of?
- use / camera or cell phone?
- Why / not like / it?
- edit / it / at all?
- What / do / with it / in the end?

**travel by plane?**
- How many times?
- Where / go?
- Who / go with?
- How old / be / you?
- be / scared?

**win a competition?**
- What kind?
- What / do?
- be / difficult?
- What / win?

**meet anyone famous?**
- Who?
- Where / be / you?
- What / say?
- take photo / together?

*66 Have you ever taken a bad photo?* **Yes...** *Where were you? ... 99*

# 1 Reading 🔊

**A. Listen, read and answer the questions.**

- Where are the dialogues taking place?
- What is the relationship between the people?

HAVEN'T WE MET BEFORE?

YEAH, I USUALLY HANG AROUND HERE.

**A:** Excuse me. Haven't we met before?

**B:** No, sorry. You don't look familiar.

**A:** Isn't your name Deborah?

**B:** That's my sister. We look alike. I'm Susan.

**A:** I'm Gwen. Deborah and I used to work at Westhill High. By the way, how is she? I haven't seen her for ages.

**B:** She's great. She hasn't changed much. She's still a Math teacher.

**A:** Tell her I said hi.

**B:** Sure. I'm sorry, I didn't catch your name.

**A:** Gwen Fisher.

**B:** OK, Gwen. This is my floor. It was nice talking to you. Bye.

---

**C:** Do you mind if I join you? There aren't any tables available.

**D:** No, go ahead.

**C:** I'm Francesca.

**D:** Jessica. Nice to meet you. What do you do?

**C:** I'm a hairstylist. I have my own salon on Garner Street.

**D:** Really? I go past there almost every day. How's business?

**C:** It could be better. What about you?

**D:** I'm unemployed. I graduated last year, but I haven't found a job yet.

**C:** Good luck with that. It's not easy at the moment.

**D:** Tell me about it. I've already been to three interviews this week and nothing.

---

**E:** Steve! Long time no see!

**F:** Hello, Ken. Good to see you again.

**E:** How long has it been since we last saw each other?

**F:** I think it was at your brother's barbecue.

**E:** That was a year ago.

**F:** Yeah. So, how have you been? Are you still working at that art gallery?

**E:** No, I work at the National Museum now. I've been there since March.

**F:** Oh, here comes the A19. Got to go. Give me a call sometime, OK?

---

**B. Read the dialogues again and answer the questions. Write A-F.**

1. Which two people know a relative of the other person? ☐ ☐
2. Who is looking for a job? ☐
3. Which two people haven't seen each other for a year? ☐ ☐
4. Who looks like someone else? ☐
5. Who wishes the other person success for the future? ☐
6. Who asks about another person? ☐
7. Who has recently changed jobs? ☐
8. Who thought the other person was someone else? ☐

**C. Find phrases in the dialogues that mean the same as the following:**

**Dialogue 1**
1. I don't recognize you.
2. for a long time.

**Dialogue 2**
3. Sure, no problem.
4. I know what you mean.

**Dialogue 3**
5. I last saw you a very long time ago.

**D. Which phrases can you use to start a conversation and which to end a conversation? Use ideas from the dialogues and also come up with your own.**

## 2 Grammar Present Perfect Simple with for, since, yet, already → p. 141

**A. Read the dialogue. When did Ted move to this neighborhood?**

> **A:** How long have you had this apartment, Ted?
>
> **B:** I've had it **for two years**, **since I moved** to this neighborhood, actually.

**for + a period of time**
e.g. two years, a week, six months, an hour, five minutes, a long time

**since + a point in time**
e.g. Sunday, yesterday, two o'clock, 2010, last week, I left school

**B. Complete with the Present Perfect Simple or the Past Simple of the verbs in parentheses and circle *for* or *since*.**

**1.**

**A:** Have you seen Rita at all lately?

**B:** I _____ (not see) her **for / since** yesterday morning.

**A:** That's strange. She _____ (not call) me **for / since** days. In fact, **for / since** the last time we _____ (go) out together.

**2.**

**A:** Hey, do you know Peter Dale?

**B:** Of course. I _____ (know) him **for / since** ages. We met in high school.

**A:** So, you _____ (know) him **for / since** you _____ (be) a teenager.

**B:** That's right. We _____ (be) friends **for / since** 1990.

**C. Read the examples and complete the rules.**

> • **A:** Have you called Tom **yet**?
>
>   **B:** No, but I've **already** told the others about the meeting.
>
> • Kelly has finished eating **already**! I haven't started **yet**.

We usually use _____ in affirmative sentences. We place it between *have/has* and the past participle or at the end of the sentence for emphasis.

We use _____ in questions and negative sentences. We place it at the end of the sentence.

**D. Say 3 things you've done so far in your life that you think are important and 3 things you haven't done yet, but want to.**

❝ *I've already gotten a degree in economics, but I haven't found a job yet.* ❞

## 3 Vocabulary

**Read the following sentences. Can you guess what the words/phrases in bold mean?**

1. Jack's gone out with his high school **buddies**.
2. This is Mike, **a childhood friend**.
3. We've invited only **close friends** and **relatives** to the wedding; no **distant relatives**.
4. Jill is **a mutual friend** of ours. I know her from school, and Tina met her at the gym years ago.
5. I've told my children never to talk to **strangers**.
6. Tom is **an old acquaintance**. I see him sometimes when I visit my home town.

## 4 Listening 🔊

**A. Listen to two people talking. What is the relationship between them?**

a. They are old acquaintances.
b. They are complete strangers.
c. They are friends with the same person.

**B. Listen again and write J for James, P for Pamela or B for Both.**

1. Who grew up in Waterville? ☐
2. Who lives in Waterville? ☐
3. Who went to Langford High School? ☐
4. Who used to go to the gas station on 8th Avenue? ☐
5. Who has worked at a gas station? ☐
6. Who has taken a Spanish class? ☐

## 5 Speaking Role play

**Talk in pairs. Go to page 133.**

# 1 Reading 🔊

**A.** Look at the ways of communicating below. Put them in order starting from the most direct to the most distant way of communicating and give reasons for your answers.

| instant messaging | face-to-face | phone call | e-mail | text message | Skype |

| direct → | → | → | → | → | → | → | → | → | → | → | → | → | → | distant |
|---|---|---|---|---|---|---|---|---|---|---|---|---|---|---|
| | | | | | |

**B.** Read the title of the text. What do you think the text is about? Listen, read and check your answers.

# Direct communication is dying out...

In the past, friends used to call or meet up to catch up on each other's news. Nowadays, with the rise of technological communication, personal contact is becoming less frequent and more distant communication methods, like e-mail, texts or instant messaging are taking its place.

Many people fear that the younger generation is losing the social skills they need to communicate. When communicating face-to-face, young people feel uncomfortable and keeping eye contact is difficult for them. They avoid making phone calls and prefer to send someone a text, even when they are in the next room.

Is this a problem? Or is this just the way that humans are evolving? A recent study has shown that two-thirds of teenagers are now more likely to text their friends than call them. Young people often prefer to text because they can hide aspects of their personality. For example, if they're shy, they can seem cooler. Also, texting is a way to stay in touch with more people as it's impossible to see lots of people face-to-face. So, many teenagers believe this distant way of communicating is actually improving communication.

There is no doubt that face-to-face communication is more than just words. When speaking to someone face-to-face, your tone of voice and body language play an important role, too. Today, many people are going against the trend of distant communication. "No e-mail" days are becoming popular in the U.S.A. and companies are encouraging people to pick up the phone and talk to another human being, or even meet face-to-face.

Are you there? 12:47

Yeah, let's talk. 12:52

What about? 12:54

Humans are social beings. Some years ago, Albert Mehrabian, a psychology professor at UCLA, came up with the following statistics for spoken communication:

7% of meaning is in the spoken words
38% of meaning is paralinguistic (the way we say the words)
55% of meaning is in facial expression and body language

**C. Read again and answer the questions. Choose a, b or c.**

1. According to the text, why is face-to-face communication becoming less frequent?
   a. Because people are busier than they used to be.
   b. Because modern communication methods are faster.
   c. Because technological communication is becoming more popular.

2. How do you know when a young person is losing his/her social skills?
   a. When they avoid looking at you when talking.
   b. When they stop sending you texts and e-mail.
   c. When they start making lots of phone calls.

3. According to the text, why do many young people prefer more distant communication methods?
   a. Because they think distant communication is cool.
   b. Because it's easier to communicate when you don't show who you really are.
   c. Because they don't want others to know their identity.

4. What is true about "no e-mail" days?
   a. They make people use more direct communication.
   b. They are against face-to-face communication.
   c. Companies feel that they are a waste of time.

5. According to A. Mehrabian, what is the most important part of spoken communication?
   a. The words you say.
   b. The way you say the words.
   c. The way you behave when you speak.

**D. Look at the highlighted words/phrases in the text and match them with their meanings.**

1. catch up on ☐
2. frequent ☐
3. generation ☐
4. evolve ☐
5. impossible ☐
6. encourage ☐

a. cannot be done
b. all the people of about the same age
c. happening often
d. to suggest that someone does something that would be good
e. to find out about what has happened
f. to develop slowly

**E. Discuss.**

- Do you disagree with any of the opinions expressed in the text? Which one(s)?
- Do you prefer sending text messages and e-mails, or talking to others face-to-face?
- What do you think the future of communication will be like?

## 2 Vocabulary

**Read the sentences below. What do the words/phrases in bold mean?**

1. I **lost touch** with Jamie after college, and I haven't spoken to him for years.
2. Have you **kept in contact** with any of your old school buddies?
3. I left a message on Dean's voicemail, but he hasn't **returned the call** yet.
4. Do you know how I can **get hold of** Julian?
5. Mr. Freeman, can I **have a word with** you after the meeting?
6. I sent an e-mail to the company, but I haven't **received a reply** yet.
7. You can **reach** me any time during the week at this number.

## 3 Listening

**Listen to three people talking about instant messaging and match the names with the statements.**

| | |
|---|---|
| Lucy | I'm not going to use instant messaging a lot in the future. |
| Jerry | There are better methods of communication than instant messaging. |
| Heather | I don't know what I'd do without instant messaging. |

## 4 Speaking Survey

**A. Talk in groups of three. Interview each other and complete the survey below. Then complete it for yourself.**

| SURVEY | Student 1 | Student 2 | YOU |
|---|---|---|---|
| How many hours a day do you spend using social media? | | | |
| What do you use social media for? | | | |
| Which sites do you usually use? | | | |
| How many people do you communicate with in a day? | | | |
| Do you think you spend too much time in front of a screen? | | | |
| Who do you usually talk on the phone to? | | | |
| What do you usually talk about? | | | |
| How long do your phone calls usually last? | | | |
| How many people do you talk to in a day? | | | |
| Do you think you spend too much time on the phone? | | | |

**B. Report the results of your group's survey to the rest of the class. Discuss the results.**

# 1 Vocabulary 🔊

**Listen and read. Which are positive and which are negative qualities?
Do you know anyone with these characteristics?**

A **bossy** person likes telling others what to do all the time.

An **outgoing** person is friendly, and enjoys meeting other people.

An **easygoing** person is relaxed and happy, and not easily upset, annoyed or worried.

A **selfish** person doesn't think about other people's feelings or needs.

A **confident** person feels sure about what he/she can do.

A **quick-tempered** person gets mad quickly, without having a good reason.

A **trustworthy** person is someone you can trust and rely on.

A **stubborn** person doesn't change his/her opinion easily.

A **forgetful** person often forgets things.

An **optimistic** person is very positive and expects good things to happen.

# 2 Listening & Speaking 🔊

**A. Listen to a brother and sister talking about roommates. Does the brother find the questionnaire useful?**

**B. Listen again and check the options in the questionnaire according to what the speakers say.**

## CHOOSE THE RIGHT ROOMMATE

> **TIP**
> Before you listen, always read the information given and make sure you don't have any unknown words.

**Do you want to live with...?**

a male ◯    a female ◯

a smoker ◯    a non-smoker ◯

someone younger ◯    someone older ◯    someone your age ◯

someone with a pet ◯    someone without a pet ◯

**What do you definitely want your new roommate to be like?**

trustworthy ◯    cheerful ◯    neat ◯    active ◯

confident ◯    outgoing ◯    easygoing ◯    helpful ◯

pleasant ◯    optimistic ◯

**What do you definitely NOT want your new roommate to be like?**

messy ◯    bossy ◯    forgetful ◯    stubborn ◯

noisy ◯    quick-tempered ◯    moody ◯    selfish ◯

unpleasant ◯    negative ◯

**Which of the following do you consider important?**

having similar sleeping habits ◯    sharing the bills ◯

having similar study habits ◯    respecting privacy ◯

sharing housework ◯    having similar interests ◯

**C. Talk in pairs. Imagine you are looking for a roommate. Think about the kind of person you want to share your apartment with. Discuss the questions in the questionnaire above.**

# 3 Writing A description of a person

**A. John has written about his new roommate, Freddie. Read the description and check the topics he has mentioned.**

1. The qualities he doesn't like about Freddie. ☐
2. How he feels about Freddie. ☐
3. What other people think of Freddie. ☐
4. The qualities he likes about Freddie. ☐
5. The things he does that annoy Freddie. ☐
6. How they know each other. ☐
7. People they both know. ☐

**B. Read the note below and find examples of intensifiers in the description on the right. Can you rephrase the sentences in the description using other intensifiers?**

**Use intensifiers to emphasize adjectives.**

| Sally is | very really extremely so pretty kind of a little (bit) | selfish. |
|---|---|---|

Freddie is my new roommate at college. I've only known him for a couple of weeks, but so far, we get along fine.

Freddie is very easygoing and has a great sense of humor so he manages to cheer me up when I'm down or stressed. In addition, he's pretty outgoing and confident and loves meeting new people. So, of course, we know almost everyone on campus already.

Unlike me, however, he isn't very active and doesn't like sports. That's a little annoying because I enjoy watching and playing sports while he just likes getting together with other students and watching DVDs. Something else I've noticed is that he's kind of quick-tempered. Not with me, but with other people. They seem to get on his nerves for no reason.

I don't know if Freddie and I are going to become best friends. However, he is definitely a good person to know, especially when you're starting off in college.

**C. Think about a person you've recently met. Look at the questions below and make some notes.**

- Who is this person?
- How did you two meet?
- What is he/she like?
- What do you like about him/her?
- What do you dislike about him/her?
- Do you think you get along well with him/her?
- Do you think you are going to become good friends?

> **TIP**
> - Before you start writing, think of the ideas you are going to write about and plan your paragraphs.
> - Use a variety of adjectives as well as intensifiers to describe the person's personality.
> - Remember to give examples to show what you mean.

**D. Write a description of a person you have recently met. Use your ideas from activity C and follow the plan below.**

## Plan
### A description of a person

**INTRODUCTION**
**Give some general information about the person (name, how you know each other).**

**MAIN PART (2 PARAGRAPHS)**
**1 Describe his/her good qualities and try to give some examples. Use phrases like:**
- *He/She is very/really/pretty...*
- *The best thing about him/her is that he/she...*
- *Another thing I like about him/her is...*
- *First of all,...*
- *Also / In addition / Apart from that,...*

**2 Describe his/her bad qualities and try to give some examples. Use phrases like:**
- *He/She is very / a little / kind of...*
- *The worst / most annoying thing about him/her is that he/she...*
- *However,...*
- *I can't stand him/her when he/she...*
- *Something else I've noticed is that he/she...*

**CONCLUSION**
**Give your general opinion of this person.**

## Vocabulary

**A. Choose a, b or c.**

1. My roommate is a little ____. One moment he is cheerful and the next he is sad.
   **a.** quick-tempered **b.** annoyed **c.** moody

2. Have you talked to Jerry lately? I e-mailed him yesterday but I never received a ____.
   **a.** result **b.** meaning **c.** reply

3. In the end, it ____ out to be a very beautiful day.
   **a.** stood **b.** turned **c.** took

4. Teachers should ____ students to talk face-to-face with their friends more.
   **a.** encourage **b.** manage **c.** notice

5. Alex has been ____ since May, but he hasn't started looking for a job yet.
   **a.** uncomfortable **b.** unemployed **c.** unpleasant

6. Tina is very easygoing. Everyone ____ her.
   **a.** catches up on **b.** gets hold of **c.** gets along with

**B. Complete the sentences with the words in the box.**

> acquaintances  mutual  privacy  extremely
> social  rely  avoid

1. Steve spends too much time alone. He really has to try to improve his _____ skills.

2. People say that it's better to have a few good friends than lots of _____.

3. A real friend is someone you can trust and _____ on. He or she should also respect your _____ and try to cheer you up when you're not feeling well.

4. **A:** Do you two know each other?
   **B:** Well, we have some _____ friends.

5. It's _____ hot today. Why don't we stay home?

6. Dr. Brady says we should _____ eating just before going to bed.

## Grammar

**C. Complete with the Past Simple or the Present Perfect Simple of the verbs in parentheses.**

**A:** Your photos are fantastic! 1 _____ you _____ (ever / take) a photography class?
**B:** No, but last year, my brother and I 2 _____ (go) to the Annual Photography Festival. 3 _____ you _____ (ever / be) there?
**A:** No, I 4 _____ (not hear) of it before.
**B:** Anyway, we 5 _____ (see) the work of many photographers and 6 _____ (talk) to a few of them. I 7 _____ (learn) lots of useful things. They also 8 _____ (teach) us some tricks on how to use the light.
**A:** Wow! You 9 _____ (improve) a lot since then. Is your brother also good at photography?
**B:** Yeah, he 10 _____ (become) a professional photographer already and he 11 _____ (take) thousands of photos! He sells them online to a photo bank website. I 12 _____ (upload) some of mine too, but nobody 13 _____ (buy) any yet.
**A:** Well, good luck!

**D. Circle the correct words.**

1. Have you eaten **just / already**?
2. **A:** How long have you known each other?
   **B: Since / For** ages, **since / for** we were in school, actually.
3. Have you talked to this person **before / never**?
4. How many years **before / ago** did you move here?
5. **A:** Are the Simpsons here?
   **B:** No. You've **recently / just** missed them. They've **been / gone** to the Tech Show.
6. Now, where have I seen this man **before / since**?
7. I haven't met Miss Jones **already / yet**. Where is she?
8. Ted has been on the phone since you **left / 've left**.

## Communication

**E. Complete the dialogues with the phrases in the box. There is one extra phrase which you will not need to use.**

> **a.** I didn't catch your name.
> **b.** Tell me about it.
> **c.** Long time no see!
> **d.** It was nice talking to you.
> **e.** How long has it been?
> **f.** How's business?
> **g.** We've lost touch.

1. **A:** Jack?
   **B:** Owen! 1 _____
   **A:** Hi! Good to see you again.
   **B:** Yeah. 2 _____
   **A:** Ten years, I think. Have you kept in touch with any of the guys from school?
   **B:** Yes, with Jim and Mike.
   **A:** What about Ben?
   **B:** I haven't seen him for years. 3 _____

2. **A:** Hi, Ken. Do you remember me? I'm Suzie.
   **B:** Sorry, I'm not Ken, but I have a brother named Ken.
   **A:** Oh, wow. You look a lot like him!
   **B:** 4 _____ Everybody tells me the same thing.
   **A:** Oh, I'm sorry. Well, I haven't seen him for years and... Anyway, tell him I said hi.
   **B:** 5 _____
   **A:** It's Suzie Myers. 6 _____ Bye!

## Self-assessment

**Read the following and check the appropriate boxes. For the points you are unsure of, refer back to the relevant sections in the module.**

### NOW I CAN...

- talk about experiences I have had ☐
- use tenses to link the past with the present ☐
- use language to start, maintain and end a conversation ☐
- use time expressions related to the Present Perfect Simple ☐
- describe the positive and negative qualities in people ☐
- emphasize adjectives ☐
- write a description of a person ☐

**Task 1&2 p. 127**

quad biking

unusual food

**Discuss:**

- Look at the pictures. Have you ever tried or experienced anything similar?
- Do you like trying new things or do they frighten you?
- Is there something you've always wanted to try, but haven't?

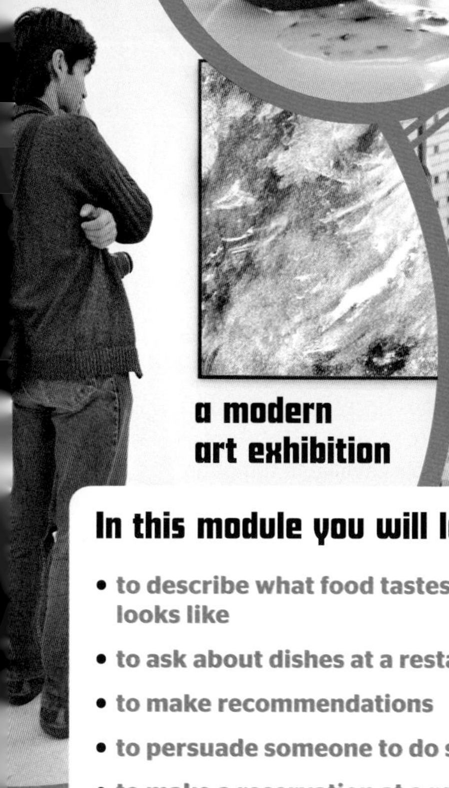

acupuncture

a modern art exhibition

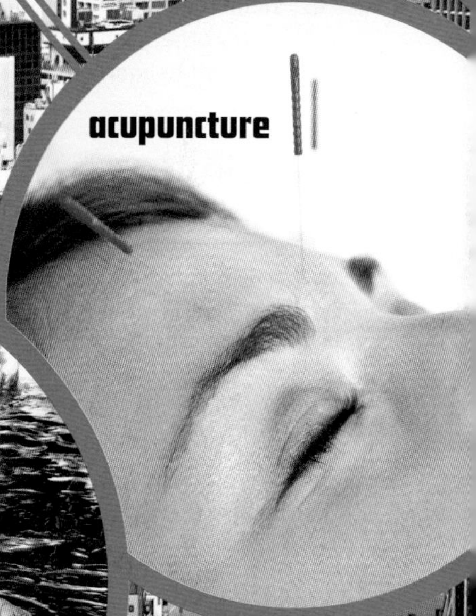

ice swimming

## In this module you will learn...

- to describe what food tastes and looks like
- to ask about dishes at a restaurant
- to make recommendations
- to persuade someone to do something
- to make a reservation at a restaurant
- to use quantifiers
- to define people, things and places by using relative pronouns and adverbs
- what a phrasal verb is
- to read dictionary entries
- to talk about different forms of art
- to form nouns (ending in –ion and –ation) from verbs
- to give news
- to respond to news by showing surprise and enthusiasm, and to ask for details
- to write an e-mail giving news
- set phrases for informal letters/e-mails

an extreme hairstyle

# 1 Reading 🔊

## A. Discuss.

- Have you ever tried food from other countries?
- If yes, what have you tried? Did you like it?
- If not, would you like to? Why/Why not?

## B. Read and put the dialogues in order. Then listen and check your answers.

**a**

**Brian** So, how was your duck?

**Lucy** It was delicious! And it came with some pancakes, so it was similar to eating Mexican fajitas. And that sauce was nice and sweet. I liked it a lot.

**Brian** I see that you've finished it all. Was it worth coming?

**Lucy** Yep, and the service was excellent. I'm definitely coming back to this restaurant to try other dishes.

**Brian** I'm glad to hear it.

**b**

**Waitress** Are you ready to order?

**Lucy** I had a look at the menu, but I'm confused. I have very little knowledge of Chinese food. What do you recommend?

**Waitress** Well, few people can resist our Peking Duck.

**Lucy** Does it contain any nuts? I'm allergic to them.

**Waitress** Don't worry. It has no nuts. It's crispy duck with tianmianjiang. That's a sweet bean sauce.

**Lucy** So, it isn't hot. I don't particularly like spicy food, you see.

**Waitress** No, don't worry.

**Lucy** I'll have that, then.

**Waitress** Certainly.

**c**

**Brian** I'm going to the Dragon Palace with a few friends tonight. Would you like to join us?

**Lucy** The Dragon Palace?

**Brian** Yes, and don't worry about the money. It's my treat.

**Lucy** It's not that. I'm just not sure about Chinese food.

**Brian** Oh, come on, Lucy. You really should try it! What do you have to lose?

**Lucy** But I don't like it.

**Brian** How do you know that? You've never tasted it. So, what do you say?

**Lucy** Umm...

**Brian** I don't have much time, Lucy. I need to book a table.

**Lucy** OK, just this once.

**d**

**Host** Dragon Palace. How may I help you?

**Brian** I'd like to reserve a table for this evening.

**Host** For how many people?

**Brian** Five.

**Host** We don't have many tables available tonight. Could you be here at 7 p.m.?

**Brian** Sure, that's fine.

**Host** All right. May I have your name, sir?

**Brian** My name's Brian Hughes.

**Host** OK, Mr. Hughes. Thank you.

## C. Read again and write T for True or F for False.

1. This is the first time Lucy has had Chinese food. ☐
2. Brian is paying for Lucy's meal. ☐
3. Brian booked a table for 7 p.m. ☐
4. Brian went to the restaurant with four friends. ☐
5. Lucy doesn't usually eat spicy food. ☐
6. Lucy didn't really enjoy her meal. ☐
7. Lucy left some of her food on her plate. ☐

## D. Read the dialogues a-d again and answer the questions. In which dialogue is someone...

1. trying to persuade someone to try something new? ☐
2. making a reservation? ☐
3. asking for information? ☐ ☐
4. giving their opinion about a dish? ☐
5. giving information about a dish? ☐
6. asking someone to suggest something? ☐

## E. Discuss.

- Have you ever had Peking Duck? If yes, what do you think of it? If not, would you like to try it?
- Have you ever ordered something at a restaurant that you didn't like? What did you do?

# 2 Vocabulary & Speaking

**A. Read the sentences below. Can you guess what the words in bold mean?**

1. Dark chocolate has a **bitter** taste. Milk chocolate contains sugar and milk and is **sweet**.
2. The fries were **disgusting**. They were too **greasy**. I like my fries nice and **crispy**, without too much oil.
3. For an appetizer, I ordered mushroom soup. It was nice and **creamy**. Then for the main course, I had a delicious, **juicy** steak with vegetables.
4. The sauce is **bland**, totally **tasteless**. I'd like it to be **spicy**.
5. At the end of our meal, they brought some **mouth-watering** cakes. I just couldn't resist. I ate three!
6. Add **fresh** vegetables to the soup. Oh, and make sure you don't make it too **salty** this time.

**B. Talk in small groups. Describe the food in the pictures and give your opinion.**

> **❝** *That cake looks delicious and the whipped cream looks very fresh.*
> *I don't like whipped cream very much. It's usually too sweet for me.* **❞**

# 3 Grammar Quantifiers: some, any, no, much, many, a lot of, lots of, (a) few, (a) little → *p. 142*

**A. Read the dialogue below and complete the rules.**

> **A:** Is there **any** apple pie left?
> **B:** Of course. Have **some**.
> **A:** Can I have **some** ice cream?
> **B:** Sorry, there's **no** ice cream left.
> **A:** How about whipped cream?
> **B:** Sorry, we don't have **any**.

Use _____ in affirmative sentences, offers and requests.

Use _____ in questions and negative sentences.

Use _____ in affirmative sentences to give a negative meaning.

**B. Read the examples and complete the rules with *much, many, a few* and *a little*. Which of the words in blue can we replace with *a lot of / lots of*?**

> • Do you have any milk? I'd like **a little** in my coffee.
> • We don't have **many** carrots for the soup.
> • There wasn't **much** traffic on the roads so I got here early.
> • Can you answer **a few** questions for me?

Use _____ and _____ before plural countable nouns.

Use _____ and _____ before uncountable nouns.

Use **a lot of / lots of** before uncountable or plural countable nouns.

**C. Read the examples and notice the words in blue. Which of them means *enough* and which means *not enough*?**

> • I have **a little** money on me; perhaps I can buy a sandwich.
> • I don't think I can go shopping; I have very **little** money on me.

**D. Read and circle the correct words.**

1. **A:** When does our flight leave?
   **B:** In an hour. So, we have **a little / little** time before we leave.
   **A:** Yes. Do you want to get **any / some** coffee?
   **B:** Yeah, there are **a few / few** coffee shops over there, I think.

2. My mother makes **much / many** nice desserts. She has **a lot / lots of** recipes but **a few / few** people know that the recipes are actually my grandmother's. My mother doesn't like using **any / no** new recipes. She says the old ones are the best. I don't mind because I like her desserts **much / a lot**.

# 4 Speaking Role play

**Talk in pairs. Go to page 133.**

## 1 Reading 🔊

**A. Look at the dictionary entry and discuss.**

- What do you use a dictionary for?
- Do you find the information dictionaries give you useful?
- Apart from the information shown below, what other information do dictionaries give?

entry  **couch potato** *n.*  ← part of speech

a person who is not active and spends a lot of time in front of a TV
*A lot of children nowadays are overweight couch potatoes.*

definition  example sentence

**B. Below is a text about neologisms. Listen and read. Then look at the words in blue below. What do you think they mean? Read and find out.**

When people want to find the meaning of unknown words, they usually look them up in a dictionary. However, the English language is constantly changing and new words and expressions enter the language every year. These words are called *neologisms* and come from a variety of fields that affect our daily life. For example, the word *vlog* is a blog where you can post videos. Dictionaries have a hard time keeping up with neologisms. Luckily, most dictionaries have online versions and updating them is a simple task. However, it can take many years for dictionaries to accept a word, so you can sometimes come across a word which exists but isn't in dictionaries yet. Check out the following recent entries to dictionaries. The year which is in parentheses refers to the time the word first appeared and not when it entered the dictionary.

**brain candy** *n.* (2005)
an activity that is entertaining but doesn't make you think too much

**frenemy** *n.* (1977)
a person who pretends to be a friend but is actually an enemy

**hangry** *adj.* (2005) *more hangry, most hangry*
annoyed and angry because you are feeling hungry

**mouse potato** *n.* (1993)
a person who is not active and spends a lot of time in front of a computer

**nonversation** *n.* (2009)
a conversation about nothing

**photobomb** *v.* (2009)
*photobombs, photobombing, photobombed*
to enter the background of a photograph without the subject of the photograph knowing

**webinar** *n.* (1998)
a live online educational seminar or presentation

**C. Read again and answer the questions.**

1. Where do new words entering the English language come from?
2. What does *vlog* mean?
3. According to the text, why is an online version of a dictionary useful?
4. Which two words were used to make the following words?
   frenemy   hangry   nonversation   webinar

# 2 Vocabulary

**A. Read the sentence below. What's the meaning of the phrase in bold?**

*When people want to find the meaning of unknown words, they usually **look** them **up** in a dictionary.*

> The phrase in bold is a **phrasal verb**. A phrasal verb consists of a verb (e.g. *get, break*) and an adverb (e.g. *back*) and/or one or more prepositions (e.g. *for, on with*). The meaning of the phrasal verb is different from the meaning of the verb it includes.

**B. Find phrasal verbs in the text in activity 1 and match them with the meanings below.**

1. to start, be born or be made somewhere: _____

2. to continue to learn about a particular subject so that you always know about the most recent events, facts, etc.: _____

3. to meet or find something or someone by chance: _____

4. to look at something that seems interesting: _____

# 3 Grammar Relative pronouns (who, which, that), Relative adverb (where) → p. 142

**A. Read the examples below. What do the words in blue refer to?**

> It's a restaurant for people who/that love ethnic food.
>
> Last week I bought a pair of boots which/that were really expensive.
>
> It's a word (which/that) you can't find in dictionaries yet.
>
> That's the school where I taught English.

**B. Read the examples again and complete the rules.**

> **Use:**
>
> • _____ and **that** for people.
>
> • _____ and **that** for things, animals and ideas.
>
> • _____ for places.

> We can omit **who**, **which** and **that** when they are the object of the verb in the relative clause.
>
> *The girl (who/that) we saw on the bus is my cousin.*

**C. Complete with *who*, *which*, *that* or *where*. If they can be omitted, put them in parentheses.**

1. **A:** Do you know a store _____ I can get a good dictionary?

   **B:** There's a mall on Graham Avenue _____ has three bookstores.

   **A:** Great.

   **B:** But there are lots of good online dictionaries _____ you can use. The Internet is the place _____ you should look first.

   **A:** You think?

   **B:** Yeah, I have a friend _____ is a writer, and he uses them all the time.

   **A:** Maybe I don't need to buy one, then.

2. **A:** Is that the camera _____ you had with you the other day?

   **B:** No, this is Jeremy's camera.

   **A:** Who's Jeremy?

   **B:** He's the neighbor _____ looks after my cat when I'm away.

   **A:** It looks like a good camera.

   **B:** It is. He also has one _____ you can use underwater.

   **A:** Awesome.

# 4 Listening 🔊

**A. Listen to 3 teenagers playing a game. The aim of the game is to describe four words on a card without saying the words on the card. Listen and guess which words are being described. Write the words on the card.**

**B. Now listen to the continuation of the dialogue. The three teenagers are discussing the answers. How many words did the girl find? How many did the boy find? How many did you find?**

# 5 Speaking Guessing game

**Student A:** Choose one of the words below or think of your own, without telling Student B. Describe it to him/her.

**Student B:** Guess what Student A is describing.

> passport
> waiter
> salesperson   market   shopping mall
> lifeguard   college   medicine
> MP3 player
> fast food restaurant   menu
> coffee shop   teenager

**66** *It's something that you take when you are sick. Is it...?* **99**

# 1 Reading 🔊

**A. Discuss.**

- Do you like art?
- Do you often visit museums or art galleries?
- What famous artists do you know of?

**B. What do you know about installation art? Listen, read and find out more.**

# Be part of the art

Installation art isn't just about making paintings or sculptures. It's a kind of art that uses the area it's in to help people enjoy it. It includes exhibits with sound, live performances, video and even the Internet. People who experience installation art often have to use different senses at the same time, not only sight, but also hearing, smell and touch. You can find installation art in galleries, but also in public places, and it can be permanent or last for just a few hours, days or weeks. The main point is not only to look at the art but to experience it and feel part of the art, too.

In 2012, the contemporary art studio **Random International** turned one of the rooms at the Barbican Centre in London into a *Rain Room*. Rain fell from the ceiling of the room non-stop. Visitors could hear, see and even smell the rain, but when they walked through the room, they didn't get wet. Eight digital cameras followed each visitor and a computer stopped the rain above them. This made the people feel they were in control of the rain. Random International saw the installation as a social experiment and were interested in people's reactions.

In 2009, Brazilian artist **Néle Azevedo** created an installation called *Melting Men*. She created a thousand tiny ice sculptures of men and placed them in a sitting position on steps in a square in Berlin. They quickly began to melt and were soon just a puddle of water. The Melting Men installation has appeared in various cities, like Paris, Florence, Havana and Sao Paulo. Azevedo's installation is more than just art. She wants people to become aware of the melting ice caps at the poles and how this can cause water levels to rise. Her art sends a warning to humanity.

**C. Read again and answer the questions. Write MM for Melting Men, RR for Rain Room or N for Neither.**

**Which installation...**

1. appeared in more than one place? ☐
2. needed special equipment to work? ☐
3. got people wet? ☐
4. could people take home with them? ☐
5. encouraged people to think about important environmental issues? ☐
6. changed over time? ☐

**D. Find words in the text and match them with their definitions below:**

1. objects or works of art put in a public place for people to see (para. 1).
2. lasting for a long time or forever (para. 1).
3. very small (para. 2).
4. a small pool, especially of rainwater (para. 2).
5. people in general (para. 2).
6. modern (para. 3).
7. the top surface of the inside part of a room (para. 3).
8. what you feel or do because of something that has happened (para. 3).

**E. Discuss.**

- Do you know of any other installation art works?
- Would you like to experience some installation art?

# 2 Vocabulary & Intonation 🔊

**A. Read the note. Then look at the nouns below and write the verb which they derive from.**

> A lot of nouns are formed by adding a suffix (e.g. *-ion, -ation*) to a verb.
>
> react → reaction    create → creation
> install → installation    prepare → preparation

| VERB | NOUN |
|---|---|
| 1. _____ | → information |
| 2. _____ | → exhibition |
| 3. _____ | → invention |
| 4. _____ | → cancelation |
| 5. _____ | → invitation |
| 6. _____ | → discussion |
| 7. _____ | → imagination |
| 8. _____ | → pollution |

**B. Listen and repeat. Notice the syllable that is stressed in words *a* and *b*.**

**a.** in**form**    **b.** infor**ma**tion

**C. Read the verbs and nouns in activity A above and underline the stressed syllable. Then listen and check your answers. Where is the stress in nouns ending in *-ion* and *-ation*? What do you notice about the pronunciation of the last syllable?**

# 3 Speaking

**Look at the activities below and discuss.**

sculpture    painting    photography

jewelry making    pottery    knitting

origami

- Which of them do you consider forms of art?
- How creative are you?
- Would you like to take up any of these activities as a hobby? Why/Why not?

# 4 Listening 🔊

**Listen to three short dialogues and answer the questions. Choose picture a, b or c.**

**1.** Which exhibit are the people looking at?

**2.** Where is the installation?

**3.** Which class did the woman join?

33

# 1 Listening 🔊

**A.** Listen to two friends talking. Which of the following is the woman doing?

1. making plans

2. giving news

3. describing an event

4. giving details

5. apologizing

**B.** Listen again and write the three questions the man asks to get more information.

1. _____

2. _____

3. _____

**C.** Listen again and complete the woman's answers to the questions above.

1. Because my old apartment was _____.

2. Yes, there is, with a great view of _____.

3. My _____.

# 2 Speaking

**A.** Imagine a friend gave you the following news. What details would you like to know? Think of as many questions as you can.

*Guess what! I'm getting married!*

*Listen to this! I found a job!*

*Guess what! I've taken up judo!*

*Did I tell you about my new car?*

_____  _____  _____  _____

_____  _____  _____  _____

_____  _____  _____  _____

_____  _____  _____  _____

**B.** Talk in pairs.

**Student A:** Imagine you have some good news to tell Student B. Use the ideas from above or your own.

**Student B:** Listen to Student A's good news and respond with the phrases in the box to show surprise and enthusiasm. Show interest and keep the conversation going by asking for details.

| | |
|---|---|
| Really? You are? / You did? / etc. | You're kidding. |
| That's great news. | Are you serious? |
| How awesome/exciting! | Unbelievable! |
| Lucky you! | Get out of here! |
| How lucky! | That's the last thing I expected. |
| I can't believe it! | I'm really happy for you! |
| What a surprise! | I'm glad to hear that! |
| What wonderful news! | Good for you! |
| Congratulations! | |

**TIP**

• Speak clearly.

• Don't worry if you make a mistake. Correct yourself if you can, otherwise just continue speaking.

• If you can't remember a word, don't stop. Try to use other words.

# 3 Writing  An e-mail giving news

### A. Discuss.
- Do you write e-mails to friends?
- What do you usually write to them about?

### B. Read the e-mail below. Why is Mike writing to John?

Hello John,

How are things? Thanks for your last e-mail. It's always great to hear from you. Sorry I didn't reply sooner, but I've been really busy lately. Anyway, I'm writing because I want to tell you about a new hobby I've taken up. It's called Aikido. Have you heard of it?

It's a peaceful martial art that developed in the early 20th century in Japan. I heard about it from a friend who started classes last year. I decided to try it out, too, and it's absolutely awesome. There are many different techniques to learn, but the instructor is really helpful and I am progressing well. What I like about it is that it isn't violent at all. I'm learning how to defend myself without hurting my opponent. We have classes twice a week and sometimes even on the beach! It's really interesting and fun. I don't even realize we're exercising. But when I go home, I'm exhausted!

So what about you? Do you still go to the gym? Maybe you can check out an Aikido class. Well, that's all for now. I have to start studying. Waiting for your news!

Bye for now,
Mike

### C. Read again and answer the questions. In which paragraph (1-3) does Mike:

a. ask for John's news? ☐

b. give a reason to end his e-mail? ☐

c. give details about his news? ☐

d. refer to John's e-mail? ☐

e. say the reason for writing? ☐

f. apologize for not writing earlier? ☐

g. ask John to write back? ☐

### D. Read the plan on the right and the phrases 1-6 below. In which part do they belong? Write the phrases in the plan.

1. Well, that's all for now. I have to go.

2. I'm looking forward to hearing from you.

3. It was nice to hear from you again.

4. Well, here's the latest.

5. Sorry I haven't written for so long, but I've been busy.

6. Anyway, enough about me. What have you been up to?

### E. Write an e-mail to Mike. Say how happy you are that he's taken up a new hobby and give him your news.

## Plan
### An e-mail giving news

**GREETING**
- **Greet the person you're writing to.**
  - *Dear Kevin,* • *Hi Bill!* • *Hello Mary,* • *Dear Mom,*

**OPENING PARAGRAPH**
- **Begin your e-mail and say why you're writing. Use set phrases like:**
  - *How have you been?*
  - *Thanks for your last e-mail.*
  - *I haven't heard from you for ages.*
  - *Sorry I didn't reply sooner, but...*
  - *I'm writing to tell you about...*
  - *Guess what! I have some exciting news.*
  - _____
  - _____

**MAIN PART**
- **Give your news. Use phrases like:**
  - *The good news is...*
  - *I've recently... Can you believe it?*
  - _____

**CLOSING PARAGRAPH**
- **State anything you want to emphasize, ask for news and end your e-mail. Use phrases like:**
  - *What's happening in your life?*
  - *What about you? Do you still...?*
  - *Waiting for your e-mail/reply.*
  - *Make sure you write and tell me your news.*
  - _____
  - _____
  - _____

**SIGNING OFF**
- **Use a signature ending and your first name below that.**
  - *Yours,* • *Take care,* • *Bye for now,* • *Keep in touch,*
    Beth        Jill          Frank            Sue
  - *Speak to you soon,*
    Lee

---

**When writing an e-mail giving news:**
- use the appropriate layout (see page 138).
- organize it into paragraphs and use set phrases as shown in the plan.
- use expressions (*e.g. well, of course, anyway, you know, by the way*).
- use standard grammar and spelling conventions. Don't use forms such as *wanna, CU L8R*, etc.
- use short forms (*e.g. I'm, don't*).
- use exclamations (*e.g. Guess what!*) and direct questions (*e.g. What have you been up to?*).

*TIP*

## Vocabulary

**A. Circle the correct words.**

1. Todd is trying to **persuade / affect** us to go to the art gallery with him.

2. Just add some **greasy / whipped** cream to the chocolate cake and enjoy.

3. I don't eat fish. I'm **allergic / permanent** to it.

4. Many **confused / contemporary** artists sell their work online.

5. I'm not sure which restaurant to choose. What do you **reserve / recommend**?

6. I'm paying tonight. It's my **task / treat**.

7. I don't often eat chips because they are too **salty / bitter**.

8. Your painting is awesome. You have a great **knowledge / imagination**.

**B. Complete the sentences with prepositions.**

1. Which dictionary do you use to look _____ unknown words?

2. You should take _____ a sport. You need exercise.

3. I came _____ a really old photograph while cleaning the basement.

4. The exhibition has beautiful works _____ art. Check it _____.

5. I don't think you are fully aware _____ the problem.

6. That couch turns _____ a bed.

## Grammar

**C. Complete the sentences with *who*, *which*, *that* or *where*. If they can be omitted, put them in parentheses.**

1. That's the waiter _____ helped me order.

2. Knitting is a hobby _____ my mother enjoys.

3. I don't understand the definition _____ I found in the dictionary.

4. Is this the office _____ Mr. Brown works?

5. The teacher _____ I like the most is Miss Jones.

6. Where did you get the sculpture _____ is on the table?

7. The coffee shop _____ is on Bell Street is very popular. It's the place _____ my friends and I usually meet.

**D. Circle the correct words.**

1. **A:** Would you like **much / some / any** sugar in your tea?

   **B:** Yes, please and **little / a little / a few** milk.

2. There are very **little / few / no** places where you can find good sushi in my neighborhood. However, in the downtown area, there are **some / lots / few** of Japanese restaurants worth going to.

3. **A:** My sister likes making jewelry and has made **many / much / a lot** bracelets for her friends.

   **B:** Really? She hasn't given me **some / no / any** jewelry.

4. **A:** Come on, we don't have **little / no / much** time left. I've booked the table for 8 p.m.

   **B:** Give me **few / many / a few** more minutes. I'm almost ready.

## Communication

**E. Put the dialogue in the correct order. Write 1-6.**

☐ You're right. I'm calling them tomorrow.

☐ Hey, Jake! What have you been up to?

☐ Well, guess what! I got a job at the arts center on campus.

☐ You should ask. What do you have to lose?

☐ Nothing much. I'm looking for a job, but no luck.

☐ Get out of here! Congratulations! Do you think they have anything for me?

**F. Match.**

1. How was the chicken? ☐
2. So, are you coming? ☐
3. I'm getting married! ☐
4. Is there any soup left? ☐

a. Just a little.

b. That's the last thing I expected.

c. Just this once.

d. A little bland.

## Self-assessment

Read the following and check the appropriate boxes. For the points you are unsure of, refer back to the relevant sections in the module.

### NOW I CAN...

▸ describe what food tastes and looks like ☐

▸ ask about dishes at a restaurant ☐

▸ make recommendations ☐

▸ persuade someone to do something ☐

▸ make a reservation at a restaurant ☐

▸ use quantifiers ☐

▸ define people, things and places by using relative pronouns and adverbs ☐

▸ read dictionary entries ☐

▸ talk about different forms of art ☐

▸ form nouns (ending in -ion and -ation) from verbs ☐

▸ give news ☐

▸ respond to news by showing surprise and enthusiasm, and ask for details ☐

▸ write an e-mail giving news ☐

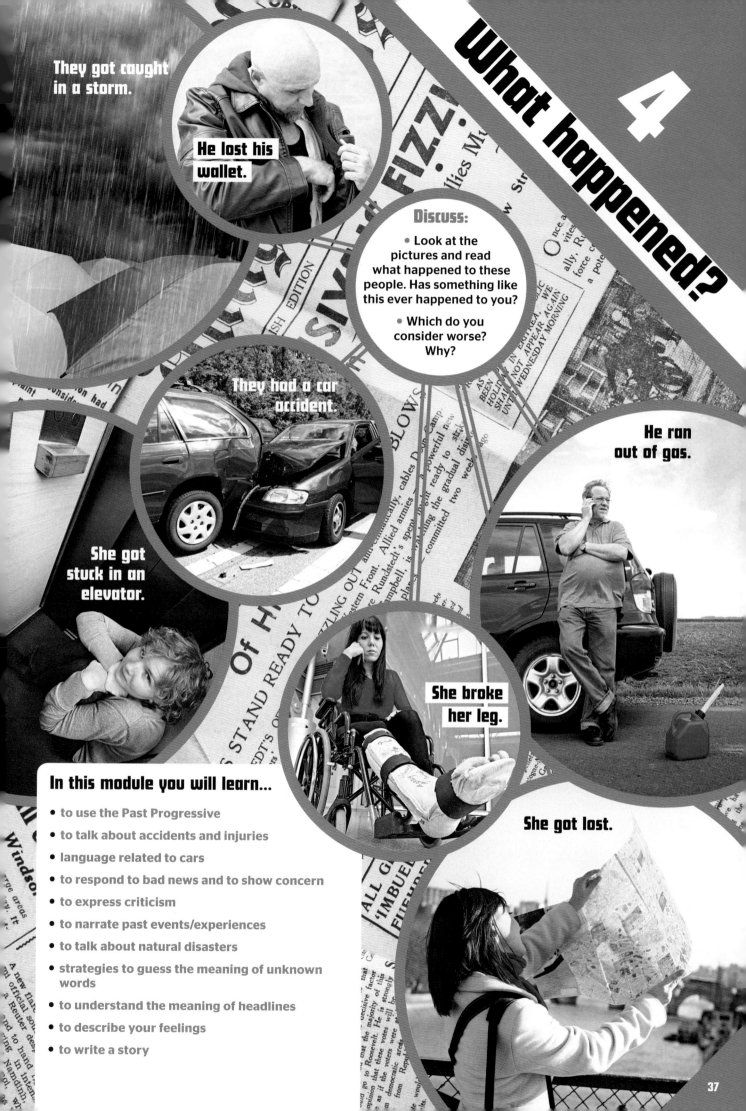

They got caught in a storm.

He lost his wallet.

**Discuss:**
● Look at the pictures and read what happened to these people. Has something like this ever happened to you?

● Which do you consider worse? Why?

They had a car accident.

He ran out of gas.

She got stuck in an elevator.

She broke her leg.

She got lost.

## In this module you will learn...

● to use the Past Progressive
● to talk about accidents and injuries
● language related to cars
● to respond to bad news and to show concern
● to express criticism
● to narrate past events/experiences
● to talk about natural disasters
● strategies to guess the meaning of unknown words
● to understand the meaning of headlines
● to describe your feelings
● to write a story

# 1 Reading 🔊

**A. Discuss.**

- Have you ever been in a blackout?
- What did you do?

**B. Read the comic strip. Choose the best last line for Mr. Baxter to say. Then listen and check your answers.**

**a.** Somebody usually has an accident during a blackout.

**b.** Someone please fix the lights before we have any more accidents!

**c.** Do you really think we can work during a blackout?

## The Blackout

**Mr. Baxter:** Listen everyone. Sorry, but we have to stay a little longer tonight... **1**

OW! MY HEAD!

AHHHH! THAT'S HOT!!!!

LOOK OUT!

... Oh no, a blackout!

DON'T WORRY, I'M COMING!

SOMEBODY GET A FLASHLIGHT... OUCH! **2**

**Jake:** I'm so sorry, Mr. Baxter. Here you are. Are you injured?
**Mr. Baxter:** You knocked me over, Jake. Why were you running? **3**

**Jake:** I was trying to help. I heard someone scream.
**Linda:** That was me. **4**

**Mr. Baxter:** What happened to you, Linda?
**Linda:** I was sitting at my desk. I wasn't doing anything. I was waiting for the lights to come back on. Suddenly, someone spilled boiling hot tea all over me. It burned my face. That's why I screamed. **5**

**Ken:** Sorry about that, Linda.
**Mr. Baxter:** Ken? You're bleeding. What happened to you?
**Ken:** I was coming back from the cafeteria with some tea for my sore throat. I tripped over something and grazed my head on a desk. **6**

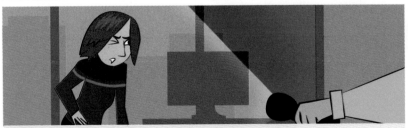

**Penny:** So, that was you?
**Ken:** What do you mean, Penny? Where were you?
**Penny:** Well, I was carrying some boxes to my desk over there. Suddenly, I stepped on something, lost my balance and fell, and I think I've sprained my ankle. Then, I heard someone trip over the boxes. **7**

**Mr. Baxter:** I don't believe this. ___?___ **8**

**C. Read the second frame of the comic strip again. Who says each phrase?**

**D. Read again. What happened when the lights went out? Put the sentences in order. Write 1-6.**

- [ ] Ken tripped.
- [ ] Jake knocked over Mr. Baxter.
- [ ] Linda screamed.
- [1] Penny fell down and sprained her ankle.
- [ ] Jake ran to help Linda.
- [ ] Ken spilled hot tea over Linda.

## 2 Grammar Past Progressive → *p. 142*

**A. Read the examples, notice the words in blue and match them with the rules.**

> 1. I **was watching** TV all evening yesterday.
> 2. I **watched** the news and a movie.

**a.** an action that was completed in the past. [ ]

**b.** an action that was in progress in the past. [ ]

**B. Read the examples and complete the rule about the formation of the Past Progressive.**

> - It **was raining** all evening.
> - My wife and I **weren't working** yesterday.

| Past Progressive |
|---|
| _____ or _____ + verb +_____ |

**C. Complete with the Past Progressive of the verbs in parentheses.**

1. **A:** Hey, Sophie. I _____ (call) you all day yesterday. Where were you? _____ you _____ (sleep)?

   **B:** No. I was at home but my cell wasn't on. I _____ (work) on an important assignment.

   **A:** So, you _____ (not take) any calls from anyone.

   **B:** That's right. I _____ (try) to finish the assignment. I wanted to hand it in this morning.

2. Yesterday afternoon Randy and Brenda _____ (cook). Suddenly, Randy cut his finger. It _____ (bleed) a lot and he couldn't stop it, so they went to the hospital.

3. **A:** How did Greg break his leg? What _____ he _____ (do) again?

   **B:** Well, he _____ (run) down the stairs to answer the phone. He lost his balance and fell.

## 3 Vocabulary & Speaking

**A. Match the verbs related to accidents with the pictures. Write the correct number next to the words.**

- spill [ ]
- slip (on) [ ]
- knock over [ ]
- trip over [ ]
- drop [ ]
- step on [ ]
- bump into [ ]

**B. Label the picture using the injuries in the box. Which of the injuries can we use as verbs?**

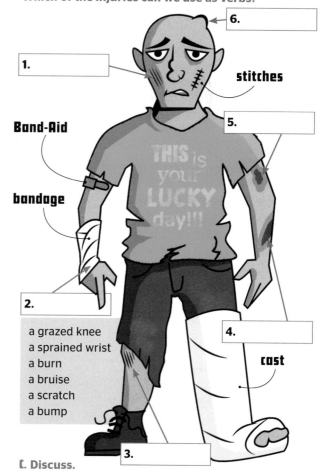

1. _____
Band-Aid
bandage
2. _____
a grazed knee
a sprained wrist
a burn
a bruise
a scratch
a bump
3. _____
4. _____
cast
5. _____
stitches
6. _____

**C. Discuss.**

- Have you ever had any of the above injuries?
- How did you get them? What were you doing?

# 1 Vocabulary 🔊

Match the words below with the items in the picture. Write the correct number next to the words. Then listen and check your answers. Do you know any other parts of a car?

| | | |
|---|---|---|
| seat belt ☐ | trunk ☐ | engine ☐ |
| windshield ☐ | spare tire ☐ | passenger seat ☐ |
| headlights ☐ | steering wheel ☐ | license plate ☐ |

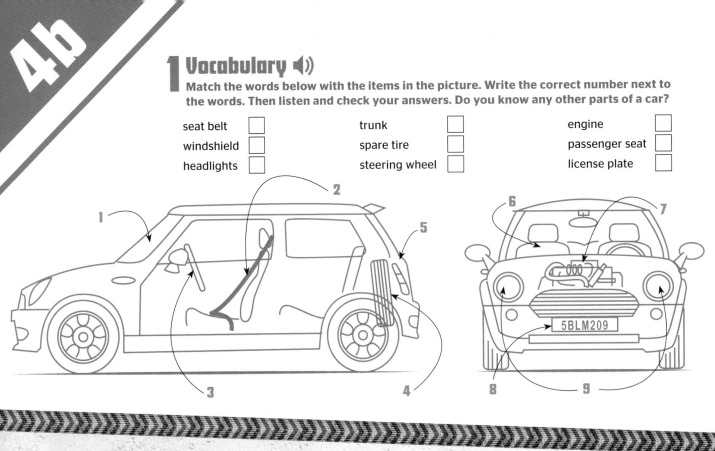

# 2 Reading 🔊

## A. Discuss.

• Can you drive?    • Do you have a car?    • Do you like traveling by car?    • Do you think it's dangerous?

## B. Listen, read and match the dialogues with the pictures a-d on the right. There is one extra picture you will not need to use.

### 1 ☐

**A:** Where have you been?

**B:** Don't ask. I got a flat tire on Alder Street as I was coming home. When I realized it, I slammed on the brakes and almost lost control of the car.

**A:** Are you all right?

**B:** Yeah. Anyway, as soon as I opened the trunk, I saw that I had no spare.

**A:** How unlucky! Did you call AAA?

**B:** I wanted to, but guess what! My phone was dead. I couldn't even call you to come and pick me up. So, I just took a cab.

**A:** Oh, you poor thing! Is there anything I can do to help?

**B:** Well, I'm going to need someone to drive me to my car tomorrow.

**A:** No problem.

### 2 ☐

**C:** You look upset. What's up?

**D:** The police pulled me over yesterday.

**C:** Why? Were you speeding?

**D:** No, I was talking on my cell phone while I was driving.

**C:** You should know better than that! What now? Are they going to take your license away?

**D:** No, but they gave me a ticket and I have to pay a fine. It's my own fault. I know it's illegal.

**C:** Yes, and very dangerous. What were you thinking?

### 3 ☐

**E:** Hey! Excuse me!

**F:** What's the matter? Why are you honking your horn?

**E:** What do you think you're doing?

**F:** I'm trying to get into this parking space. Is it illegal to park here?

**E:** No, just watch where you're going.

**F:** Why is that?

**E:** You bumped into my motorcycle and almost knocked me over while you were reversing.

**F:** Did I? I'm really sorry. I didn't see you. Is everything all right?

**E:** Yeah, I think so.

## C. Listen again and answer the questions. Write A-F.

1. Who hit something with their car? ☐
2. Who is annoyed with the other person? ☐ ☐
3. Who needed help but couldn't get any? ☐
4. Who broke the law? ☐
5. Who didn't realize what happened? ☐
6. Who offers help? ☐
7. Who regrets what he/she did? ☐ ☐
8. Who feels sorry for the other person? ☐

## D. Find phrases in the dialogues that can be used to:

1. respond to bad news
2. show concern
3. express criticism

# 3 Grammar Past Simple vs. Past Progressive - Time Clauses (when, while, as, as soon as) → *p. 143*

**A.** Read the examples and notice the words in blue. Then match them with a-c.

1. I **was going** really fast when I **lost** control of the car. ☐
2. While Tina **was driving**, Diane **was sleeping** in the passenger seat. ☐
3. As we **were trying** to find a parking space, it **started** raining. ☐
4. As soon as I **saw** Mike, I **crossed** the street to talk to him. ☐

**a.** The two actions were happening at the same time.

**b.** The two actions happened one after the other.

**c.** One action was in progress when the other happened.

**B.** Complete the sentences with the Past Simple or the Past Progressive of the verbs in parentheses.

1. Roger _____ (slam) on the brakes as soon as he _____ (notice) the cat on the road. He _____ (not want) to hit it.

2. Luckily, my sister _____ (wear) a seat belt when she _____ (crash) into another car, and _____ (not get) injured.

3. While we _____ (wait) at the traffic lights, a car _____ (run) through a red light.

4. Last summer, Brian _____ (travel) to the south of the country when his car _____ (break) down. Then, as he _____ (come) back home, he _____ (run) out of gas twice. It's unbelievable!

5. My dad _____ (listen) to the news while he _____ (drive) to work.

# 4 Speaking & Writing

**A.** Talk in groups of three.

**Student A:** Imagine you were involved in one of the situations below. Tell Students B and C about your experience, explaining what happened, what you did and how you felt.

> **You had a car accident.**    **Your car broke down.**
>
> **You went through a red light and the police stopped you.**
>
> **You ran out of gas.**

**Students B and C:** You see your friend (Student A), and realize that something is troubling him/her. Ask what is wrong and respond to his/her bad news. Show concern and, if necessary, criticize his/her actions. Ask questions to find out more about his/her experience.

> **TIP**
> When talking to another person, listen carefully to what he/she is saying so that you can respond appropriately. Also, remember that a good way to maintain the conversation is by asking Wh-questions (*e.g. Why did you do that?, When did it happen?*) to find out about certain details. Avoid asking Yes/No questions.

**B.** Write a short paragraph describing the situation you discussed in activity A above.

# 1 Vocabulary 🔊

**A. Read and match the paragraphs with the pictures. Listen and check your answers. Then try to guess the meaning of the words in bold.**

**a.** The tsunami hit a town on the west coast. The huge **wave** caused serious **damage** to buildings and roads, and whole areas have **flooded** with water.

**c.** Many buildings **collapsed** during the earthquake last Friday. The ground was **shaking** for a whole minute and there have been lots of **aftershocks** since then.

**b.** Firefighters are still trying to **put out** the wildfire which **broke out** yesterday morning, and is still **burning** one of the most beautiful forests in the country. You can see the cloud of black **smoke** from miles away.

**d.** The strong winds and heavy storms destroyed several houses. Many people are now **trapped** and the **authorities** are doing what they can to **rescue** them. This was a category two hurricane.

 1.
 2.
 3.

**TIP**

To guess the meaning of unknown words, use the following strategies:
• Read the words before and after the unknown word and think of the context.
• Try to figure out what part of speech (verb, noun, etc.) the unknown word is.
• See if the unknown word is similar to other words in English or in your own language.

**B. Discuss.**
• Do you remember hearing about any major natural disasters?
• What happened?
• How did you find out about them?

THE DAILY NEWS / Saturday, March 11, 2011

# 2 Reading 🔊

**A. Look at the pictures and the headline of the news article. What do you think happened? Listen, read and check your answers.**

# DOUBLE DISASTER IN JAPAN

Yesterday, the fourth largest earthquake since records began hit the northeast coast of Japan. The 9.0 magnitude earthquake occurred at 2:46 p.m. local time and caused serious damage and deaths. However, soon after the quake, a tsunami hit the coast, causing even more chaos.

Eyewitnesses are saying the waves from the tsunami were over 30 feet high at Miyako City and the water traveled 6 miles inland in the Sendai area. The tsunami destroyed entire towns and completely flooded Sendai airport. There have been tsunami warnings in countries all around the Pacific coast, and in California, people have reported 8-feet-high waves. A wave even broke off enormous icebergs from the Sulzberger ice shelf in Antarctica, 8,100 miles away.

Already thousands of Japanese people have lost their lives, thousands are injured, thousands are missing and hundreds of thousands are now homeless. Rescue teams are doing what they can to help the people who are trapped. However, rescue operations are extremely difficult, especially as there are continuous major aftershocks.

The people are terrified. "I can't believe how we survived. Many houses collapsed and then as we were trying to help others, the wave arrived. Let's just hope the aftershocks don't continue," a Sendai resident told us.

One of the main worries at the moment is the state of the Fukushima nuclear power plant. There are reports that the earthquake damaged the plant and experts are worried there could be a huge nuclear disaster.

**B. Read again and answer the questions.**

1. When did the earthquake occur?

2. What damage did the tsunami cause to the Sendai area?

3. How far did the wave that reached Antarctica travel?

4. What is causing extra problems for the rescue teams?

5. What are the people of Sendai afraid of?

6. What do experts fear?

**C. Look at the highlighted words in the text and try to guess what they mean.**

> **TIP**
> Keep in mind that a text will most probably include unknown words. Try to understand which of the words are really important. Try to guess the meaning of as many of these words as possible from the context.

**D. Match the highlighted words with the definitions below.**

1. without a home: _____

2. to happen: _____

3. someone who actually saw something happen: _____

4. very scared: _____

5. a person who lives in a particular place: _____

6. whole or complete: _____

7. huge: _____

**E. Discuss.**

• Do you remember anything about this event?
• Do you know what happened at Fukushima?

## 3 Pronunciation 🔊

**A. Listen and repeat. Notice the difference in pronunciation.**

| /tʃ/ | rea**ch** | ca**tch** | sculpture |
|------|-----------|-----------|-----------|
| /dʒ/ | re**g**ion | bri**dge** | **j**ust |

**B. Say the words below. In which category would you add them? Listen and check your answers.**

injured    damage    chance    actually

major    century    manage    object

research    knowledge

## 4 Listening & Speaking 🔊

**A. Listen to four news bulletins and match them with the headlines below. Write 1-4. There are three extra headlines which you do not need to use.**

FIRE DESTROYS NATIONAL MUSEUM ☐

QUAKE DESTROYS SMALL TOWN ☐

RESCUE TEAM SAVES SCHOOLCHILDREN FROM FLOOD ☐

HUNDREDS HOMELESS AFTER HURRICANE ☐

20 TRAPPED AFTER BUILDING COLLAPSES ☐

HEAVY SNOW CAUSES CHAOS ON ROADS ☐

ISLAND RESIDENTS SURVIVE TSUNAMI ☐

**B. Listen again and answer the questions for each news bulletin.**

1. a. When did the disaster happen? _____

   b. Where can the homeless go? _____

2. a. How many days have schools been closed? _____

   b. When is the bad weather going to end? _____

3. a. What caused the building to collapse? _____

   b. Does the rescue team know where the survivors are? _____

4. a. What is Kingsley High School close to? _____

   b. Was anybody injured? _____

**C. Talk in pairs or small groups. Read the newspaper headlines in activity A and use your imagination to describe what happened in each of the situations.**

❝ *Yesterday afternoon a fire broke out at the National Museum. Luckily, there weren't many visitors in the building so nobody was injured. Unfortunately, the fire destroyed many paintings...* ❞

# 1 Vocabulary

**A. Read the speech bubbles. What's the difference between the adjectives *bored* and *boring*?**

*I'm bored!*

*Yeah, this lecture is boring.*

**B. Circle the correct words.**

1. Were you **surprised / surprising** to see Jonathan at the airport?

2. The 7-hour trip back home was really **exhausted / exhausting**.

3. We were all **shocked / shocking** when we heard the news.

4. I travel a lot and visit lots of **amazed / amazing** places.

5. The children were very **disappointed / disappointing** when we canceled the trip to the beach.

6. The boys were **frightened / frightening** when they saw someone outside the window.

7. One of the most **embarrassed / embarrassing** moments of my life was when I sang in front of the whole school.

**C. Make sentences using the adjectives below.**

| interested/interesting | relaxed/relaxing |
| --- | --- |
| tired/tiring  excited/exciting | annoyed/annoying |

# 2 Listening 🔊

**A. Discuss.**

- Have you ever been lost? If yes, how did you feel? What did you do?
- Have you ever heard a story about a missing person?

**B. You will hear Noreen telling a friend a story about a missing person. Before you listen, look at the picture and guess which of the words below will be mentioned.**

*Before you listen, try to imagine the situation and predict what the speakers are going to talk about.*

**TIP**

| rescue | police | helicopter | search party |
| --- | --- | --- | --- |
| disappear | news bulletin | description | |
| photograph | recognize | hospital | alive |

**C. Now listen and check your answers to B. Who was the missing person in the end?**

**D. Listen again and put the events in the correct order. Write 1-6.**

a. The driver called the police. ☐

b. Noreen changed her T-shirt. ☐

c. The driver realized a passenger wasn't missing. ☐

d. Noreen spoke to the driver. ☐

e. Noreen searched the area with the others. ☐

f. The bus stopped. ☐

# 3 Speaking
**Tell a story**

Talk in groups.
Go to page 134.

# 4 Writing A story

## A. Read the story and answer the following questions.

1. When did the story take place?
2. Where did the story take place?
3. Who are the main characters?
4. What tenses does the writer use throughout the story to narrate what happened?
5. How does Peter feel throughout the story?
6. Why do you think the writer uses direct speech?

## A chance meeting

Peter woke up early that Monday morning. He was feeling very confident about his job interview. He left his apartment, got a coffee from a coffee shop and went to the bus stop.

As he was waiting, he suddenly remembered that the buses and taxis were on strike. He was worried. "I can't be late!" he thought and started running. As he was passing by a trash can, he tried to get rid of his coffee cup, but he missed, and it landed on a man in a blue suit. He shouted "Sorry!" and continued running. He arrived at the offices of Gravener Inc. fifteen minutes late. Luckily, the manager was also late. However, when he walked in, Peter was surprised to see that he was wearing a blue suit with a huge coffee stain on it. "I hope he doesn't recognize me," Peter thought. Mr. Gravener sat down and said, "Coffee? Or maybe you had some earlier?" Peter felt so embarrassed!

Amazingly, Mr. Gravener had a great sense of humor. After Peter apologized about ten times, the interview started and in the end Peter even got the job. He felt so relieved!

## B. Read the note below and complete the sentences with an adverb or adverbial phrase. In some cases, there is more than one answer.

### Adverbs and adverbial phrases

When narrating, it is a good idea to use adverbs and adverbial phrases:

suddenly = all of a sudden
fortunately = luckily
unfortunately = unluckily
amazingly = to one's surprise
immediately = at once
then = after that
finally = in the end

1. We were walking in the forest when _____ we saw a snake. _____, it didn't come towards us. It disappeared seconds later.

2. My brother had his credit card with him yesterday, but _____ he lost it. When he realized it, he _____ called the bank to inform them.

3. The search party was searching for hours, but couldn't find the missing child. _____, a helicopter took part in the search and _____ the pilot found the child alive and well.

## C. Read the plan and TIP below. Then look at the pictures and the prompts on page 134 and write the story. Use the ideas you discussed in activity 3.

### Plan

**A story**

**INTRODUCTION**
Describe the setting of the story (time, place, weather, etc.) and introduce the main character(s).

**MAIN PART**
Mention what happened, what the character(s) did, saw, heard, etc. and how they felt.

**CONCLUSION**
Describe what happened in the end and how the character(s) felt.

**TIP**

When writing a story:
- write the events in chronological order. Use past tenses (*Past Simple and Past Progressive*).
- use time linkers (*when, while, as, as soon as, etc.*).
- use adverbs and adverbial phrases (*suddenly, fortunately, in the end, to my surprise, etc.*).
- use adjectives describing feelings (*surprised, frightened, upset, worried, etc.*).
- use direct speech, questions and exclamations to make your story more interesting.
- try to organize it into paragraphs using the plan above as a guide. However, sometimes you may not be able to follow it strictly. You may, for example, need to introduce a character or change the setting in the main part.

45

## Vocabulary

**A. Match.**

| | |
|---|---|
| **1.** grazed | **a.** tire |
| **2.** seat | **b.** seat |
| **3.** steering | **c.** space |
| **4.** passenger | **d.** wheel |
| **5.** parking | **e.** knee |
| **6.** news | **f.** belt |
| **7.** flat | **g.** bulletin |

**B. Choose a, b or c.**

**1.** The police asked the eyewitness for information, but he was too _____ to speak.
 **a.** shocking   **b.** frightened   **c.** relieved

**2.** Jason _____ over a cable and hurt his knee.
 **a.** tripped   **b.** knocked   **c.** pulled

**3. A:** Why is he honking his _____?
 **B:** Because there's a boy in the middle of the street.
 **a.** trunk   **b.** horn   **c.** engine

**4.** A lot of houses _____ during the earthquake.
 **a.** collapsed   **b.** injured   **c.** occurred

**5.** Mark broke his leg and now it's in _____.
 **a.** a bruise   **b.** stitches   **c.** a cast

**6.** Don't you know that it's _____ to run through a red light?
 **a.** embarrassing   **b.** enormous   **c.** illegal

**7.** Were you _____ when you had the accident?
 **a.** bleeding   **b.** speeding   **c.** spilling

## Grammar

**C. Complete the dialogue with the Past Progressive of the verbs in parentheses.**

**A:** What happened to you?

**B:** I had an accident.

**A:** Again? 1 _____ you _____ (ride) your bike in the rain?

**B:** No, I 2 _____ (not ride) my bike and I 3 _____ (not jog) in the rain either. It's funny, really. Last night, I 4 _____ (watch) TV while I 5 _____ (work out) on the treadmill. At around 11 p.m., Julie called.

**A:** And you answered the phone while you 6 _____ (run) on the treadmill. That's dangerous.

**B:** I know that now. Anyway, we 7 _____ (talk) and 8 _____ (laugh) about something funny when suddenly, my cell phone rang. I got so confused! I didn't know what to do, lost my balance and fell. You can imagine the rest.

**A:** Unbelievable!

**D. Use the prompts and the words given to write sentences.**

**1.** Rob / read / book / he / fall / asleep   **when**

_____

**2.** Jane and Tina / come over / they / hear / the news   **as soon as**

_____

**3.** I / make dinner / I / cut / finger   **while**

_____

**4.** We / drive / highway / we / run out of / gas   **as**

_____

**5.** Owen / clean / garage / Ben / watch / the news   **while**

_____

## Communication

**E. Match.**

**1.** How did the accident happen? ☐
**2.** Why did you walk all the way from downtown? ☐
**3.** Watch where you're going. ☐
**4.** I had a car accident this morning. ☐
**5.** What did the police officer tell you? ☐
**6.** Why are you exhausted? ☐

**a.** My car broke down and I didn't have money for a taxi.

**b.** Oh, no. Is there anything I can do to help?

**c.** Nothing. He just gave me a ticket.

**d.** I was driving in the rain when I lost control of the car.

**e.** I was running around all morning.

**f.** I'm sorry. I didn't see you coming.

## Self-assessment

**Read the following and check the appropriate boxes. For the points you are unsure of, refer back to the relevant sections in the module.**

### NOW I CAN...

| | |
|---|---|
| ▶ use the Past Progressive | ☐ |
| ▶ talk about accidents and injuries | ☐ |
| ▶ use language related to cars | ☐ |
| ▶ respond to bad news and show concern | ☐ |
| ▶ express criticism | ☐ |
| ▶ narrate past events/experiences | ☐ |
| ▶ talk about natural disasters | ☐ |
| ▶ use strategies to guess the meaning of unknown words | ☐ |
| ▶ describe my feelings | ☐ |
| ▶ write a story | ☐ |

**Task 3&4 p. 128**

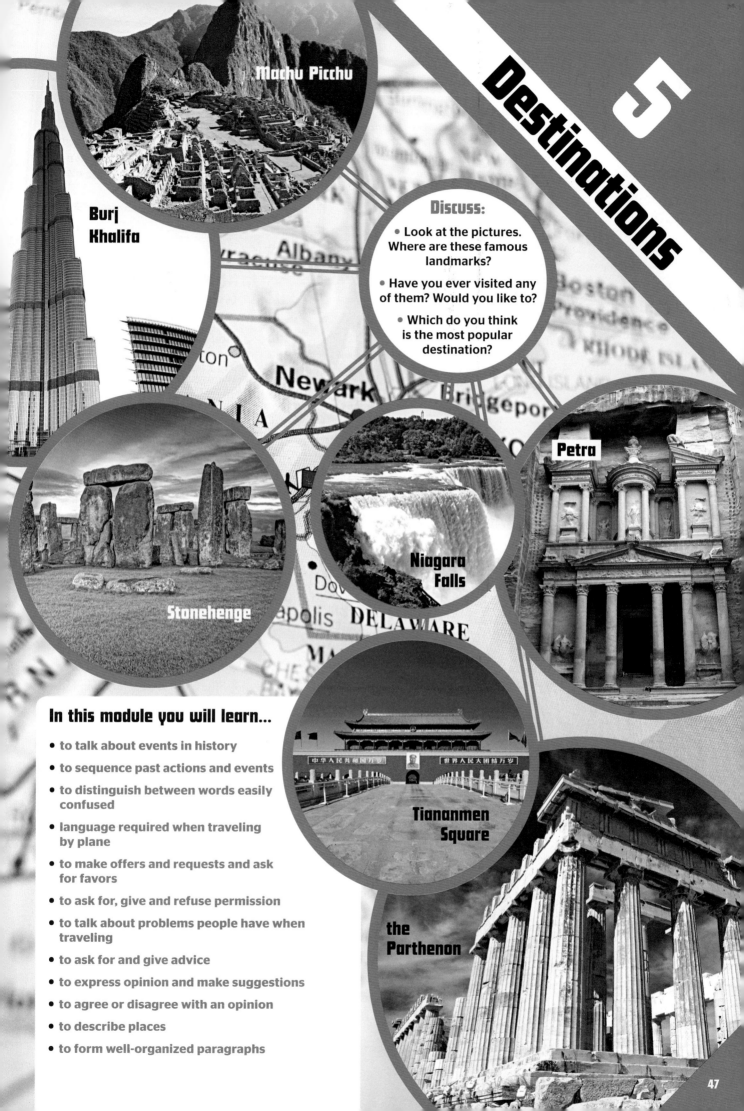

# 5 Destinations

Machu Picchu

Burj Khalifa

**Discuss:**

- Look at the pictures. Where are these famous landmarks?
- Have you ever visited any of them? Would you like to?
- Which do you think is the most popular destination?

Petra

Niagara Falls

Stonehenge

Tiananmen Square

the Parthenon

## In this module you will learn...

- to talk about events in history
- to sequence past actions and events
- to distinguish between words easily confused
- language required when traveling by plane
- to make offers and requests and ask for favors
- to ask for, give and refuse permission
- to talk about problems people have when traveling
- to ask for and give advice
- to express opinion and make suggestions
- to agree or disagree with an opinion
- to describe places
- to form well-organized paragraphs

5a

## 1 Reading

**A.** Look at the reward announcement on the right, the map and the newspaper clipping. What do you think the explorers tried to do? Did they succeed? Then listen, read and find out more about the expedition from Burke's journal.

**£2,000**
**REWARD**
for the
**FIRST SUCCESSFUL SOUTH-NORTH CROSSING OF THE CONTINENT**
issued by the
**South Australian Government**
**1859**

# The journal of Robert O'Hara Burke

*August 20th, 1860*

We set off early. A large crowd had gathered in Royal Park. The expedition consists of 19 men, 26 camels, 23 horses and 6 wagons. Around 20 tons of equipment and food for 2 years. We are all very excited.

*September 24th, 1860*

Loaded the camels with supplies and ordered the men to walk.

*November 2nd, 1860*

Have received word that John McDouall Stuart has taken up the challenge. I am worried about our slow progress. I had expected to travel faster. Stuart is a more experienced explorer than I am. My second-in-command, Wills, and I have decided to take the seven strongest men and horses, and continue quickly to Cooper's Creek. The others can catch up later.

*December 15th, 1860*

Everyone is safe and settled here in Cooper's Creek. Tomorrow, Wills and I are going to take some men and camels and go north, so Brahe is in charge until we return.

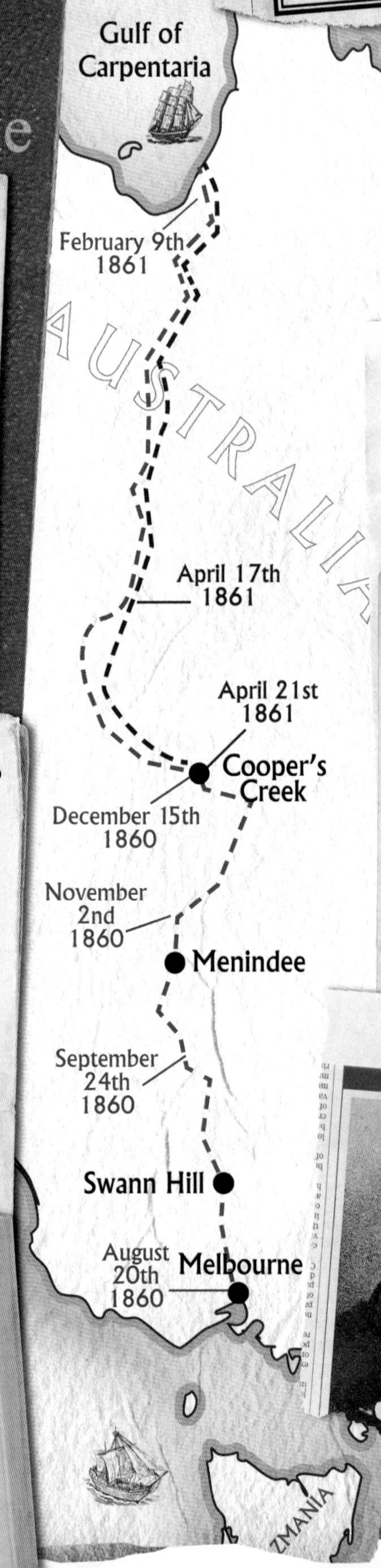

Gulf of Carpentaria
February 9th 1861
AUSTRALIA
April 17th 1861
April 21st 1861
Cooper's Creek
December 15th 1860
November 2nd 1860
Menindee
September 24th 1860
Swann Hill
August 20th 1860
Melbourne


*February 9th, 1861*

Reached the swamps today. Good weather. Journey was easier than I had thought. Finally, the Gulf of Carpentaria is very near. But we are running out of supplies.

*April 17th, 1861*

The return journey is getting harder. The heat is unbearable. We have lost a lot of camels and some good men. It's very sad.

*April 21st, 1861*

We finally managed to get to Cooper's Creek. Very disappointed. Brahe and the others left this morning. I had told them to wait 13 weeks. It's been 18. They left a note and buried some supplies under a tree.
It's late evening now. We are exhausted and very weak, so no hope of catching up with them.

The Sydney Morning Herald Aug 12th, 1862

### Tragic end for first explorers to cross the continent

An expedition returned yesterday with the bodies of Robert O'Hara Burke and William Wills. They died shortly after they had reached Cooper's Creek on their way home. They were the first Europeans

**B. Read the text again and answer the questions.**

1. Who is the leader of the expedition?
2. What supplies did they start their journey with?
3. Who else decided to cross the continent?
4. Why was Burke worried when he found out about Stuart?
5. Who arrived at Cooper's Creek first?
6. Why was the return journey difficult?
7. What did Brahe and the others do before they left Cooper's Creek?
8. Why couldn't Burke and Wills catch up with the others?

**C. Match the words/phrases below from the text with their meanings.**

| 1. set off ☐ | 6. unbearable ☐ |
|---|---|
| 2. crowd ☐ | 7. bury ☐ |
| 3. wagon ☐ | 8. weak ☐ |
| 4. supplies ☐ | 9. catch up (with sb.) ☐ |
| 5. challenge ☐ | |

a. a vehicle with four wheels, usually pulled by a horse
b. a difficult task that tests sb.'s ability
c. to begin a journey
d. to hide something in the ground
e. a large group of people who have gathered together
f. to reach sb. who is in front of you by going faster
g. not strong
h. so unpleasant or annoying that you can't accept it
i. food, clothes, medicine, etc. that are necessary for a particular purpose

**D. Discuss.**

• Do you know of any other famous explorers?
• What did they discover?

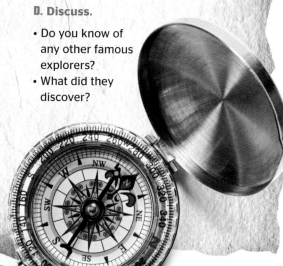

# 2 Vocabulary

**Complete the sentences with the correct form of the words in the boxes.**

explore    discover    invent

1. Percy Spencer _____ the first microwave oven in the 1940s.
2. The best way to _____ Barcelona is on foot.
3. William Herschel _____ the planet Uranus in 1781.

arrive    get    reach

4. When we finally _____ our destination, we were exhausted.
5. The train _____ at the station an hour late yesterday evening.
6. It took the explorers over five hours to _____ to the north coast of the island.

manage    succeed

7. Luckily, the rescue team _____ to find the missing girl.
8. In the end, the climbers _____ in reaching the top of the mountain.

# 3 Grammar Past Perfect Simple → *p. 143*

**A. Read the examples and find which actions happened first and which happened second. Then complete the rule.**

• They **had gathered** lots of supplies before they **left** Royal Park.
• By the time Burke **arrived** at Cooper's Creek, the others **had left**.
• We **went** to Royal Park yesterday. We **hadn't been** there before.

| Past Perfect Simple |
|---|
| _____ + past participle |
| We use the Past Perfect Simple for an action which had happened _____ another action in the past. |

**B. Complete with the Past Simple or the Past Perfect Simple of the verbs in parentheses.**

1. By the time the climbers _____ (reach) the top of the mountain, it _____ (start) raining.
2. When I _____ (arrive) at the office, I _____ (realize) that I _____ (not take) my cell phone with me.
3. My sister _____ (be) angry when she _____ (come) home because her car _____ (break down).
4. The men _____ (load) all the supplies on the ship before they _____ (leave) the port.
5. After Jamie and his friends _____ (explore) the old part of the town, they _____ (go) to the beach.

# 4 Speaking Information gap activity

**Talk in pairs.**

Student A go to page 134. Student B go to page 137.

# 1 Reading 🔊

## A. Discuss.

- Have you ever traveled by plane? If not, would you like to?
- Is there anything you like / don't like about flying?

## B. Listen and read. Where are the dialogues taking place? Match.

| | |
|---|---|
| Dialogue 1 | on a plane |
| Dialogue 2 | at a tourist information desk |
| Dialogue 3 | at a check-in desk |
| Dialogue 4 | at a car rental desk |

## C. Read again and answer the questions. Write A-H. You will not need to use all the letters.

1. Who asks for permission to do something?
2. Who asks to see some official documents?
3. Who offers to help another person?
4. Who requests some information?

### — 1 —

**A:** Good afternoon. Could I see your passport, please?

**B:** Certainly. Could I take this carry-on with me? I don't have anything else.

**A:** Sure, no problem.

**B:** Umm, can I ask you something else? Is there a delay?

**A:** No, the flight is running on time.

**B:** Good.

**A:** Here's your boarding pass. Check the TV monitors for your gate number. Enjoy your flight.

**B:** Thank you very much.

### — 2 —

**C:** Hello, I made a reservation for a mid-size.

**D:** Name, please?

**C:** Larry Kramer.

**D:** I'm sorry, but there's been a mix-up. There aren't any mid-size vehicles available here at the airport. However...

**C:** Excuse me? I made a reservation.

**D:** You can rent a larger vehicle at the same price.

**C:** OK, then. And I'd like insurance, too.

**D:** Of course. Can I see your driver's license?

**C:** Here you go.

### — 3 —

**E:** Good morning, sir. How may I help you?

**F:** Hello, I'd like some information, please. Where is the exhibition center?

**E:** Let me show you on this map. Here it is, on the other side of town.

**F:** Could you tell me how to get there from the airport?

**E:** Well, there's no bus service, but you can take the subway to Green Park station and walk from there. Or you can take a taxi.

**F:** OK. May I keep this map?

**E:** Yes, of course.

### — 4 —

**G:** Excuse me, will you please help me put my bag in the overhead compartment?

**H:** Of course. There you go. Anything else?

**G:** Yes, I have an aisle seat, but there's nobody by the window. Can I sit there?

**H:** I don't think there are any more passengers, so yes. Go ahead.

**G:** Thank you.

**H:** Would you like me to put your coat up there, too?

**G:** No, thanks. What time are we leaving?

**H:** We're taking off very soon.

# 2 Vocabulary

Complete the sentences with the words in the box.

| boarded | arrival | luggage | flight attendant | landed |
|---|---|---|---|---|

1. The _____ told us to fasten our seat belts.
2. We _____ at Terminal 1 and went to collect our bags.
3. You can see _____ and departure times and gate numbers on the TV monitors.
4. **A:** How much _____ are you checking in?
   **B:** Just this suitcase.
   **A:** Please put it on the conveyor belt.
5. Members of the cabin crew welcomed us and gave us newspapers as we _____ the plane.

NAME OF PASSENGER

FROM LONDON          LHR
TO WARSAW           WAW

CARRIER / FLIGHT    CLASS / DATE    TIME
282        M  16AUG  1040

GATE    GATE CLOSES    SEAT        SMOKE
17      1030          23D          XX

PCS.  CK. WT.   UNCK. WT.   SEQ. NO.
1 17   0 101

PASSENGER TICKET AND BAGGAGE CHECK

4A

## 3 Pronunciation 🔊

**A.** Look at the words below containing consonant clusters. Listen and repeat.

A consonant cluster is a group of two or three consonants that appear together in a word without any vowels between them. When reading, each letter within the cluster is pronounced individually.

problem    departure    information desk
conveyor belt    attendant    ground    compartment

**B.** Listen. Then practice saying these sentences.
*The train went through the tunnel at twenty to three.*
*On Friday Frank flew from Florence to Frankfurt.*
*Professor Blake took a plane from Bristol to Brazil.*

GATES

## 4 Grammar can, could, may, will, would → *p. 143*

**A.** Read the examples below. What do the words in blue express? Complete the rules using *requests*, *favors*, *permission* and *offers*.

- To ask for _____, use:

  Can I
  Could I  } take this on the plane?
  May I

  Yes, you can/may.
  Yes, of course. Go ahead.
  Certainly.
  Sure, no problem.

  No, you can't.
  I'm afraid not.
  No, sorry.

- To make requests and _____, use:

  Can I
  Could I  } see your boarding pass?
  May I    } help you?

- To make _____ and ask for _____, use:

  Can you
  Could you  } bring me a magazine?
  Will you   } lend me your cell phone?
  Would you

**B.** Think of four things you want from a classmate and four things you want from your teacher. Make requests or ask for permission.

❝ *Could I borrow a pen, please?*
*May I go out, please?* ❞

## 5 Listening 🔊

Listen to five short announcements and answer the questions.

1. Where do passengers on flight R217 to Calgary need to go?
2. What is happening soon?
3. What should the passengers do with their carry-on?
4. Why can't the plane land?
5. Has the plane landed or taken off?

## 6 Speaking Role play

Talk in groups of three using the ideas in the boxes.

**1.**
**Student A:** You are a check-in agent at the airport.
**Students B + C:** You are tourists checking in luggage.

see / passports?
have aisle or window seats?
put luggage / conveyor belt?
check in / this bag?
show me / carry-on?
take / laptop / on plane?
go / gate…

**2.**
**Student A:** You are a flight attendant.
**Students B + C:** You are passengers on a plane sitting next to each other.

have / water?
borrow / newspaper?
turn off / cell phone?
use / laptop / now?
get up?
fasten / seat belt?
put / carry-on / overhead compartment?
change / seats?

**3.**
**Student A:** You are a clerk at a tourist information desk.
**Students B + C:** You are tourists who have just landed at the airport.

help / you?
give us / information about…?
inform us / sights?
tell us / how / get there?
keep / brochure and map?
show us / bus stop?

## 1 Reading 🔊

**A. Discuss.**
- Do you like traveling?
- What modes of transportation do you usually use?
- Have you ever had problems while traveling?

**B. Listen, read and choose the best title.**

a. HOW TO TRAVEL SAFELY

b. TOP TIPS FOR A COMFORTABLE TRIP

c. WAYS TO MAKE YOUR VACATION ENJOYABLE

When you've planned a vacation, you don't want anything to ruin it, especially problems like jet lag and motion sickness. Whether you are traveling by plane, going on a cruise or taking a road trip, there are things you can do to prevent these problems.

I go on many overseas business trips and used to suffer badly from jet lag. I had difficulty adjusting to the new time zone after a long flight. I felt tired, sleepy and sometimes just plain sick for days. I've learned to deal with it and have managed to reduce the symptoms. Here's what I do. When I get on an airplane, I always set the time on my watch to the new time zone. I sleep according to my new schedule and not when my body feels like it, which means you should stay awake during the daytime. Food is important, too. Don't eat whatever they serve you. You should eat very little and lightly, and only when you're hungry, not because you're bored. I eat lots of fruit and drink plenty of water. Avoid coffee, tea or sodas with caffeine. They mess up your wake/sleep patterns and cause dehydration. Also, during the flight you should get up and walk around often. It helps.

Motion sickness is another problem some travelers have when traveling by car or boat, and can make them feel nauseous or dizzy. I used to take motion sickness medicine, but it wasn't a good solution because it didn't really work and it had a lot of side effects, including drowsiness. My advice? Well, even before you start feeling sick, you should try to focus on a distant point on the horizon, and avoid reading. Sitting in the front seat of a car can help and when on a boat, try to find a seat near the middle on the lower levels. I like drinking a lot of coffee, but I have noticed that it makes the symptoms worse, so you'd better avoid it. You shouldn't eat too much food, but the truth is that traveling on an empty stomach doesn't help much either. There is one thing that seems to work for me: green apples.

**C. Read again and write T for True or F for False.**

1. The writer doesn't have a serious problem with jet lag anymore. ☐
2. The writer starts following a new sleeping pattern days before his flight. ☐
3. According to the writer, eating during the flight reduces the symptoms of jet lag quickly. ☐
4. The writer stopped taking motion sickness medicine because it did more harm than good. ☐
5. According to the writer, your position and where you look affect motion sickness. ☐
6. The writer recommends green apples for motion sickness. ☐
7. According to the writer, coffee is bad for both jet lag and motion sickness. ☐

**D. Complete the sentences with the correct form of the words in capitals. All the missing words are in the text.**

1. Helen has been off work for two weeks because of _____.    **SICK**
2. The _____ from Paris to Los Angeles is boarding now.    **FLY**
3. I can't keep my eyes open. I'm very _____.    **SLEEP**
4. I'm having _____ finding a book to take with me on my trip.    **DIFFICULT**
5. Harry enjoys chatting with other _____ on a long journey.    **TRAVEL**
6. Have you found a _____ to the problem yet?    **SOLVE**
7. I'm telling you the _____. I'm not lying!    **TRUE**

**E. Discuss.**
- Have you ever experienced jet lag or motion sickness? What did you do?
- What sort of things can ruin a vacation?

# 2 Vocabulary

**A.** Look at the nouns below from the text. What other kinds of trips can you think of?

road trip     business trip

**B.** Read the note and find more compound nouns in the text in activity 1.

> A compound noun is a combination of two nouns that function as one word. The first noun defines the second one (e.g. bus stop = a stop for buses).

**C.** Match the nouns on the left with the nouns on the right to make compound nouns.

| | |
|---|---|
| 1. tourist | **a.** station |
| 2. travel | **b.** guide |
| 3. ski | **c.** agency |
| 4. train | **d.** shopping |
| 5. souvenir | **e.** destination |
| 6. tour | **f.** resort |

# 3 Grammar should, had better → p. 143

**A.** Read the examples. Are the statements 1-6 below true or false?

> I think you **should** book your vacation at the local travel agency.
>
> You **'d better** see a doctor about your headaches.
>
> You **shouldn't** drink so much caffeine. It's bad for you.
>
> You can borrow my car but you**'d better not** crash it.

1. *Should* and *had better* are followed by *to + base form*. ☐
2. We use *should* and *had better* to give advice. ☐
3. *Should* and *had better* refer to the past. ☐
4. The negative form of *should* and *had better* is formed by adding *not*. ☐
5. We use *should* and *had better* to give our opinion or make a suggestion. ☐
6. *Had better* can sometimes imply a warning. ☐

**B.** Rewrite the sentences using the words given.

1. Don't forget to set the alarm clock for tomorrow morning. (**had better**)
   You _____

2. It's a good idea to take sunscreen with you. (**should**)
   You _____

3. We have to leave for the station right now because we're going to miss our train. (**had better**)
   We _____

4. It's not a good idea to drive when you're feeling dizzy. (**should**)
   You _____

# 4 Listening 🔊

**A.** Discuss.

- Do you find packing for a trip stressful?
- How do you decide what to take and what not to take with you?

**B.** Listen to a radio show about packing. Which of the following are mentioned?

iron     chewing gum     towels     jewelry     cell phone     passport     sunscreen     shoes

**C.** Listen again and answer the questions.

1. How many suitcases do airlines lose every year?
2. Where shouldn't you put valuable items?
3. What can't you take with you to Singapore?
4. Where should you call before you leave?
5. What should you wear while you're traveling?

# 5 Speaking

Talk in pairs.

**Student A:** Imagine that this is the first time you are going to visit a friend (Student B) who lives in another city/country. Call him/her asking about the following:

> - What / weather / like?
> - What / pack?
> - bring / warm clothes?
> - What / do / while / there?
> - visit / museums?
> - anything else?

**Student B:** Imagine that your friend (Student A) who lives in another city/country is going to visit you for the first time. He/She calls you to ask for advice. Answer his/her questions, give advice and make suggestions.

66 *I have great news! I'm coming next week!*
   ***Really? I can't wait!***
*Listen, I have some questions for you. What's the weather like at this time of year?*
   *...*
*So, what should I pack?*
   ***You should definitely bring... and you'd better not forget...*** 99

# 1 Vocabulary

**A. Read the sentences 1-7 below and match the adjectives in bold with the definitions a-g.**

1. Don't forget to visit the old town where there are lots of **historic** buildings. ☐
2. Yesterday we explored a cave. It was an **unforgettable** experience. ☐
3. The locals are very kind and **hospitable** to tourists. ☐
4. Life in the village is so **peaceful**, nothing like the busy city. ☐
5. From my hotel window, I had a **breathtaking** view of the ancient ruins. ☐
6. The well-known island of Santorini in Greece has **unique** beaches, with white, red or even black sand. You've never seen anything like it! ☐
7. Take the ferry and go to the island. It's the **ideal** place for swimming. ☐

a. quiet and calm
b. that you cannot forget
c. being the only one of its kind; very unusual or special
d. friendly and welcoming to visitors
e. very beautiful, impressive or surprising
f. perfect, most suitable
g. important in history

**B. Use some of the adjectives to describe the place where you live.**

# 2 Listening 🔊

**A. Someone is calling a travel agency and is listening to a recorded message. Listen and check the topics that are mentioned.**

| | | |
|---|---|---|
| prices | weather | sightseeing |
| modes of transportation | food | hotels |
| time schedule | | |

**B. Listen again and answer the questions. Choose a, b or c.**

1. Which destination does the person calling want information about?
   a. Costa del Sol
   b. Morocco
   c. Tunisia

2. What does the day trip include?
   a. breakfast and dinner
   b. lunch and dinner
   c. lunch only

3. What can tourists do in the old city?
   a. They can visit a traditional market.
   b. They can visit a cave.
   c. Both of the above.

4. How much does each member of a group of five students have to pay?
   a. 30 euros
   b. 40 euros
   c. 50 euros

# 3 Speaking

**Talk in pairs. Imagine you work for a travel agency. Look at the three groups of people below and read the information given about the day trips. Discuss the day trips and decide which one is the most suitable for each group. Give reasons for your choices. Use the phrases in the box.**

**A family with young children**   **A group of teenagers**
**A group of elderly people**

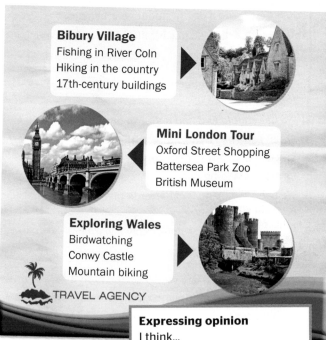

**Bibury Village**
Fishing in River Coln
Hiking in the country
17th-century buildings

**Mini London Tour**
Oxford Street Shopping
Battersea Park Zoo
British Museum

**Exploring Wales**
Birdwatching
Conwy Castle
Mountain biking

🌴 TRAVEL AGENCY

**❝** *I think Exploring Wales is more suitable for the family because...*
*I don't agree. I think the ideal day trip for them is... because...* **❞**

**Expressing opinion**
I think...
Personally, I believe...
In my opinion,...
They should/shouldn't...

**Agreeing/Disagreeing**
I agree/disagree with you.
I think so, too. / I don't think so.
You're right/wrong about that.
You have a point.
I'm not so sure about that.

# 4 Writing
## A description of a place

**A.** Read the description and find:

1. general information about the city.
2. three sights the writer recommends.
3. examples of factual information describing the sights.
4. the place the writer recommends for shopping.
5. some adjectives the writer uses to describe the place.
6. examples of the writer's opinion.

**B.** Read the note. Then find and underline the four topic sentences in the description.

### Topic sentences
The sentence that introduces the central idea of a paragraph is called a topic sentence. This is usually the first sentence in the paragraph. The other sentences develop the idea expressed in the topic sentence by expanding on it, giving examples or explaining it.

---

## Travel routes blog

HOME    PHOTOS    **FORUM**    SPECIAL OFFERS

**TravelMan**
✗✗✗✗
Messages: 483
Last post: 03/12/2012

My destinations
My maps
My photos

## Alexandria

Alexandria is one of the most impressive cities I've ever visited. Its nickname is the *Pearl of the Mediterranean*. It is the second largest city in Egypt and the country's main port.

Alexandria has many interesting sights as it is rich in history. One of the most well-known is Fort Qaitbey. This impressive 15th-century building stands on the site where one of the Seven Wonders of the Ancient World once stood – the famous Lighthouse of Alexandria. The Montazah Palace is also worth visiting. Its beautiful gardens and museum attract many tourists. Another top attraction is the Bibliotheca Alexandrina, a modern library with impressive architecture.

There are many things to do in Alexandria. The local open markets, or souks, are great for shopping as you can find some real bargains there. Also, go for a walk along the *Corniche*, the road which runs along the coast. Don't leave without trying the seafood in one of the many restaurants the city offers. You should also visit one of Alexandria's beautiful beaches.

Alexandria is a fascinating city and I had an unforgettable time there. Personally, I believe that everyone should visit this place at least once in their lifetime.

⟨ ▢ ⟩

---

**C.** Think of an interesting place you have visited and know well. Look at the questions below and make some notes.

What's the name of this place?
Where is it?
Is there anything special about it?
What are some of the most interesting sights?
Do you know anything about them?
Do they attract many tourists?
What can visitors do there?
What did you like the most about this place?
Is this place worth visiting?

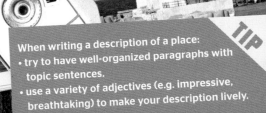

### TIP
When writing a description of a place:
• try to have well-organized paragraphs with topic sentences.
• use a variety of adjectives (e.g. impressive, breathtaking) to make your description lively.

**D.** Write a description of an interesting place you have visited and know well for a travel blog. Use your notes from activity C and follow the plan below.

## Plan
**A description of a place**

**INTRODUCTION**
**Give some general information about the place (name, location, most interesting features).**

**MAIN PART (2 PARAGRAPHS)**
**1 Mention some of the sights but don't just list them. Try to give some information about each sight. Use phrases like:**
   • *One of the most interesting/well-known places is...*
   • *There's also...*
   • *Another place worth visiting is...*
   • *... also attracts many tourists.*
   • *... is another top attraction.*
   • *You can also visit...*
   • *Don't forget to visit...*

**2 Mention what visitors can do there. Use phrases like:**
   • *You can...*
   • *Don't leave without...*
   • *Another thing you can do is...*
   • *You should also...*

**CONCLUSION**
**Give your general opinion of this place.**

55

## Vocabulary

**A. Circle the correct words.**

1. The plane **set off / took off** at 8 a.m. so we're landing in about two and a half hours.

2. This website explains how you can prevent motion **sickness / symptoms**.

3. There's a two-hour **delay / departure**, so I guess we can take a look around the stores.

4. During your stay in Mexico, don't forget to visit the **elderly / ancient** ruins of the old city of Palenque.

5. The cabin **crew / compartment** helped us with our carry-ons.

6. How long did it take the explorers to reach their **expedition / destination**?

7. What kind of food did they **solve / serve** on the plane?

**B. Complete with the words in the box.**

| supplies   difficulty   weak   official |
|:---:|
| hospitable   consists   deal |

1. Why do you have _____ sleeping? Is there any particular reason?

2. The palace _____ of three main buildings and an impressive garden.

3. I don't know how to _____ with this problem. Any ideas?

4. Before you leave on the camping trip, make sure you have enough _____ for three days.

5. Do I need to have any _____ documents with me?

6. We were amazed by how _____ the locals were. We really felt at home.

7. I have been sick for four days and now I feel very _____ .

## Grammar

**C. Rewrite the sentences using the words in parentheses.**

1. Is it OK to take a bottle of water on the plane? (could)

   _____

2. Do you mind helping me carry these bags? (can)

   _____

3. Don't leave your luggage here. (had better)

   _____

4. Is it possible for me to use your cell phone for a minute? (may)

   _____

5. Jake, please give me Maria's number. (will)

   _____

6. It is a good idea to avoid drinking coffee before your flight. (should)

   _____

**D. Complete with the Past Simple or the Past Perfect Simple of the verbs in parentheses.**

1. We _____ (check in) our luggage and then _____ (get) something to eat from a coffee shop. When we _____ (reach) the gate, we _____ (realize) we _____ (leave) our boarding passes at the coffee shop.

2. When we _____ (hear) the announcement about the delay, we _____ (not be) surprised. The information desk clerk _____ (inform) us about it.

3. By the time the flight attendants _____ (serve) the meal, most of the passengers _____ (fall) asleep.

4. The flight attendant _____ (ask) the passengers to fasten their seat belts after everyone _____ (board) the plane.

## Communication

**E. Complete the dialogue with the phrases in the box.**

| a. You should. |
|:---|
| b. You have a point. |
| c. Here you go. |
| d. Would you like me to show you? |
| e. Personally, I believe that's the best one. |

**A:** Can I take a look at that brochure you have there?

**B:** Sure. **1** _____

**A:** Thanks. Seattle, huh? My wife and I really want to go there.

**B:** **2** _____ But not in the winter, that's for sure. It doesn't stop raining.

**A:** **3** _____ Anyway, which attractions would you recommend?

**B:** There's Pioneer Square, Pike Place Market, Elliott Bay and of course the unbelievable Space Needle. **4** _____

**A:** Really?

**B:** Oh, yes. The view from up there is unique. You can check it out on the Net. The official website has a live camera and you can see the view from the top live!

**B:** Unbelievable!

**A:** **5** _____ I have my laptop with me.

**B:** Thanks.

## Self-assessment

**Read the following and check the appropriate boxes. For the points you are unsure of, refer back to the relevant sections in the module.**

### NOW I CAN...

- sequence past events and actions ☐
- use language required when traveling by plane ☐
- make offers, requests and ask for favors ☐
- ask for, give and refuse permission ☐
- ask for and give advice ☐
- express opinion and make suggestions ☐
- agree or disagree with an opinion ☐
- describe places ☐

no ice cap at the North Pole

a hotel on the moon

**Discuss:**

● Look at the pictures. Which of these exist now? Which do you see existing in the future?

flying cars

robots doing housework

houses using only solar power

holographic touchscreen

## In this module you will learn...

- to make predictions about the future
- to talk about various aspects of modern life (environmental issues, technology, space)
- to refer to the future using appropriate tenses
- to make offers, promises, on-the-spot decisions and requests
- to understand language used in advertisements
- to express ability
- to discuss the positive and negative aspects of an issue
- to express your opinion
- linking words/phrases used when listing or adding points
- to write a paragraph expressing your opinion

# 1 Reading 🔊

**A. Discuss.**

- What kind of environmental problems exist in your area/town/city?
- What do you do to protect the environment?

**B.** Read the text quickly and decide which futurologist's set of predictions is pessimistic and which is optimistic. Then listen, read and discuss your answers.

# Life on Earth

## a hundred years from now…

Since the 1950s, we have destroyed more than a third of the natural world. Our way of life has caused many serious environmental problems. We use huge quantities of natural resources and produce too much garbage. Pollution is affecting the climate and our planet is getting warmer. The question is: will things ever change for the better?

Some scientists are optimistic and believe that, with the help of science, today's environmental problems will disappear. Other scientists are pessimistic and believe that soon it will be too late to save the planet. We asked two futurologists their views about life on Earth a hundred years from now…

- The global population will increase and reach approximately 16 billion. There won't be enough food or resources for everyone.
- Temperatures will be higher than they are today. As a result, the Amazon rainforest will disappear completely and the area will turn into a desert.
- The ice at the poles will melt and sea levels will rise. As a result, some cities in coastal areas, as well as islands that are not very high above sea level, will flood and disappear.
- Air pollution will keep increasing and people will suffer from lung diseases because of the polluted air.

Jake Davis

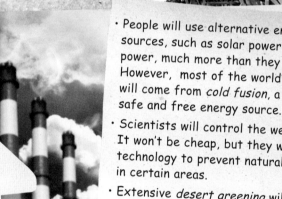

- People will use alternative energy sources, such as solar power and wind power, much more than they do today. However, most of the world's energy will come from *cold fusion*, a clean, safe and free energy source.
- Scientists will control the weather. It won't be cheap, but they will use technology to prevent natural disasters in certain areas.
- Extensive *desert greening* will take place and most of the world's deserts will turn into forests.

Nicola Brand

**C. Read again and complete the sentences.**

1. _____ exist because of our way of life.

2. Humans produce a lot of _____.

3. According to Davis, people won't have enough _____ or _____.

4. He also believes that _____, the ice at the poles, _____ and some islands won't exist 100 years from now.

5. According to Brand, scientists will manage to create better _____ conditions and as a result, we will have fewer _____.

6. She also believes that the Earth will be greener and will have fewer _____.

**D.** Look at the text again and find:

**synonyms for the words/phrases below.**

1. amounts = _____ (intro.)
2. trash = _____ (intro.)
3. opinions = _____ (intro.)
4. worldwide = _____ (Davis)
5. for example = _____ (Brand)

**antonyms for the words below.**

6. decrease ≠ _____ (Davis)
7. exactly ≠ _____ (Davis)
8. low ≠ _____ (Davis)
9. clean ≠ _____ (Davis)

> **TIP**
> You can increase your vocabulary by also learning synonyms and/or antonyms of new words.

## 2 Grammar The Future *will* → *p. 143*

**A.** Read the examples. Do the phrases in blue express plans or predictions about the future?

- I think I **will live** to be a hundred.
- The Maldives **will** soon **disappear** under water.
- In a hundred years, there **won't be** enough resources for everyone.

> We use the **Future *going to*** and the **Present Progressive** for future plans and arrangements.
> *I'm going to take part in "Plant-A-Tree Day" next Saturday.*
> *We're traveling to the Maldives this summer.*

**B.** Complete the sentences with the Future *will* of the verbs in the box.

| invent | do | increase | not be | become |
|--------|----|----------|--------|--------|
| | win | not do | get | |

1. Experts predict that e-waste, such as old gadgets, devices and appliances that people throw away, _____ in the next few years by 500%.

2. Charlie and Jill _____ probably _____ married next year. We just have to wait and see.

3. I think the Mariners _____ the game tonight. What do you think?

4. Scientists believe that there _____ any clean air to breathe in the future.

5. _____ scientists ever _____ flying cars?

6. I think you _____ a very successful businessman one day.

7. In the future, people _____ any housework. Robots _____ everything.

## 3 Listening 🔊

**A.** Have you ever heard of the term "carbon footprint"? Read the definition. What sort of activities increase your carbon footprint?

> **carbon footprint:** The amount of carbon dioxide ($CO_2$) a person produces by using fossil fuels or products that come from fossil fuels.

**B.** Read the questions in the quiz below and try to guess the answers.

1. A flight from London to Hong Kong has the same carbon footprint as using...
   - **a.** 100,000 plastic bags.
   - **b.** 200,000 plastic bags.
   - **c.** 300,000 plastic bags.

2. When shopping, which packaging should you choose for a smaller carbon footprint?
   - **a.** paper
   - **b.** plastic
   - **c.** cardboard

3. Which of the following increases your carbon footprint more than the others?
   - **a.** buying a flower out of season
   - **b.** buying locally produced food
   - **c.** buying 9 pounds of imported bananas

4. What produces 2 pounds of carbon dioxide?
   - **a.** traveling in a plane for 4 miles
   - **b.** using a computer for 32 hours
   - **c.** both a and b

**C.** Listen to two friends discussing the quiz above. How many questions did you answer correctly?

## 4 Speaking & Writing

**A.** Talk in pairs. Make predictions about the future in fifteen years' time. Talk about:

- your own future (family, job, etc.)
- the environment
- technology
- transportation

> 66 *What will your life be like in fifteen years' time?*
> **I think I will be married and have two kids.**
> *Will you still live here?*
> **I don't know. Perhaps I'll...** 99

**B.** Write some of your predictions about the future in fifteen years' time.

# 1 Reading

**A. Read the Internet advertisement below. Would you like to buy the product? Why / Why not?**

# SOLAR CAP!

## $45

### The ideal accessory for your outdoor excursions

During the day, it protects you from the sun, and at the same time it charges up. At night, it's perfect for finding your way in the dark, or simply reading a book.

The batteries last for up to 5 hours. Say goodbye to flashlights! The cap has 2 superbright LED lights and a dimmer switch so you can adjust the brightness.

**Get one for your next camping trip. You won't regret it.**

You will love our product! Not 100% satisfied? We will give you your money back. Guaranteed!

Allow 7 days for delivery.

**Order online now and get a 15% discount!**

---

**B. Below is a conversation between two friends. Listen and read. Is Phil going to buy the solar cap?**

**Phil**  Hey, Mark. Check out this cap. It looks really cool and useful. It has lights, and the batteries last for 5 hours.

**Mark**  You don't believe that, do you? Those companies just want to make money. There's no way the batteries can last for 5 hours.

**Phil**  It only costs $45, and I'm making plans to go camping. So, I'll get one.

**Mark**  OK, but I think you're making a mistake. You'll remember me when you try it out.

**Phil**  Don't worry. It's more likely you'll ask to borrow it...

**Mark**  We'll see.

**Phil**  I want to order online and get the discount. Will you lend me your credit card? I'll give you the money back as soon as I have the cash.

**Mark**  OK, but before you order, will you make sure that the site is safe?

**Phil**  Sure, I'll check it now. Look, it's safety-guaranteed.

**Mark**  All right. Go for it.

**C. Read the advertisement and the dialogue again and answer the questions.**

1. How long do the batteries last?
2. What does the advertisement promise to do if you buy the cap and realize you don't like it?
3. When do you receive a 15% discount?
4. Who doesn't believe the advertisement is telling the truth?
5. What does Phil think Mark will want to do when he gets the cap?
6. What does Phil ask Mark to do?
7. What does Mark ask Phil to do?
8. What decisions does Phil make while talking to Mark?

> Use **will/won't** to make offers, on-the-spot decisions, requests and promises.
> *I'll carry that for you.*
> *I like the red dress. I'll buy it.*
> *Will you show me how this works?*
> *I won't borrow your things again without asking first.*

**D. Discuss.**

• Have you ever bought anything over the Internet? What?

## 2 Vocabulary

Complete the sentences with the words in the box to form expressions with "make."

| mistakes | a decision | sense | sure | a difference | predictions | plans | promises | money |

1. Make _____ you read the advertisement carefully before you buy anything over the Internet.

2. Greg and Susan are making _____ for their wedding next year.

3. Everyone makes _____ when they're learning a new language. It's only natural.

4. My uncle is a successful businessman and makes lots of _____.

5. I just can't make _____. Where should I go on vacation? Mexico or Brazil?

6. It's difficult to make _____ about the weather.

7. I don't understand this sentence. It doesn't make _____.

8. Don't make _____ you can't keep.

9. Everyone should help protect the environment. Everyone can help make _____.

## 3 Grammar Time Clauses → p. 144

**A. Read the example and complete the rule.**

> As soon as they *deliver* the product, *I'll call* you.

| Time Clause (referring to the future) | Main Clause |
|---|---|
| when, after, before, until, as soon as<br>+ _____ Simple | Future *will* |

**B. Complete with the Present Simple or the Future *will* of the verbs in parentheses.**

1. **A:** Hey, Tony. Are you going to work?

   **B:** Yes, I am, Jake.

   **A:** 1 _____ (you / check) the engine of my car before you 2 _____ (leave)? It was making a funny noise last night.

   **B:** I don't really have time. I 3 _____ (do) it as soon as I 4 _____ (get) home from work.

   **A:** Don't worry about it. I 5 _____ (ask) my cousin who knows about cars to come over. Maybe I 6 _____ (take) him out to lunch when he 7 _____ (finish).

2. **A:** I want to buy something over the Internet, but I've never done it before. 8 _____ (you / help) me, please?

   **B:** I 9 _____ (show) you how to do it after I 10 _____ (do) the dishes.

   **A:** Oh, come on, Kate. That 11 _____ (take) you more than half an hour.

   **B:** Don't worry. I 12 _____ (not be) long.

   **A:** All right. I 13 _____ (continue) searching on the Net until you 14 _____ (join) me.

## 4 Pronunciation 🔊

**A. Listen and repeat. Notice the difference in pronunciation.**

**a. I go** to college.     **b. I'll go** to college.

**B. Read the pairs of sentences below aloud. Then listen and check your pronunciation.**

1.
a. We have dinner at 6 p.m.     b. We'll have dinner at 6 p.m.
2.
a. I help my brother with his homework.     b. I'll help my brother with his homework.
3.
a. You love my desserts.     b. You'll love my desserts.

**C. Listen and circle what you hear.**

| 1. | | 3. | |
|---|---|---|---|
| a. We | b. We'll | a. They | b. They'll |
| 2. | | 4. | |
| a. I | b. I'll | a. I | b. I'll |

## 5 Speaking Role play

Talk in pairs. Act out some of the situations below. Try to use the Future *will* as much as possible.

Student A is organizing a barbecue and needs help. Student B offers to help.

Student A owes Student B some money, but can't pay him/her back until next week.

Student A has to go to the airport. Student B is free and offers to take him/her.

Student A wants to borrow Student B's laptop, but Student B is worried Student A will break it.

Student A finds a new gadget on the Net and decides to buy it. Student B thinks it isn't a good idea.

# 1 Reading 🔊

**A. Discuss.**

• Would you like to travel to space?
• Do you think people will travel to space as tourists soon?

**B. Read the text quickly and match the questions a-f with the paragraphs 1-5. There is one extra question which you do not need to use. Then listen and check your answers.**

a. Why do people want to travel to space?
b. What do we mean by "space tourism"?
c. Why is space tourism so expensive?
d. Do space tourists need to train before their journey?
e. Is space tourism only for millionaires?
f. Is the trip dangerous?

# SPACE TOURISM

Is it a distant dream for the very wealthy or something that we will all be able to enjoy in the future? We were able to interview a representative from ExploreSpace, Jeff Hilburn, and get some answers.

**1** ☐ There are two types: orbital and sub-orbital, but at present only orbital is available. Russian space companies offer individuals the opportunity to travel on one of their spacecraft for up to 2 weeks in orbit around the Earth. Sub-orbital flights will be available soon and will take space tourists directly outside the Earth's atmosphere, where they will stay for ten minutes or so.

**2** ☐ For two reasons: the spectacular view and zero gravity. Looking down on our beautiful blue planet from space is a sight that only few people have ever witnessed. Also, imagine looking out into space where the stars are closer and brighter than when you're on Earth. It's something the majority of people want to experience along with weightlessness. Floating around is simply fun!

**3** ☐ Well, they certainly don't need to be professional astronauts. However, both types of space tourism require training. For orbital space flight, space tourists need at least six months and for sub-orbital not more than a week. Also, space travelers will need to have medical check-ups.

**4** ☐ It's for those who can afford it. At the moment, orbital space tourism costs over $30 million for a two-week experience, and only one tourist is able to travel with the Russian team every year. When the sub-orbital flights become available, they will cost about $200,000. Some space tourism companies hope that they will be able to lower the price to $100,000.

**5** ☐ Space travel has come a long way and technology has improved, so I believe it is safe enough to introduce to the public. However, it is not without risk. People who are eager to find out what it's like in space don't mind taking that risk. For them, it's a dream come true.

62 miles (boundary of space)

orbital

sub-orbital

**C. Read again and write T for True or F for False.**

1. One of the differences between orbital and sub-orbital space tourism is the time they last. ☐
2. The stars seem different when you look at them from space. ☐
3. Sub-orbital space tourism will require one week to six months of training. ☐
4. Russia offers a member of the public one orbital trip a year. ☐
5. Space tourism companies are hoping that orbital flights will soon cost $100,000. ☐
6. Jeff Hilburn believes that space travel has made great progress but should only be available to astronauts. ☐

**D. Find words/phrases in the text that mean the same as the following:**

1. chance (para. 1)
2. very impressive, breathtaking (para. 2)
3. the largest part of a group (para. 2)
4. to move slowly in the air (para. 2)
5. to need sth. (para. 3)
6. to have enough money to pay for sth. (para. 4)
7. to make progress (para. 5)
8. all ordinary people (para. 5)
9. the possibility of sth. bad happening (para. 5)
10. very interested and wanting very much to do sth. (para. 5)

**E. Discuss.**

• Do you think space tourism is worth the money?

# 2 Vocabulary

**Complete the sentences with the phrases in the box.**

> at last    at least    at the beginning
> at the end    at once    at present
> at first    at the latest    at the moment

1. All visitors should leave the space center by 5:15 _____, because we are closing.
2. For a good telescope, you need to pay _____ $150. Don't get anything cheaper.
3. _____ of the race, Brad was doing well, but _____ of the race, he was exhausted and almost didn't finish.
4. Linda will call you later, OK? She's watching a documentary about space exploration _____.
5. _____, I thought my brother was joking, but then I realized that he was serious.
6. _____, after four days, the scientists were able to find what was polluting the river.
7. _____, children are not allowed on space flights.
8. I need to speak to Mary immediately. Tell her to come here _____!

> at the beginning/end of = the time when sth. begins/ends
> in the beginning = at first
> in the end = finally

# 3 Grammar be able to → *p. 144*

**A. Read the examples below and answer the questions.**

1. No one **is able to** live on Mars.
2. People **aren't able to** predict the future.
3. It was a successful trip. Scientists **were able to** collect rocks from the bottom of the ocean.
4. Astronauts **weren't able to** travel to the moon a century ago.
5. We **will be able to** go to the moon for a vacation very soon.

a. Which sentence(s) express(es) ability or inability in the present?
b. Which sentence(s) express(es) ability or inability in the past?
c. Which sentence(s) express(es) ability in the future?
d. Which phrase can we replace with "can"?
e. Which phrase can we replace with "couldn't"?
f. Which phrase can we replace with "can't"?

> **Could** expresses general ability in the past.
> **Was/were able to** expresses ability in a particular situation in the past.
> I *could* swim at the age of five.
> The rescue team *was able to* save the boy who fell into the river.
> ~~The rescue team could save the boy who fell into the river.~~

**B. Rewrite the sentences using the correct form of *be able to*.**

1. Two years ago, Jack couldn't speak a word of Spanish.

   _____

2. In a few years' time, the team will have the ability to take part in the championship.

   _____

3. I'm very upset and I can't talk to you right now.

   _____

4. While Sue was in London, she had the ability to do a business course.

   _____

# 4 Listening 🔊

**Listen to a radio interview with an expert on Mars and answer the questions. Choose a or b.**

1. When did the first probe land on Mars?
   a. in 1970
   b. in 1976
2. Where is the *Viking 1 Lander* now?
   a. on Mars
   b. on Earth
3. What is a sol?
   a. a Martian day
   b. a Martian year
4. Which of the two is longer?
   a. an Earth year
   b. a Martian year
5. What is *terraforming*?
   a. looking for life on a planet
   b. turning a planet into a place where humans can live

# 5 Speaking & Writing

**Work in groups. Make a list of things you think we will be able to do 100 years from now which are not possible today. Then compare lists with other groups. Are any of your ideas similar?**

66 *We will be able to speak and understand all languages that exist.* 99

# 1 Vocabulary

**A.** Read the note. Which adjectives can you form using the words below?

> A lot of adjectives are formed by adding a suffix (-ful, -less) to a verb or noun.

beauty    peace    home    help

**B.** Read the speech bubbles. What's the difference between the adjectives *careful* and *careless*?

Be careful with those dishes!

Oops! I'm so careless sometimes.

**C.** Complete with the correct form of the words in capitals.

**1.** The map you gave us was very _____ and we didn't get lost.          **USE**

**2.** Most snakes are _____, but people are still afraid of them.          **HARM**

**3.** Richards is a very _____ player. I think he'll become one of the best on the team.          **SKILL**

**4.** Agatha Christie was a very _____ writer of crime novels.          **SUCCESS**

**5.** I always thought this painting was worth a lot of money, but in actual fact it's _____!          **WORTH**

**6.** Smoking is _____ to your health and to the health of those around you.          **HARM**

**7.** Since I bought a smartphone, my camera seems _____. I take all my photos with my phone now.          **USE**

# 2 Listening & Speaking 🔊

**A.** Listen to four people talking about the Internet and match the names with the statements a-e. There is one extra statement which you do not need to use.

Beth

   Jack

Julie

   Frank

**a.** The Internet can be dangerous.

**b.** The Internet is making our brains lazy.

**c.** The Internet has more advantages than disadvantages.

**d.** I think the Internet is convenient.

**e.** I think the Internet is bad for my health.

**B.** Talk in groups of four. Discuss the positive and negative aspects of the Internet using the ideas and vocabulary in the boxes. Keep notes and then use your notes to present your arguments to the class. Give reasons for your answers.

**Talk about:**
- what people use it for
- how it has improved our lives
- the dangers it involves
- whether it's harmful to people's health

| | |
|---|---|
| get informed | steal personal details |
| educational purposes | inappropriate sites |
| save time | false information |
| have (easy) access to | become addicted |
| viruses | waste time |
| hackers | not socialize |

❝ Personally, I believe...
   I disagree. In my opinion,...
*You have a point. I also think that...*
   *The way I see it...* ❞

- Think of as many ideas as you can.
- Express your opinion and give reasons.
- Don't worry if you disagree with someone else. Remember, no answer is right or wrong, as long as it is justified.

TIP

# 3 Writing A paragraph expressing an opinion

## A. Discuss.

• Do you think a GPS device is useful? Why?/Why not?

## B. Read the texts below and answer the questions.

1. In which text does the writer have a positive opinion about GPS devices? How can you tell?
2. Which words/phrases do the writers use to list their points? Underline them.
3. Which phrases do the writers use to state their final opinion? Circle them.

http://www.yourviews.com/search/

## YOUR VIEWS:

Home   Forum   Maps   Contact

### How useful are GPS devices?

**Peter Jefferson**
**Age: 39**

*Messages: 1082*

It is true that GPS devices are very popular nowadays, but in my opinion, life was better without them. To begin with, I think they are dangerous. A GPS distracts you from your driving as you have to pay attention to the directions it's giving and check the screen. Secondly, there's that annoying voice. I can't stand listening to it. What's more, you need to spend money updating it often, so that you have the latest map of your city/country with the new streets or the streets that have closed down, for example. Lastly, people rely on this device too much and when it fails for some reason, they feel totally helpless. The way I see it, there's not much point in owning a GPS. What's wrong with a good old map and road signs?

*Posted 09:23*

**John Bennett**
**Age: 22**

*Messages: 47*

The GPS is a wonderful invention that helps drivers get to different locations. It has many advantages. Firstly, it is easier to use and more reliable than a regular map, so you hardly ever get lost. Also, you don't really have to look at the screen. You can just listen to the voice. I love downloading famous people's voices for my device. In addition, a GPS chooses the best and quickest route to a destination, so you actually save time. What is more, it can give you valuable information like traffic updates, and even where the nearest supermarket or hotel is. Finally, you can use a GPS for playing MP3 files, or even for looking at photos. Personally, I believe that a GPS device is something useful that all drivers should have.

*Posted 12:47*

## C. Read the note and complete the text on the right.

### Linking words/phrases

When you want to list or add points, use the linking words/phrases below:

Firstly, / First of all, / To begin with,

↓

Secondly, / Also, / In addition, / What is more,

↓

Finally, / Lastly,

---

In my opinion, the MP4 player is not a very useful invention.
**1** _____ of all, you can listen to music on your cell phone these days so you don't really need an MP4 player. What is **2** _____, they are very small devices and you can lose or break them easily. They are **3** _____ pretty expensive, and become outdated very quickly. **4** _____, they don't usually connect to the Internet, so you can't download songs directly, something which is not very practical.

## D. Imagine that a magazine has asked you to write your opinion about the Internet. Write a paragraph using the ideas in activity 2B.

## Vocabulary

**A. Choose a, b or c.**

1. It is extremely important to find ____ energy sources.
   a. ordinary     b. spectacular     c. alternative

2. Don't listen to him. He always makes ____ he can't keep.
   a. predictions     b. mistakes     c. promises

3. You need to finish your assignment by Monday ____, otherwise you'll get a D.
   a. at least     b. at last     c. at the latest

4. How much money do you ____ Tina?
   a. own     b. afford     c. owe

5. Almost everyone has ____ to the Internet nowadays.
   a. access     b. power     c. attention

6. You will soon need to get rid of this cell phone. It's so ____.
   a. practical     b. addicted     c. outdated

**B. Complete with adjectives ending in -ful or -less.**

1. I really like this painting. It's very _____. **COLOR**

2. People can be so _____! They throw garbage everywhere. **CARE**

3. I can't eat this food. It's completely _____. **TASTE**

4. I couldn't find my hotel, but luckily some very _____ locals gave me directions. **HELP**

5. Eating too much candy can be _____ to your health. **HARM**

6. Alex has become a _____ driver. **SKILL**

## Grammar

**C. Join the following sentences using the words in parentheses. Make all the necessary changes.**

1. First I will wash all the plastic bottles. Then I will recycle them. (as soon as)

   _____

2. Type in the address on the GPS. Then it will give you the quickest route. (after)

   _____

3. First I'll fix the computer screen for you. Then I'll leave. (before)

   _____

4. Jack will get a job. Then he will pay Tony back. (when)

   _____

**D. Choose a, b or c.**

1. Soon, it ____ possible for everyone to travel to space.
   a. going to be     b. will be     c. will be able to

2. You ____ use the printer today. It doesn't work.
   a. won't     b. don't     c. won't be able to

3. ____ me your GPS? I need to find the quickest route to a place.
   a. Do you lend     b. Will you lend     c. Are you lending

4. I like this telescope. I think I ____ it.
   a. will be able to buy     b. will buy     c. buy

5. Three years ago, Mark ____ speak a word of French.
   a. can't     b. won't be able to     c. wasn't able to

6. When the scientist ____ his talk on space tourism, he'll answer your questions.
   a. finishes     b. will finish     c. is going to finish

## Communication

**E. Complete the dialogue with the phrases a-e.**

> a. The way I see it
> b. What is more
> c. I can't see much point in them
> d. To begin with
> e. Go for it then

**A:** Hey, why don't you have any e-books on your tablet?

**B:** To tell you the truth, 1 ____.

**A:** Why do you say that?

**B:** Well, for many reasons. 2 ____, I like holding the book in my hands and turning the pages.

**A:** But you can hold the tablet and turn the pages on the screen. 3 ____, you can save many books on just one device.

**B:** Yeah, but it's not the same. 4 ____, there's nothing like the real thing.

**A:** You're old-fashioned.

**B:** Maybe.

**A:** Take a look at this website. Their e-books are really cheap. I think I'll buy one or two.

**B:** 5 ____.

## Self-assessment

**Read the following and check the appropriate boxes. For the points you are unsure of, refer back to the relevant sections in the module.**

### NOW I CAN...

- make predictions about the future ☐
- refer to the future using appropriate tenses ☐
- make offers, promises, on-the-spot decisions and requests ☐
- express ability ☐
- discuss the positive and negative aspects of an issue ☐
- express my opinion ☐
- use linking words/phrases when listing or adding points ☐
- write a paragraph expressing my opinion ☐

Task 5&6 p. 129

summer winter

jogging

gym

book

movie

theme park

museum

a night in

a night out

**Discuss:**

- Look at the pictures. Which of the two options do you prefer and why?
- Do you find it easy to make choices?

## In this module you will learn...

- to express possibility and certainty in the present and future
- to express preference
- to understand signs and messages
- to talk about conditions and their results
- to compare and contrast people and situations
- to talk about lifestyle changes and intentions
- to form opposites using prefixes (un-, dis-)
- to take notes
- to invite and accept or refuse an invitation
- to make suggestions and arrangements
- to write an e-mail based on prompts

# 7a

## 1 Reading 🔊

**A. Listen, read and match the dialogues with the statements.**

a. Both people decide to go somewhere.
b. Both people decide not to go somewhere.
c. One of the people decides to go somewhere.

**1. Lee** Hey, Mike. I might go to the sculpture exhibition tomorrow. Are you interested?

**Mike** Tomorrow? No, thanks. It's likely to be really crowded on a Saturday. I'd rather go on a different day, when it's quiet.

**Lee** You may be right. Perhaps we could go on Monday. It's my day off.

**Mike** Yes, it will definitely be quieter on Monday. Are you sure it's open then?

**Lee** I'm positive. Look here, it says so on this flyer.

**Mike** OK, good. Do you want me to pick you up on Monday morning?

**Lee** I think I might go on my bicycle.

**Mike** OK, let me know when you make up your mind.

**2. Tina** Hey, look at what's opened at the Golden Mall. I've never been ice skating before. Why don't we give it a try?

**Mary** No way. You know how clumsy I am. I will most likely fall over the minute I step onto the rink!

**Tina** Oh, come on. It'll be fun! There will probably be instructors there who can show us how to skate.

**Mary** Do you think it might be cold in there?

**Tina** I'm sure you'll survive.

**Mary** I don't know. I also have studying to do.

**Tina** Fine. I give up. Do as you please. I'm thinking of checking it out later today. Call me if you change your mind.

**3. Ted** I think that Jerry Watson will win the race today.

**Brad** I'm not so sure. Don't forget about Massimo Langella. There's a good chance he will do very well, too.

**Ted** I doubt it. He drives better in dry conditions, and it may rain later.

**Brad** That's true. So, do you feel like going down to the race track?

**Ted** No, I'd prefer to watch the race from the comfort of my own home. A few friends might drop by later. You're welcome to join us, too.

**Brad** No, I'd like to watch it up close and enjoy the whole atmosphere.

**Ted** In the rain? It'll be nice and dry at my place. What's more, I'm going to order pizzas. It's up to you.

**Brad** Pizzas? In that case, count me in!

**B. Match the phrases from the dialogues with their synonyms.**

1. I'd rather
2. I'm positive
3. I give up
4. I doubt it
5. It's up to you

a. I don't think so
b. I'm certain
c. It's your choice
d. I'd prefer
e. I'm going to stop trying

6. make up your mind
7. do as you please
8. feel like
9. drop by
10. count me in

f. want
g. include me
h. do whatever you like
i. visit someone or a place
j. decide about something

**C. Read again and find sentences to prove the following:**

**Dialogue 1**

1. Saturday is not a good day to visit the museum.
2. The museum is open on Mondays.
3. Lee hasn't decided how he's going to get to the museum for sure.

**Dialogue 2**

4. Mary thinks she'll have an accident while ice skating.
5. Tina stops trying to persuade Mary.

**Dialogue 3**

6. Ted and Brad disagree with each other.
7. Ted invites Brad to his house.
8. Brad changes his mind about something.

# 2 Grammar may, might, could → *p. 144*

**A.** Read the examples below from the dialogues. What do the words in blue express in all cases? Choose a, b or c.

> • You **may** be right.
> • I **might** go on my bicycle.
> • We **could** go on Monday.

**a.** Something that is likely to happen.

**b.** Something that is not likely to happen.

**c.** Something that will certainly happen.

> We use **may not / might not** to express improbability in the present or future. **Could not** expresses lack of ability.
> *Susan may not / might not go out tonight, but she isn't sure yet. She couldn't find a babysitter.*

**B.** Rewrite the sentences using the words given.

1. Perhaps the Bears will lose this game.   (might)

   _____

2. It's likely that we will go to Spain on vacation.   (may)

   _____

3. It is possible that Ted won't enjoy car racing.   (might)

   _____

4. I'm thinking of buying a car, but I haven't made up my mind yet.   (may)

   _____

5. I don't think Linda will come with us tomorrow.   (may)

   _____

6. The coffee shop is likely to be noisy at this time of day.   (could)

   _____

# 3 Listening & Speaking ◀))

**A.** Look at the flyers below and listen to two friends, Eddie and Mark, talking. Which event do they decide to go to?

ALL STAR BOWLING ALLEY TOURNAMENT

contests for beginners, kids and experts

9 p.m. Saturday March 16th

Free entry!

HAYFIELD GALLERY
Glenn Hunt
wildlife photographer of the year

Over 200 photos from his 20-year career

Tickets $15 | Closed on Sundays

The Regal Movie Theater presents the

14TH SILENT MOVIE FESTIVAL

March 16th, 17th
Showings: 2p.m., 5p.m. & 8p.m.
Tickets $10

SUPER CUP FINAL      Saturday, March 16th

Falmouth United VS. Leyton Town

kick-off **7:45p.m.**
Tickets $45      from Kingston Stadium or online www.supercupfinaltickets.net

**B.** Listen again and write T for True or F for False.

1. There is information about the events in the newspaper. ☐
2. They think the tickets for the game are too expensive. ☐
3. They think United will win the game. ☐
4. Eddie isn't very good at bowling anymore. ☐
5. Mark's sister finds black-and-white movies boring. ☐
6. Eddie and Mark don't know who Glenn Hunt is. ☐
7. Mark's sister may not go out for dinner with them. ☐

**C.** Look at the flyers above again. In pairs, discuss the events and decide which of them you'd like to go to.

> 66 *So, what are you doing this weekend?*
> ***I may/might go... Do you want to go together?***
> *Not really. It'll probably be boring. Let's do something else.*
> ***OK. Do you feel like going...? It may/might/could be interesting.***
> *I doubt it. I'd rather go / I'd prefer to go... I'm sure it'll be fun.* 99

# 1 Reading

**A. Read the signs and messages below and choose the best explanation for each.**

## LOST
Answers to the name Twinkle

Please call 555-879-8686

**1**

**STARSHIP**

HEIGHT RESTRICTIONS:

minimum: 40 inches

Check before you pay for ride

**2**

## Admission is free

But remember: your donation is what keeps us open

Recommended:

$7      €6      £5

Thank you for your support

**3**

**4**

## → HEATHROW Express
Non-stop from Heathrow Airport to Central London

### SPECIAL DEAL!
Heathrow Express Carnet
12 single tickets for the price of 11
(valid for a year)

£198

**5** **FIRE**
IN CASE OF FIRE BREAK THE GLASS ↓

**6**

Next-day delivery $6.99

Standard delivery FREE
(3-5 business days)

Please ring bell for attention **7**

**Complaints or comments?**
Please fill out form anonymously

**8**

1. **a.** If you find Twinkle, you should call 555-879-8686.
   **b.** You should call 555-879-8686 if you want to find out more about Twinkle.
   **c.** If you call 555-879-8686, you will help find Twinkle.

2. **a.** Children over 40 inches tall are not allowed on the ride.
   **b.** Children can't go on the ride if they are taller than the minimum height.
   **c.** Children have to be at least 40 inches tall to go on the ride.

3. **a.** Everyone has to pay to enter.
   **b.** Ticket prices depend on the country you are from.
   **c.** It's up to you whether you give money or not.

4. **a.** The Heathrow Express Carnet is valid for 11 journeys.
   **b.** You have to use the Heathrow Express Carnet within the year.
   **c.** It's cheaper to get 12 single tickets than the Heathrow Express Carnet.

5. **a.** Be careful. The glass might break when there is a fire.
   **b.** You should break the glass if there is a fire.
   **c.** If you break the glass, you may cause a fire.

6. **a.** People who pay extra receive the item sooner.
   **b.** If you pay $6.99, you will receive the item in 3-5 business days.
   **c.** Everyone has to pay extra for delivery.

7. **a.** If you think someone needs your attention, ring the bell.
   **b.** Ringing the bell won't help you get someone's attention.
   **c.** When you need to get someone's attention, you should ring the bell.

8. **a.** Satisfied customers don't need to fill out the form.
   **b.** Every customer has to fill out the form.
   **c.** Only customers who want to remain anonymous can fill out the form.

**B. Read the signs and messages again. Where would you most likely find them? Discuss.**

## 2 Listening 🔊

Listen to three short dialogues. Which sign/ message from activity 1 are the people looking at?

Dialogue 1 _____

Dialogue 2 _____

Dialogue 3 _____

## 3 Grammar Conditional Sentences Type 1, if vs. when → *p. 144*

**A.** Read the examples and complete the rule.

- If you **buy** two products, you **will get** a third one for free.
- If you **want** to complain, you **should fill** out the form.
- If Betty **needs** help, **tell** her to ask at the information desk.

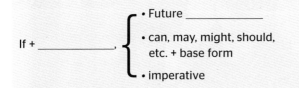

If + _____, {
- Future _____
- can, may, might, should, etc. + base form
- imperative
}

**B.** Read the examples and answer the questions.

- John: I'll order something **if** I get hungry.
- Lisa: I'll order something **when** I get hungry.

1. Do the sentences refer to the present/future or past?
2. Is John sure he will get hungry?
3. Who is sure that he/she will get hungry?

**C.** Circle the correct words and complete the boxes with *if* or *when*.

1. **A:** What are you doing tomorrow?

   **B:** Well, I'm going on a day trip with my cousin Richard. [     ] the weather **is / will be** good, we **go / may go** hiking, too. Do you want to join us?

   **A:** I'd love to, but my brother is coming to visit me tomorrow.

   **B:** Tell him to come along, too.

   **A:** OK, I **ask / 'll ask** him [     ] he arrives, and I'll let you know.

   **B:** Sure.

2. **A:** Hi, it's Jamie. Is Danny there?

   **B:** No, he isn't. He's in the garage. [     ] he **gets / will get** back, I **tell / 'll tell** him to give you a call. OK, Jamie?

   **A:** OK, but [     ] he **tries / will try** to call me and I'm not home, he **calls / should call** me on my cell phone, because I'm going out later.

   **B:** OK, then.

## 4 Intonation 🔊

Listen and repeat. Notice the intonation and rhythm.

1. If you aren't satisfied, you should talk to the manager.
2. If we book the tickets online, we will get a discount.
3. If you see a fire, call the fire department.
4. If it doesn't rain, we may go swimming.
5. If they go to the theme park, they will go on all the new rides.

## 5 Speaking

Look at the poster below advertising an aquarium. Think of a good name for the aquarium and complete the missing information. Then talk in pairs. Discuss your posters and try to persuade each other that your aquarium is the better place to visit.

**Visit** [     ] **for an unforgettable experience!**

- See hundreds of [     ]
- Feed the [     ]
- Swim with [     ]
- Watch the [     ] show
- Adopt a baby [     ]
- Have something to eat at [     ]

Tickets: Adults [     ] Students [     ] Children [     ]

❝ *If we choose to go to AquaWorld, we will see whales.* **Yeah, but if we go to AquaPark, we can feed the... What do you say?** ❞

# 1 Reading 🔊

**A. Discuss.**

- Do you know of any people who have made major changes in their lives?
- What makes people want to change their lives?

**B. Look at the picture. What do you think happened? Listen, read and find out.**

# What happened to Nicholas Baines?

HD TV

CHANNEL 8

NICHOLAS BAINES

We all remember the anchorman Nicholas Baines. Last year, millions of people were watching the news on Channel 8, the title sequence ended and there was Baines. He looked into the camera ready to speak, paused and looked down at the desk. Then he did something unexpected. He said: "I'm sorry, I can't do this anymore!" He then stood up and left the studio. He quit his job and his career in television. But what led him to this major decision?

It seemed like Baines had the perfect life. He had achieved the success he'd always wanted and had a loving family. However, behind the scenes, he was unhappy. At that time, he was working 13 hours a day, sometimes more. He hardly ever had time to spend with his family and, whenever he did, he was exhausted. His lifestyle was also affecting his health. His doctor had told him to work fewer hours, but he was unable to do so. In addition, he was constantly arguing with the producer because of the quality of the news bulletins. It was all gossip and celebrities and had very few stories about the real issues in the world. He strongly disapproved of this and, that night, it all seemed too much to cope with.

A year later, Baines is living a less complicated life in the countryside. He has just published his first book *The Best Time Is Now!* and also writes a blog. He gives advice to people who live stressful lives and shows them how to change their lifestyle in a few steps. Baines told us, "I want people to believe that anything is possible. I turned my life around and it's been the most important decision I've ever made." Baines spends a lot of time with his children and he also grows his own vegetables. He isn't as stressed as he used to be and he is healthier and more energetic than ever. Many people ask Baines why he chose to quit on air. Baines explains, "When you realize you need to make a change in your life, you shouldn't keep putting it off. The best time to do it is now."

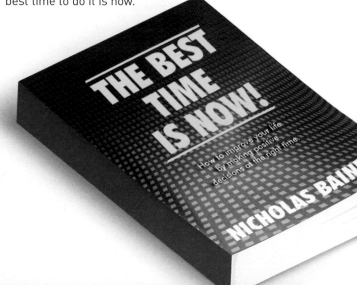

THE BEST TIME IS NOW!

How to improve your life by making positive decisions at the right time

NICHOLAS BAINES

**C. Read again and answer the questions. Choose a, b or c.**

1. Why does the writer expect everybody to know who Nicholas Baines is?
   a. He often did unexpected things on live TV.
   b. He's the country's most famous anchorman.
   c. He made an announcement on live TV that surprised everyone.

2. What is true about Baines' life before he quit his job?
   a. He was unhappy because of medical reasons.
   b. He was feeling dissatisfied with his life.
   c. His home was the only place where he felt relaxed and happy.

3. What did Baines believe about the news bulletins?
   a. They weren't serious enough.
   b. They weren't what the public wanted.
   c. The public wasn't interested enough in them.

4. What is **NOT** true about Baines a year after he quit?
   a. He has more spare time.
   b. He misses his old life.
   c. He has become a writer.

5. What advice does Baines give?
   a. Think hard before you make any decisions.
   b. When you've made up your mind, don't delay.
   c. Talk to lots of people before you make a decision.

**D. Discuss.**
- Do you think Nicholas Baines made the right decision?
- What would you do if you were Baines?

## 2 Vocabulary 🔊

**A. Find the opposites of the following words in the text in activity 1.**

| expected | happy | able | approve |

**B. Read the note. Find the opposites of the words in the box and complete the table. Then listen and check your answers.**

> The opposites of many English words are formed by adding a negative prefix (e.g. un-, dis-) to the words.

| healthy | appear | suitable | agree |
| natural | necessary | advantage | friendly |
| | like (v.) | certain | |

| un- | dis- |
| --- | --- |
| | |
| | |
| | |
| | |
| | |
| | |

## 3 Grammar Comparisons → p. 144

**A. Look at the examples and answer the questions.**

> - Baines is **healthier** now.
> - Life in the city is **more stressful than** life in the country.
> - **The most difficult** part was telling his friends and family.
> - This is **the happiest** time of his life.

1. Which of the examples above include adjectives in the comparative form and which in the superlative form?

2. Which word do we usually use **after** adjectives in the comparative form and which **before** adjectives in the superlative form?

**B. Read the example and decide what it means. Choose a, b or c.**

> His new job isn't **as stressful as** his old job.

a. His new job is more stressful.
b. His old job was more stressful.
c. The two jobs have the same amount of stress.

**C. Read the example. Which of the sentences that follow are true and which are false?**

> I think golf is **less exciting than** soccer, but tennis is **the least exciting** of the three.

1. Soccer is more exciting than golf and tennis. ☐
2. Tennis isn't as exciting as golf and soccer. ☐
3. Golf is the most exciting of the three sports. ☐

**D. Complete with the correct form of the adjectives in parentheses. Add *the* where necessary.**

1. Since I started going to the gym, I don't feel as _____ (exhausted) as I used to. I am _____ (active) and feel _____ (energetic) than before.

2. The town I live in is _____ (quiet) and _____ (peaceful) than the city. Life here might not be as _____ (exciting) as life in the city, but it certainly is _____ (little) stressful. For me, the city is _____ (bad) place a person can live in.

3. My friend Jack is _____ (outgoing) person I know. He has _____ (many) friends than me and everybody likes him. I'm not as _____ (good) as he is at making friends, but I'm really trying to change and become _____ (warm) and _____ (friendly) than I already am.

## 4 Speaking & Writing

**A. Discuss lifestyle changes you would like to make. Think about the ideas in the box and give reasons for your answers.**

| health / exercise |
| eating habits |
| personality |
| entertainment habits |
| social life |
| education |
| work |

> 66 *I want to start exercising more so that I can become healthier.*
> *I'm not as optimistic as I'd like to be, so I might...*
> *I want my college assignments to be the best, so I'm going to...* 99

**B. Write a few sentences about lifestyle changes you would like to make.**

# 1 Listening 🔊

**A. Discuss.**

- In which situations do people take notes?
- What kind of information do notes usually include?

**B. Listen to two voicemail messages and complete the notes below.**

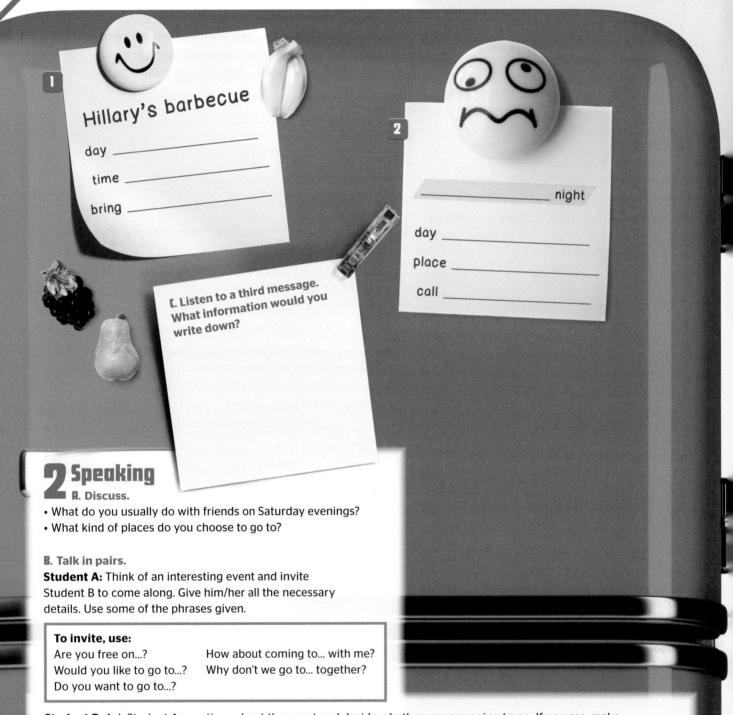

**1**

Hillary's barbecue

day _____

time _____

bring _____

**2**

_____ night

day _____

place _____

call _____

**C. Listen to a third message. What information would you write down?**

# 2 Speaking

**A. Discuss.**

- What do you usually do with friends on Saturday evenings?
- What kind of places do you choose to go to?

**B. Talk in pairs.**

**Student A:** Think of an interesting event and invite Student B to come along. Give him/her all the necessary details. Use some of the phrases given.

| To invite, use: | |
|---|---|
| Are you free on…? | How about coming to… with me? |
| Would you like to go to…? | Why don't we go to… together? |
| Do you want to go to…? | |

**Student B:** Ask Student A questions about the event and decide whether you are going to go. If you are, make arrangements about the time and meeting place. If you aren't, refuse and give a reason. Use some of the phrases given.

| To accept an invitation, use: | To refuse an invitation, use: | To make suggestions and arrangements, use: |
|---|---|---|
| How can I say no to that? | I'm afraid I can't make it because… | How about…? |
| I'd love to come. | It was nice of you to invite me, but… | Let's… |
| Count me in! | I have other plans. Maybe some other time. | Why don't we…? |
| Sounds like a plan! | Sorry, but I have to… | What if we…? |
| Thanks for inviting me. | Unfortunately, I won't be able to make it. | We can/could… |
| Sure! Give me the details. | | Do you mind if we…? |

# 3 Writing An e-mail based on prompts

**A.** Roger has received an e-mail from his friend Jerry. Read Jerry's e-mail with the notes Roger has made and answer the questions.

1. Why is Jerry writing to Roger?
2. What does Jerry want Roger to do?

Hi Roger,

Hey, you know Tony is leaving for Australia next month. Well, I'm organizing a get-together at my house to give him a good send-off. It'll be more of a barbecue really, and I want it to be a surprise. So, what do you say? Are you coming? **definitely!**

The barbecue is in two weeks, on Saturday July 16th. Tony's sister has agreed to bring him to my house at about one. So, I need everyone to be here at ten in the morning to help out. OK? **can't / 11:30?**

I'm going to sort out most of the food and drinks, but I'd welcome any ideas in that department. Let me know, though. **Two ideas**

It's going to be great. I hope you can make it.

E-mail me when you can,
Jerry

**B.** Now read Roger's reply and underline the sentences which correspond to his notes. Is the wording in Roger's e-mail exactly the same as in his notes?

Hello Jerry,

The barbecue's an awesome idea! The weather's been perfect lately. He's going to love it, I'm sure.

I really want to see Tony before he leaves, and this gives me the perfect opportunity. So, count me in! The only problem is that I won't be able to make it at 10 o'clock. I have to drive my dad to the airport in the morning. But don't worry, I'll be there by 11:30 at the latest. I hope that doesn't ruin your plans.

I'm looking forward to one of your famous barbecues. I have two ideas for food to bring. How about a salad with corn and black beans? Or I can bring raw vegetables, like eggplants and peppers, which we can grill and serve with yogurt. Whatever you prefer.

I'm really excited now. I can't wait to see Tony's face.

Get back to me soon,
Roger

**C.** Read the note and the situations 1-5. How would you reply?

**Expanding on notes/prompts**

When writing an e-mail based on prompts, don't just copy the prompts. Try to rephrase them and add any comments and/or information that is relevant.

1. I'm thinking of going to the beach tomorrow. Do you want to come along?
   *great idea / time?*

2. How about going out tonight? Let's go for pizza.
   *sure / but not pizza again*

3. I'm afraid I can't lend you my tent for your camping trip.
   *it's OK / buy new one*

4. Will you meet me for coffee after work?
   *can't / working till late*

5. Would you like to go to a baseball game on Saturday?
   *love to / tickets?*

**D.** Imagine that you have received an e-mail from a friend. Read your friend's e-mail and the notes you have made and write a reply.

Hi there,

Guess what! I'm getting married! I'm going to send you a formal invitation soon, but I wanted to let you know so that you can book flights early. I really want you to come! **of course!**

The wedding day is April 12th. I know that's kind of soon, but we really wanted a spring wedding and didn't want to wait for next year. As for our honeymoon, we haven't decided where to go yet. Anyway, you're one of my closest friends and I really need you by my side. Could you please come a little earlier? **When?** I know I'm asking for too much, but pretty please?

I'm afraid I won't be able to put you up because there will be lots of relatives here. But I know a good hotel near my house. I can give them a call and see if they have any rooms free. **No need, can stay with friends**

Get back to me as soon as you can,
Sandy

---

When writing an e-mail based on prompts:
- use appropriate expressions to begin and end your e-mail.
- read the prompts carefully. Make sure you expand on them, instead of simply copying them. Also, make sure you include all of them in your reply.
- group related ideas together and divide your e-mail into paragraphs.
- use appropriate phrases/expressions to accept an invitation, refuse an invitation and give a reason, make arrangements and suggestions, etc.

**TIP**

## Vocabulary

**A. Complete the sentences with the words in the box.**

> feed argue unexpected valid
> clumsy achieve dissatisfied

1. If your ticket isn't _____, you will have to pay a fine.
2. Something very _____ just happened and I will be a little late for work.
3. The customers were _____ with the service and made several complaints.
4. We visited the aquarium last week, but they didn't let us _____ the dolphins.
5. Don't ask Robert to help in the kitchen. He's very _____.
6. If you try hard enough, you can _____ anything you want in life.
7. Why do you always _____ with your brothers?

**B. Complete with prepositions.**

1. **A:** Is the family get-together this Saturday?
   **B:** No, we put it _____ till next week.
2. If you have any comments, please fill _____ this form and drop it in the box.
3. I've always wondered how she can cope _____ a job and two babies.
4. **A:** Are you free tonight? Do you want to drop _____ my place? I'm having a movie night.
   **B:** Sure. Count me _____.
5. Ring the bell in case _____ fire.

## Grammar

**C. Rewrite the sentences using the words in parentheses.**

1. There is a possibility that I won't see Jamie tonight. (might)

   I _____

2. In 2011, the Metropolitan Museum of Art had more visitors than the British Museum. (as)

   In 2011, the British Museum didn't _____

   _____

3. Tony and Amy are likely to join us at the festival. (may)

   Tony _____

4. In the past, the city wasn't as noisy and polluted as it is now. (less)

   In the past, the city _____

5. I know many people who are wealthier than Jack Stannard. (the)

   Jack Stannard isn't _____

6. Carol isn't as friendly as I am. (than)

   I _____

**D. Circle the correct words.**

1. **If / When** you reach the train station, give me a call.
2. If you **don't like / won't like** your job, I think you should quit.
3. What **do you do / will you do** if Kelly **invites / will invite** you to her get-together?
4. Greg **couldn't / might not** come with us tonight if he's busy.
5. I won't go out **if / when** it rains. I don't feel very well.
6. Ted and I **may try / will try** ice skating, but we haven't decided for sure yet.
7. If you **want / will want** to make a donation, **put / will put** the money in this box, please.

## Communication

**E. Choose a or b.**

1. **A:** Feel like coming jogging with me?
   **B:** ____
   **a.** I'd rather not.
   **b.** Do as you please.
2. **A:** I'm not sure if I should buy this painting.
   **B:** ____
   **a.** Will you make up your mind?
   **b.** Will you change your mind?
3. **A:** There's a good chance we'll see your brother at the mall.
   **B:** ____
   **a.** Sounds like a plan.
   **b.** I doubt it.
4. **A:** Are you sure you have the right address?
   **B:** ____
   **a.** It's up to you.
   **b.** I'm positive.

## Self-assessment

**Read the following and check the appropriate boxes. For the points you are unsure of, refer back to the relevant sections in the module.**

### NOW I CAN...

- express possibility and certainty in the present and future ☐
- express preference ☐
- understand signs and messages ☐
- talk about conditions and their results ☐
- compare and contrast people and situations ☐
- talk about lifestyle changes and intentions ☐
- form opposites using prefixes (un-, dis-) ☐
- take notes ☐
- invite and accept or refuse an invitation ☐
- make suggestions and arrangements ☐
- write an e-mail based on prompts ☐

**Discuss:**

• Look at the sports in the pictures. Where do people play/do them? Match with the words below. Can you think of any other sports that are played at these places?

court   field   track
pool   ice rink

• How active are you?

• In your opinion, which are better, individual sports or team sports? Why?

## In this module you will learn...

• to talk about sports (equipment, rules, etc.)

• to express enthusiasm, surprise, admiration, disappointment, anger, annoyance

• to express result

• to understand information on flyers and signs

• to express obligation, lack of obligation, and prohibition

• to use the Passive Voice

• to talk about movies and express your opinion

• to write a movie review

# 1 Reading 🔊

**A. Read and label the dialogues. Then listen and check your answers.**

**Before the match...**    **During the match...**    **After the match...**

**1** _____

**A:** So, what were you saying about Pinkman lifting the trophy?
**B:** What a disappointment! He's never played like this before. He let down all his fans.
**A:** I've never seen such a terrible match in my whole life. What a shame!
**B:** I know. How embarrassing! He won the first game with those aces. How did he manage to lose?
**A:** Pinkman was playing so badly after the first game that I was glad when the match was over. What a waste of time and money!
**B:** You can say that again!

**2** _____

**A:** Phew, we made it to our seats just in time.
**B:** Yeah, look at how many people have turned out. Andy Pinkman has so many fans!
**A:** Well, who wants to miss out on such an important match?
**B:** Not me. I'm so excited! I can't wait for the match to begin.
**A:** There he is! Let's cheer him on! Andy! Andy! Yeah!

**3** _____

**A:** Did you see that? What a player!
**B:** Unbelievable! Another ace! That was such a fast serve that Wilson didn't have time to react.
**A:** Pinkman is so talented! Another point. That was so amazing!
**B:** Wilson's in serious trouble now.
**A:** There's another big serve from Pinkman. He's playing so well! One more point and that's the first game.
**B:** It's over. That was awesome! What a game!

**B. Read the dialogues again and answer the questions.**

1. Which phrases show that the two men are enthusiastic about the match?
2. How do we know that the men admire Pinkman?
3. Why didn't Wilson have time to react?
4. Why were the men glad when the match was over?
5. Which phrases show that the men are disappointed?

**C. Find phrasal verbs in the dialogues and match them with the meanings below.**

1. to disappoint: _____
2. to gather together to watch an event: _____
3. to not have the chance to do sth. that you enjoy: _____
4. to encourage sb. by shouting to him/her in a game, race or competition: _____

# 2 Grammar Exclamatory sentences, Clauses of result → p. 145

**A. Read the examples. What does the speaker want to emphasize?**

> • **How** wonderful!   • **What** a nightmare!
>
> • It's **so** cold outside!   • It's **such** an important game!

**To make exclamations, use:**
• *how* and *so* before adjectives/adverbs
• *what* and *such* before nouns or adjectives + nouns

**B. Read the examples, answer the questions and complete the rules.**

> • The game was **so** exciting **that** the fans didn't want it to end.
>
> • It was **such** an exciting game **that** the fans didn't want it to end.

**1.** What didn't the fans want to happen?

**2.** Why didn't they want this to happen?

**To express result, use:**

• so + _____ or adverb + (that)...

• such + (a/an) + (adjective) + _____ + (that)...

**C. Complete the dialogues with *how, what, so* or *such*.**

**1.**

**A:** Mark, I have **1** _____ amazing news! I've won a trip to Thailand! I can't believe it! It's been my dream to travel to Asia for **2** _____ a long time!

**B:** **3** _____ lucky!

**A:** Yeah, but I enter **4** _____ many competitions that I had to win something someday.

**B:** And **5** _____ a prize to win!

**A:** I know. It was **6** _____ a surprise when they called me that I didn't believe it!

**2.**

**A:** I had **7** _____ a bad day!

**B:** Why? What happened?

**A:** First of all, there was **8** _____ much traffic on the roads that I was two hours late for work.

**B:** **9** _____ a nightmare!

**A:** Then my boss gave me **10** _____ a lot of work to do that I left the office at 7 p.m.

**B:** **11** _____ annoying!

**A:** Then when I got home, it was **12** _____ late that I missed my yoga class.

**B:** **13** _____ a shame! I hope tomorrow won't be **14** _____ a disaster!

# 3 Listening 🔊

**A. Listen to four people talking about a hockey game and decide who each person is.**

> **TIP**
> Before you listen, read through the options given and try to imagine each person. Think about how each person might feel and what they might say.

| | |
|---|---|
| Danny | a player |
| Robert | a fan |
| Craig | a coach |
| Steve | a sports commentator |

**B. Listen again and match the people with the statements.**

| | |
|---|---|
| Danny | thinks a player can make a difference. |
| Robert | thinks the team can play better. |
| Craig | was surprised at the result. |
| Steve | thinks the fans play an important role. |

# 4 Speaking

Talk in pairs. Imagine you are in the situations below. Have two conversations, one during the event and one after. Show your enthusiasm or disappointment.

| DURING | | AFTER |
|---|---|---|
| • You're at a basketball game and your team is winning. However, the referee has started making lots of bad calls. | → | Your team lost. |
| • You're at a concert waiting for your favorite group to perform. You think the supporting groups are a waste of time. | → | You really enjoyed the concert. |

> **66** *This is such an exciting game.*
> *Look at Jameson! What a player!* **99**

> **TIP**
> Keep in mind that your tone of voice can help enhance what you are saying. You can show surprise, admiration, enthusiasm, disappointment, anger, annoyance, etc.

# 1 Reading

**A. Discuss.**

- Have you ever been skydiving?
- If yes, what was it like? If not, would you like to try it?
- Do you know of any safety precautions that you have to follow? What are they?

**B. Read the information in the texts below and the sentences 1-8. Write T for True or F for False.**

## Looking for a thrill?

Come to **Sandy Bay Skydiving Center** for a safe, exciting and unforgettable experience.

**Make the decision to jump: you won't regret it!**

- You must be between 18 and 65 yrs. old.
- You mustn't be over 200 pounds.
- You need to be in good physical condition.
- You have to complete our ground training program.
- You don't have to bring your own parachute equipment or helmet. We provide everything.

info@sandybayskydivingcenter.com

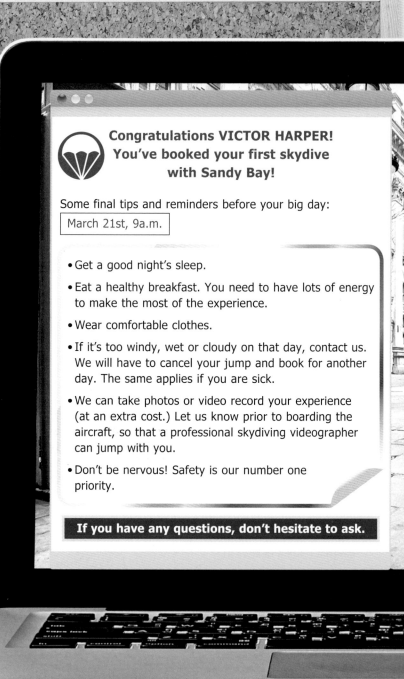

**Congratulations VICTOR HARPER! You've booked your first skydive with Sandy Bay!**

Some final tips and reminders before your big day:

March 21st, 9a.m.

- Get a good night's sleep.
- Eat a healthy breakfast. You need to have lots of energy to make the most of the experience.
- Wear comfortable clothes.
- If it's too windy, wet or cloudy on that day, contact us. We will have to cancel your jump and book for another day. The same applies if you are sick.
- We can take photos or video record your experience (at an extra cost.) Let us know prior to boarding the aircraft, so that a professional skydiving videographer can jump with you.
- Don't be nervous! Safety is our number one priority.

**If you have any questions, don't hesitate to ask.**

1. You need to be at least 18 to skydive at Sandy Bay Skydiving Center.
2. If you weigh more than 200 pounds, they won't accept you.
3. You have to buy the safety equipment before you go.
4. You can choose whether you want to do the training or not.
5. Victor has booked a jump on March 21st.
6. The center offers you breakfast.
7. If you are sick, you should contact the center.
8. Everyone receives a video recording of their experience before they leave.

## 2 Vocabulary 🔊

**Look, listen and discuss. In which sports do you need equipment like this?**

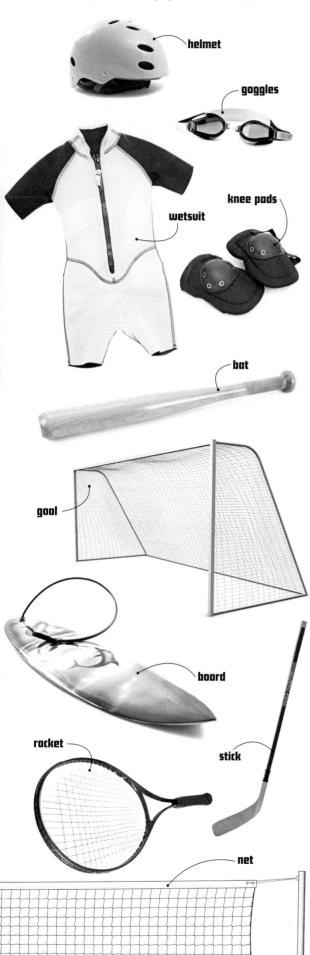

helmet

goggles

wetsuit

knee pads

bat

goal

board

racket

stick

net

## 3 Grammar have to, don't have to, must, mustn't, need to, don't need to, needn't → p. 145

**A. Read the examples and decide what each of them means. Choose a, b or c.**

1. You **have to** wear special boots to go rock climbing. ☐
2. You **don't have to** wear special clothes. ☐
3. You **must** be in good shape. ☐
4. Inexperienced climbers **mustn't** climb alone. ☐
5. Inexperienced climbers **need to** complete a training program first. ☐
6. Experienced climbers **don't need to** complete a training program. ☐
7. You **needn't** worry about anything. ☐

**a. It is necessary.**    **b. It isn't necessary.**    **c. Don't do it!**

---

- We use **must** to express obligation in the present/future. For all other tenses, we use the forms of **have to**.
  *I had to leave work early yesterday.*
  *I will have to leave work early tomorrow.*
- We can use **can't** instead of **mustn't** in situations where you are not allowed to do something, especially when a law or rule is involved.
  *You can't/mustn't park here.*

---

**B. Look at the signs and make sentences using *have to*, *don't have to*, *must*, *mustn't*, *need to* and *don't need to*.**

TICKET OFFICE →

Sports Center

**P** Parking free for members only

Westhill Swimming Pool

DOOR CLOSES AUTOMATICALLY

## 4 Speaking Game

**Work in groups of four. Look at the places below. One student chooses one of the places and the other three in the group have to find out which place it is by asking questions about what you *can, have to, don't have to, mustn't*, etc. do there. Use the ideas in the box.**

plane    hospital    museum    movie theater

theme park    stadium    train    library

buy tickets
eat
take photos
use cell phone
wear seat belt
be quiet

**66** *Do you have to be quiet there?*
    *No, you don't.*
*Can you use...?* **99**

## 1 Reading 🔊

**A. Discuss.**
- What is the most popular sport in your country?
- Is this sport played in other countries, too?

**B. Listen and read. What is the main purpose of the text?**

**a.** To explain the difference between varieties of sports called *football*.

**b.** To show the history of *football* from its origins till modern times.

**c.** To highlight the differences between *football* in the U.S.A. and the U.K.

# Football Codes

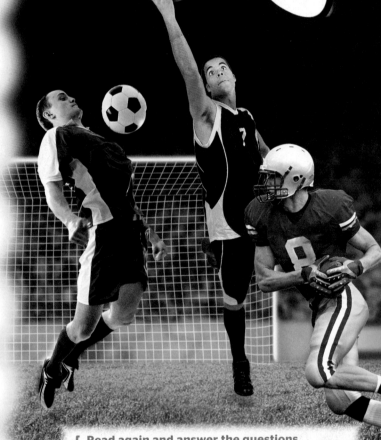

In different parts of the world, the word *football* is used to describe some very different games. These games are called *codes*, and the only things they have in common are that they are played with a ball, they are all team games and they are related to games played in medieval times.

Most people think that *football* got its name from the fact that players kick the ball, but that's not true. Different medieval games became known as *football* because they were played by peasants on foot and not on horseback as the noblemen did.

The game the British know as *football* is officially called *Association Football*. People in the U.S.A. and Australia call it *soccer*. In this game, players are allowed to use their feet, heads and bodies, except for the goalkeeper who can use his hands, too. The rules of *Association Football* were created in the late 19th century, and the first international game took place in 1872 between Scotland and England. Today, the World Cup is held every four years and is watched by millions of people.

In the U.S.A., *football* is something different. What Americans call *football*, the rest of the world calls *American Football*. In this game, players mostly use their hands. They score points by carrying the ball to score a *touchdown* or they can kick a *field goal* through the upright posts. *American Football* developed from early versions of rugby and *Association Football*.

*Football* for Australians is *Australian Rules Football* or *Aussie Rules* and players use their hands and feet to kick, pass and shoot. *Aussie Rules* began as a way for cricket players to keep in shape during the winter, and it was played on cricket fields. These fields are round and much bigger than those that are used for other types of football.

Other football codes include Canadian football, Gaelic football and rugby, which is also considered a football code. One thing's for sure, though, *football*, whichever game you're talking about, is very popular across the globe.

**C. Read again and answer the questions.**

1. Who were the first people to play a game called *football*?
2. What do Americans call *Association Football*?
3. What happened in 1872?
4. In which game do you score *touchdowns*?
5. How do you score a *field goal*?
6. What is *Aussie Rules*?
7. Why was *Aussie Rules* created?

**D. Discuss.**
Do you know any sports that are similar to football?

# 2 Grammar Passive Voice (Present Simple – Past Simple) → p. 146

**A.** Read the examples below. Do the sentences in the Active Voice have the same meaning as the ones in the Passive Voice? Which ones focus on the person doing the action? Which ones focus on the action?

| ACTIVE VOICE | PASSIVE VOICE |
|---|---|
| People **play** basketball on indoor or outdoor courts. | Basketball **is played** on indoor or outdoor courts. |
| James Naismith **invented** basketball in 1891. | Basketball **was invented** by James Naismith in 1891. |

**B.** Read the examples again and complete the rules.

| ACTIVE VOICE |
|---|
| Subject + Main Verb + Object |

| PASSIVE VOICE |
|---|
| Subject + Verb _____ + Past Participle of _____ Verb (+by...) |

**C.** Complete with the Present Simple Passive or the Past Simple Passive of the verbs in parentheses.

**1.** The new Wembley Stadium in London _____ (build) in 2007.

**2.** The Super Bowl is an event which _____ (watch) by millions of Americans every year.

**3.** Spanish _____ (speak) in Spain but also in many countries in South America.

**4.** Brandon is excited because he _____ (choose) to play on the college basketball team.

**5.** I'm dizzy because I _____ (hit) on the head with a ball.

**6.** Computers _____ (use) in most schools nowadays.

**7.** During yesterday's practice, the players _____ (ask) to run around the court for half an hour.

# 3 Vocabulary & Writing 🔊

**A.** Match the pictures with the verbs in the box. Then listen and check your answers.

| hit | shoot | catch | pass | dribble | kick | throw | bounce |
|---|---|---|---|---|---|---|---|

**B.** Think of a sport and describe some of the rules players need to follow.

*Basketball is played by two teams of five players. It is played on a basketball court. Players can dribble and pass the ball to other players. To score points, they must shoot the ball through a basket.*

# 4 Pronunciation 🔊

**A.** Below are some words that contain the schwa. Listen and repeat. Is the schwa a short or a long sound?

> The schwa (ə) is the most common vowel sound in English and it is almost always unstressed.

bənanə    əbout    commə
teləphone    refəree

**B.** In the sentences below, the schwa is highlighted. Read the sentences aloud. Then listen and check your pronunciation.

Soccer is an international sport.

I've never traveled abroad.

Ricky is Colombian. I'm Canadian.

Steve is a professional hockey player.

# 5 Speaking Sports Quiz
Go to page 135.

# 8d

## 1 Vocabulary ◀))

**A. Discuss.**

- What kind of movies do you like watching? Why?

| | |
|---|---|
| action | sci-fi |
| adventure | thriller |
| documentary | horror |
| crime drama | biopic |
| historical drama | animated |
| romantic comedy | war |

**B. Which of the words 1-9 below do you know? Match them with their definitions a-i. Then listen and check your answers.**

1. plot ☐
2. scene ☐
3. leading actor ☐
4. special effects ☐
5. costumes ☐
6. soundtrack ☐
7. cast ☐
8. director ☐
9. blockbuster ☐

a. the person who stars in a movie
b. a part of a movie
c. the person who directs a movie
d. a movie which is very successful
e. the story of a movie
f. the music which is heard in a movie
g. the clothes the actors wear
h. unusual and exciting images or sounds in a movie usually made by computers
i. all the people who act in a movie

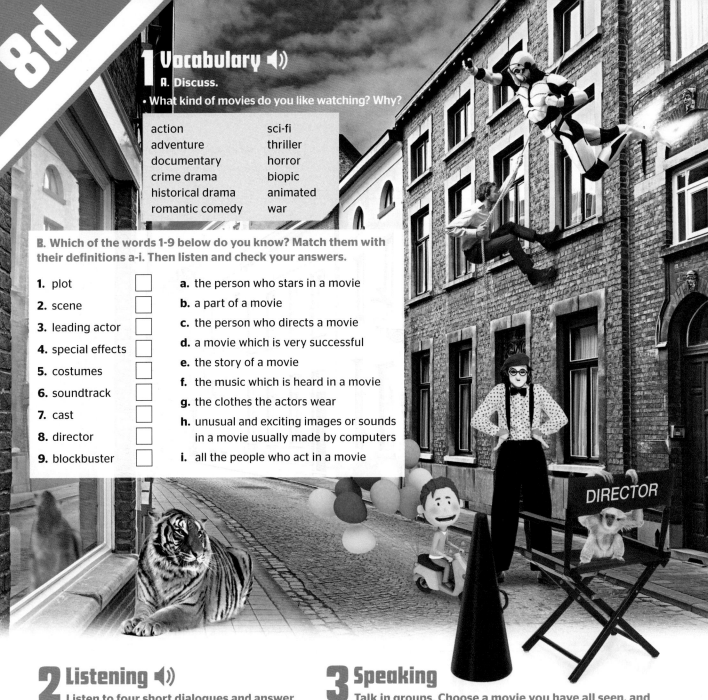

DIRECTOR

## 2 Listening ◀))

Listen to four short dialogues and answer the questions. Choose a, b or c.

1. What did they think of the movie?
   a. It was surprising.
   b. It was violent.
   c. It was disappointing.

2. Who's Thomas Balding?
   a. an actor
   b. a director
   c. a producer

3. What kind of movie are they watching?
   a. a historical drama
   b. a documentary
   c. a sci-fi movie

4. What <u>didn't</u> they like about the movie?
   a. the plot
   b. the soundtrack
   c. the costumes

## 3 Speaking

Talk in groups. Choose a movie you have all seen, and individually check the boxes in the table below according to your opinion. Then discuss your answers with your group members. Use some of the adjectives in the box.

| | excellent | OK | terrible |
|---|---|---|---|
| **plot** | | | |
| **special effects** | | | |
| **acting** | | | |
| **soundtrack** | | | |
| **ending** | | | |

❝ *I thought the special effects in the movie were awesome!*
*I disagree. I found them unrealistic, but I really liked the soundtrack.* ❞

| | | |
|---|---|---|
| awesome | exciting | awful |
| original | amazing | disappointing |
| surprising | entertaining | terrible |
| unexpected | incredible | boring |
| realistic | excellent | unrealistic |
| spectacular | fantastic | |

# 4 Writing  A movie review

## A. Discuss.

- In your opinion, what makes a movie successful?
- Do you read movie reviews? Are you influenced by them?

## B. Read the movie review and answer the questions.

1. What kind of information is included in the first paragraph?
2. In which paragraph is the plot of the movie described?
3. What tense does the writer use to describe the plot?
4. Does the writer reveal the ending of the movie?
5. Did the writer like the movie?
6. In which paragraph does the writer express her opinion?

## C. Read the plan and the phrases 1-6 below. In which part do they belong? Write the phrases in the plan.

1. I was very disappointed by the movie.
2. ... is the leading actor/actress.
3. Don't miss it!
4. It was directed by...
5. The movie is about...
6. It's suitable for children/adults.

MOVIES  SERIES  NEWS  TRAILERS  CONTACT

BRAD PITT

**Movie Review** by Zoe Winters
**Moneyball** (2011)
(original title)

⭐ **7.6** ★★★★★★★★

**Director:** Bennett Miller
**Starring:** Brad Pitt, Jonah Hill, Philip Seymour Hoffman, Robin Wright

*Moneyball* is a sports drama which was directed by Bennett Miller. Brad Pitt stars as Billy Beane, the manager of a baseball team, and his assistant, Peter Brand, is played by Jonah Hill. The movie is based on a true story that was written about in a book by Michael Lewis.

The movie is about the world of baseball in the United States but also about sports and society in general. Beane (Pitt) manages a small team with financial problems and an unsuccessful record. One day, at a game, he meets an economics graduate who has an unusual strategy for success. Beane decides to try out his strategy, and the pair work together to change the team's fortune.

I really enjoyed this movie from start to finish. I found the plot very original and entertaining. Brad Pitt was excellent as the team's manager, and overall the performances were very good. It is one of the best sports movies of recent years. I recommend it to all sports fans.

⟨ ◻ ⟩

## Plan

### A movie review

### INTRODUCTION
**Give some general information about the movie (title, type of movie, leading actors, director).**
**Use phrases like:**
- *It's a comedy / an action movie / a thriller, etc.*
- *... stars as... in this movie.*
- *... plays/has the leading role.*
- *The role of... is played by...*
- _____
- _____

### MAIN PART
**Give a general outline of the plot. Don't include too many details and don't reveal the ending. Use the Present Simple and phrases like:**
- *The movie is set in...*
- *The main character of the movie is...*
- _____

### CONCLUSION
**Write your opinion of the movie and say whether you recommend it or not. Use the Present Simple or the Past Simple, a variety of adjectives and phrases like:**
- *Overall, I found the movie hilarious/entertaining/boring, etc.*
- *The movie is action-packed/nothing special/scary, etc.*
- *In my opinion, the plot/ending/soundtrack/etc. is...*
- *I definitely recommend it.*
- *It includes some very funny/violent scenes.*
- *I enjoyed this movie from start to finish.*
- *It's a great movie for action-lovers / horror fans.*
- *It's (not) worth seeing.*
- *It was better than I expected.*
- _____
- _____
- _____

## D. Write a review of a movie you have recently seen and know well or about the one you discussed in activity 3. Follow the plan.

## Vocabulary

**A. Choose a, b or c.**

1. Who ____ the ball and broke that window?
   a. kicked    b. dribbled    c. lifted

2. One of the members of the ____ also wrote the soundtrack.
   a. cast    b. plot    c. scene

3. I made a promise and I'll try my best not to let you ____.
   a. out    b. up    c. down

4. Julian and Pedro may be brothers, but they have nothing in ____.
   a. shape    b. line    c. common

5. These ____ are ideal for scuba diving and other water sports.
   a. parachutes    b. goggles    c. helmets

6. The movie was ____. We couldn't stop laughing.
   a. hilarious    b. action-packed    c. enthusiastic

7. For this scene, we need an actor who is in very good physical ____.
   a. role    b. condition    c. character

8. Steve should become a sports ____. He's very good at describing games.
   a. coach    b. commentator    c. referee

## Grammar

**B. Circle the correct words.**

1. You **don't need to / mustn't** buy any sports equipment. The ski school will provide everything.

2. You **need / must** be over 15 to take part in the race.

3. I **must / had to** take a cab home last night because the buses were on strike.

4. You **don't have to / mustn't** put electrical appliances near water. It's dangerous.

5. Why do you **must / have to** leave so early?

**C. Rewrite the sentences using the words given.**

1. That's wonderful news!    (what)

   _____

2. The painting was so beautiful that I bought it.    (such)

   _____

3. The special effects were very realistic.    (so)

   _____

4. I didn't want to go out because I was very tired.    (so)

   _____

5. That car is very fast.    (such)

   _____

**D. Complete with the correct form of the words in parentheses.**

1. 300,000 tickets _____ (sell) for last night's baseball game.

2. Both English and Spanish _____ (teach) at my son's school.

3. This movie review _____ (not write) by Mike Crane but by Sally Fisher.

4. This bag _____ (design) by a cousin of mine.

5. Nowadays, cell phones _____ (use) by almost everyone.

6. This event _____ (organize) in a different city every year.

## Communication

**E. Complete the dialogue with a-f.**

> a. But I thought it was very unrealistic.
> b. I'm not exactly a huge fan of his.
> c. You can say that again.
> d. Overall, it was OK.
> e. It's going to be a blockbuster!
> f. They were nothing special.

A: Did you like the movie?

B: 1 ____

A: You don't sound very excited.

B: Well, the movie review said that it is based on a true story. 2 ____

A: What about Mark Fry? He's so talented!

B: He was OK, I guess. 3 ____

A: I think he's awesome! What about the costumes?

B: 4 ____ I don't understand why this movie is so popular.

A: Just popular? 5 ____

B: Whatever.

A: Well, maybe thrillers are not for you.

B: 6 ____ What a waste of time!

## Self-assessment

Read the following and check the appropriate boxes. For the points you are unsure of, refer back to the relevant sections in the module.

**NOW I CAN...**

- talk about sports (equipment, rules, etc.) ☐
- express enthusiasm, surprise, admiration, disappointment, anger, annoyance ☐
- express result ☐
- express obligation, lack of obligation, and prohibition ☐
- use the Passive Voice ☐
- talk about movies and express my opinion ☐
- write a movie review ☐

Task 7&8 p. 130

# 9 Career paths

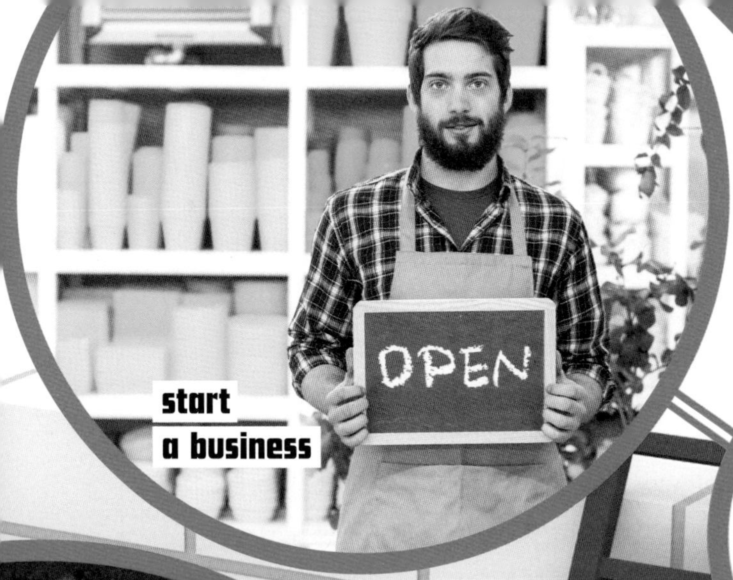
OPEN
start
a business

**Discuss:**

- Look at the pictures. What do you think young adults should do after high school? Why?
- What did you do? / What are you thinking of doing?

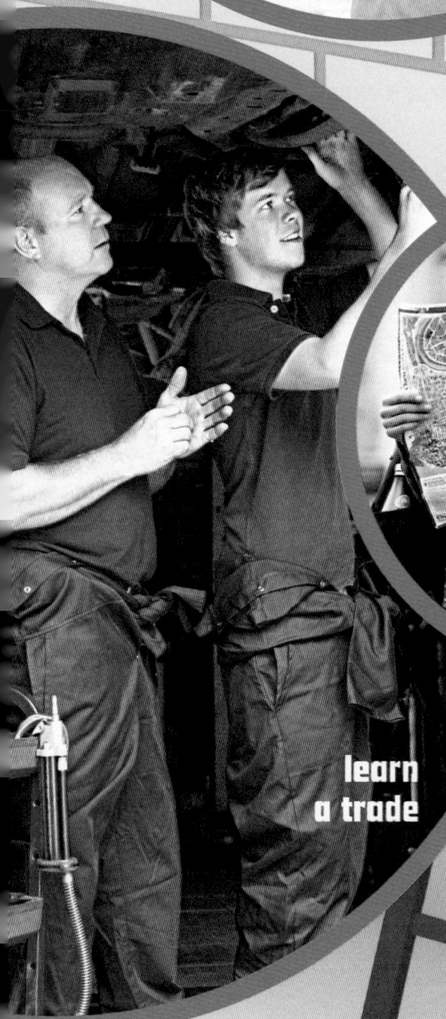
learn
a trade

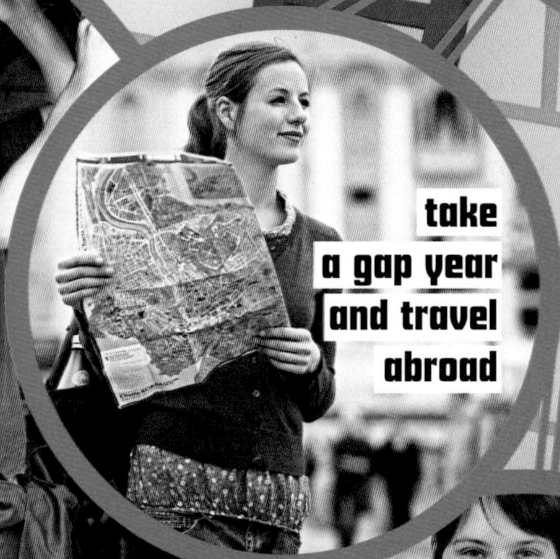
take
a gap year
and travel
abroad

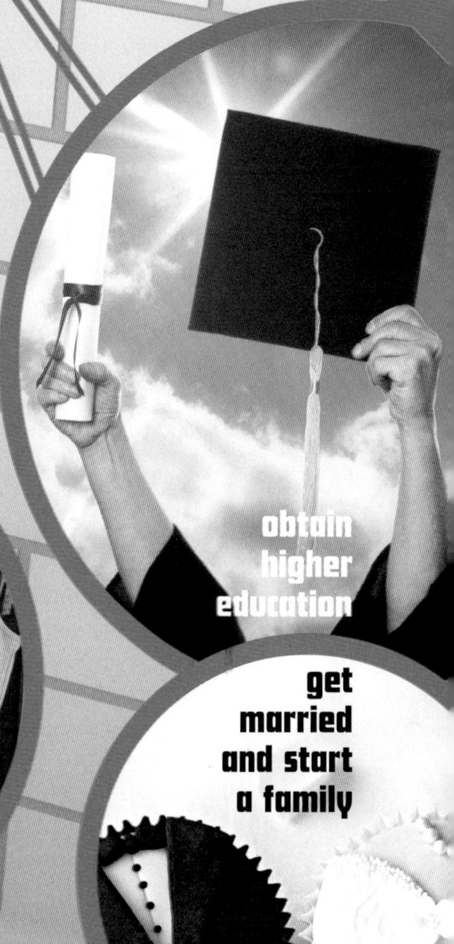
obtain
higher
education

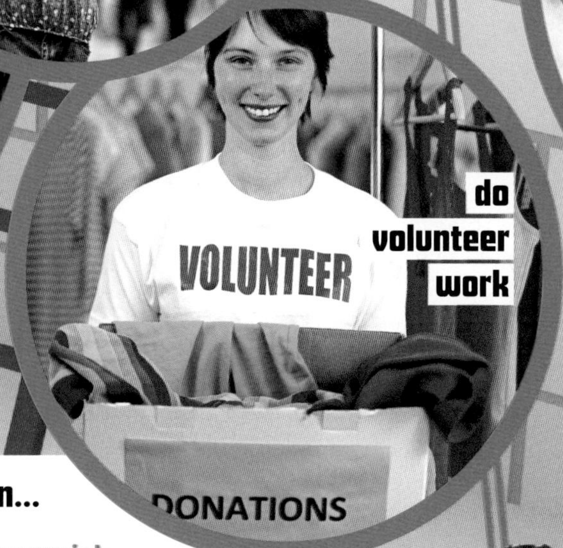
VOLUNTEER
do
volunteer
work
DONATIONS

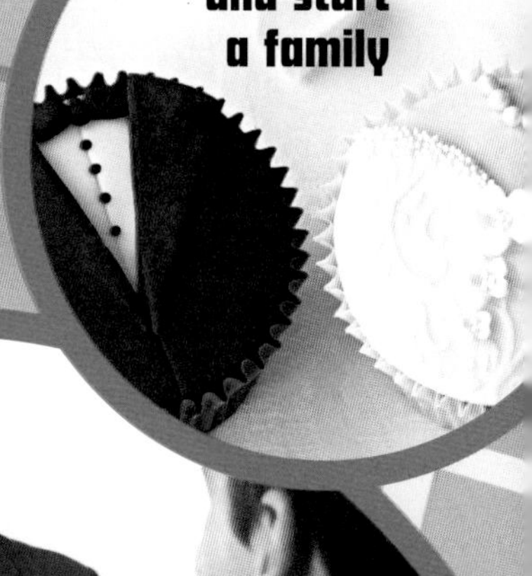
get
married
and start
a family

## In this module you will learn...

- to talk about your studies and/or your job
- to express agreement and disagreement
- vocabulary related to jobs
- to link the past with the present
- to talk about language learning experiences
- to understand information in job advertisements
- to describe your qualifications
- to distinguish between formal and informal language
- to write a cover letter

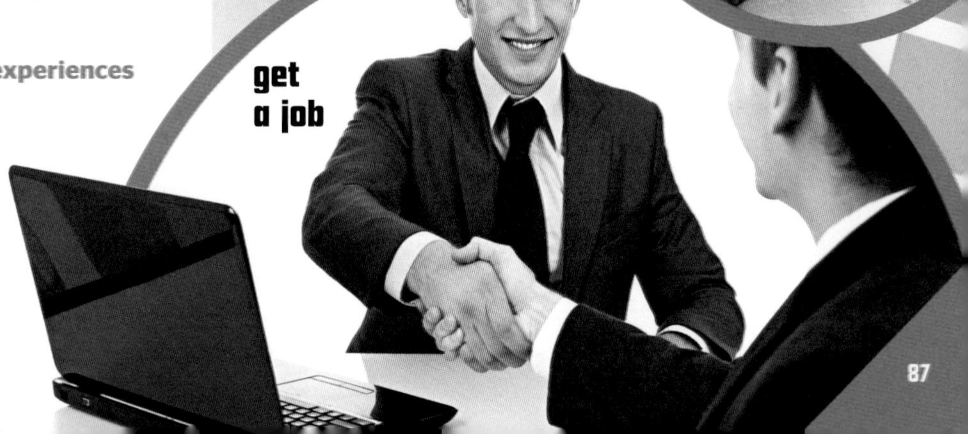
get
a job

# 9a

## 1 Reading 🔊

**A. Listen and read. Where are the dialogues taking place and what is the relationship between the people?**

**1.**

**Tim** Hey, guys. I'm thinking about taking software engineering this semester. It sounds cool.

**Roy** I find it boring.

**Lee** I do too. Why do you want to take that class?

**Tim** I want a career in the video game industry.

**Lee** I'm not sure that studying software engineering is the best way to do that.

**Roy** Neither am I. You should study graphic design, or something.

**Tim** Graphic design?

**Roy** Yeah, and I don't think software engineering is very easy, you know.

**Tim** Neither do I. But I like a challenge.

**Roy** Oh, come on! You just like sitting around playing computer games all day. I don't think you can earn a living by doing that.

**Tim** I don't either, but...

**Lee** I do. My cousin is a computer game tester, and he plays video games all day. But he says it's not as easy as it seems.

**Tim** I don't want to play video games. I want to create them.

**2.**

**Sheila** How's your first day going, Rita?

**Rita** Just fine. So, how long have you worked at this firm?

**Sheila** Almost 10 years now. Time flies when you're having fun, huh? So, where did you use to work?

**Rita** I was an accountant at a big bank downtown.

**Sheila** Really? So was I.

**Rita** But before that, I worked in retail, selling clothes. You know, to help pay the bills while I was in college. I didn't want to get a student loan.

**Sheila** Neither did I. I worked as a waitress in a coffee shop for a couple of years. So, did you study accounting at college?

**Rita** Yes, but I didn't really find it interesting.

**Sheila** Me neither. I wanted to study art.

**Rita** Really? I did too. But there were no job prospects. So, I stuck with accounting.

**Sheila** Well, you're part of our team now, and I'm sure you'll love it here.

**Rita** Thanks.

**B. Read the first dialogue again. Who agrees with the following statements?**

|  | Tim | Roy | Lee |
|---|---|---|---|
| 1. The software engineering course doesn't sound interesting. | ☐ | ☐ | ☐ |
| 2. Software engineering isn't useful for getting a job in the video game industry. | ☐ | ☐ | ☐ |
| 3. The software engineering course is difficult. | ☐ | ☐ | ☐ |
| 4. You can earn a living by playing video games. | ☐ | ☐ | ☐ |

**C. Read the second dialogue again and check what Sheila and Rita have in common.**

1. They have been at the firm for ten years. ☐
2. They used to work at a bank. ☐
3. They didn't get a student loan. ☐
4. They worked as salespeople. ☐
5. They worked as waitresses. ☐
6. They studied accounting. ☐
7. They found accounting a boring subject. ☐
8. They wanted to study art. ☐

## 2 Vocabulary & Speaking 🔊

**A. Match the occupations with the pictures. Then listen and check your answers.**

bank teller ☐   politician ☐   plumber ☐
receptionist ☐   pilot ☐   paramedic ☐
lawyer ☐   graphic designer ☐   surgeon ☐

**B.** Read the tables and talk in pairs. You can use some of the ideas given or your own.

### Talking about my studies

| | | |
|---|---|---|
| What are you studying? | I'm studying medicine at McGill University. | **Academic Subjects** |
| Have you decided on a career? | I'm studying to be a doctor. | Accounting |
| What are you majoring in? | I'm in college. | Law |
| Are you a college student? | I'm majoring in English. | Graphic design |
| | I'm a history major. | Engineering |
| | I'm thinking about a career in the tourist industry. | Media |
| | I'm graduating from McGill University with a degree in medicine. | Business and finance |
| | I'm doing a degree in finance. | Philosophy |
| | | Economics |
| | | Social and political sciences |

### Talking about my job

| | |
|---|---|
| What do you do? | I'm a lawyer. |
| What do you do for a living? | I work in an office. |
| Do you have a job? | I work for a large computer company/firm. |
| Are you employed at the moment? | I work at a bank. |
| Who do you work for? | I work with young children / with computers. |
| What kind of work do you do? | I work as a nurse in a hospital. |
| Where do you work? | I have a part-time / full-time job. |
| | I'm unemployed. |

## 3 Grammar so, neither, too, either → p. 146

**A.** Read the dialogues and match the phrases in blue with their uses a-c.

> **A:** I really enjoy my job.
>
> **B:** *So do I. / I do too. / Me too.* ☐
>
> **C:** *I don't.* I want to find a new one. ☐
>
> **A:** I'm not working this Friday.
>
> **B:** *Neither am I. / I'm not either. / Me neither.* ☐
>
> **C:** Well, *I am.* And I'm working on Saturday, too. ☐

**a.** It is used to agree with an affirmative sentence.

**b.** It is used to agree with a negative sentence.

**c.** It is used to disagree.

**B.** Complete using *so, neither, too, either* and an auxiliary verb if necessary.

**1. A:** I can't stand physics.

   **B:** I _____.

**2. A:** My brother used to work as a hotel receptionist.

   **B:** _____ mine.

**3. A:** I don't mind working in the evenings.

   **B:** _____ I.

**4. A:** I should get a driver's license.

   **B:** I _____.

**5. A:** Tom has found a job in finance.

   **B:** _____ Karen.

**6. A:** I really like playing video games.

   **B:** Me _____.

## 4 Pronunciation 🔊

**A.** Listen to the dialogue below. What do you notice about the way the two speakers pronounce *neither*?

> I'm not working today.
>
> Neither am I.
>
> Me neither.

Some words can be pronounced in more than one way, all of which are considered correct.

**B.** Look at the words below. How do you pronounce them? Can you think of another possible way of pronouncing them? Listen and check your answers.

either    often    economics    garage    adult    Caribbean

## 5 Speaking

Talk in groups of three. Discuss the issues below, expressing your opinion, agreeing and disagreeing.

- academic subjects
  *I like/liked physics.../ I find/found physics...*
- part-time jobs you had
  *I worked/used to work...*
- things you like/don't like in your life
  *I really enjoy / can't stand...*

- how easy/difficult it is to study and work at the same time
  *I think/believe it is... because...*
- your future plans
  *I want to / I'd like to / I'm going to...*

> **❝** *I found psychology boring and difficult.*
>
> ***So did I.***
>
> *I didn't. It was one of my favorite subjects.* **❞**

# 1 Reading

## A. Discuss.

- Which of the following do you think employees consider important in their job?
- Is there anything else that you consider important?

| | | | |
|---|---|---|---|
| salary | the type of work | colleagues | employer |
| workplace | working hours | benefits (e.g. car, bonus) | |

## B. Read the cartoons below. Which one do you like the most? Why?

**1** TECHNICALLY, YOU AREN'T GETTING FIRED. WE JUST WANT YOU TO TAKE A REALLY LONG VACATION WITHOUT PAY.

**2** WHY AREN'T YOU WORKING? — I DIDN'T SEE YOU COMING.

**3** DO YOU SEE YOURSELF AS PART OF THE FUTURE OF THIS COMPANY? — YES, I DO. — GOOD. YOU'RE FIRED. COME BACK IN TWENTY YEARS.

**4** LATE AGAIN, FLETCHER? — I WAS SLEEPING SO PEACEFULLY THAT I DIDN'T WANT TO WAKE MYSELF UP.

**5** ALL EMPLOYEES HAVE AIRBAGS INSTALLED, SO THEY CAN PROTECT THEMSELVES WHEN THEIR COMPUTERS CRASH.

**6** Consider yourself lucky. No other firm I've been to has hired me. Therefore, I'm available!

**7** IF YOU WORK 24 HOURS A DAY, YOU WON'T NEED TO PAY RENT FOR AN APARTMENT. AS A RESULT, YOU WILL SAVE MONEY AND I WON'T NEED TO GIVE YOU A RAISE.

**8** I've figured out the problem. We earn money 5 days a week, but we spend money 7 days a week.

## C. Read again and answer the questions. Write 1-8.

Which cartoon shows...

a. safety in the workplace? ☐

b. that the employees aren't making enough money? ☐ ☐

c. a job interview? ☐

d. a lazy employee? ☐ ☐

e. a boss who is refusing to give more money? ☐

f. someone who wants to get a job? ☐

g. an employee who is losing his/her job? ☐ ☐

h. an employee giving the boss an excuse? ☐ ☐

## 2 Vocabulary

Complete the sentences with the words in the boxes.

| work | job | career |
|---|---|---|

**1.** I went to bed late last night because I had a lot of _____ to do.

**2.** My father had a long and successful _____ taking photographs for magazines.

**3.** My first part-time _____ was delivering pizzas.

| colleague | employer | employee | staff |
|---|---|---|---|

**4.** Does your _____ know that you work so many hours at home?

**5.** Mr. Charles gathered all the _____ into the main meeting room and introduced the new manager.

**6.** A(n) _____ of mine at the office told me about this website.

**7.** As a new _____, I had to do a month's training.

| break | time off | overtime |
|---|---|---|

**8.** On Mondays, we have a lot to do, so I usually have to work _____.

**9.** We usually have a ten-minute coffee _____ at around 11 o'clock.

**10.** I need to ask my boss for some _____ next month. It's my sister's wedding.

| quit | retire | get fired |
|---|---|---|

**11. A:** Why did Danny _____?

**B:** Because he was late every day for almost a month.

**12.** I decided to _____ my old job because I found a new one with a better salary.

**13.** After 45 years working at the company, Gerald decided it was time to _____.

## 3 Grammar Reflexive pronouns → p. 146

**A. Read the examples and answer the questions.**

- **Ms. Jones** introduced **herself** to the manager of the bank.
- **The manager of the bank** introduced **her** to the employees.

In which sentence does the pronoun refer to the subject?

- Do you prefer to work **by yourself** or with others?
- Can you two work by **yourselves** for a while?

What does the phrase *by yourself* mean?
What's the difference between *yourself* and *yourselves*?

**B. Complete the sentences using the verbs in the box and reflexive pronouns.**

| make | enjoy | look at | taught | introduce |
|---|---|---|---|---|

**1.** Are you going out like that? _____ in the mirror.

**2.** Did you and Edith _____ at the beach?

**3.** I'm going to _____ a sandwich. I'm hungry.

**4.** At the beginning of the meeting, everyone _____.

**5.** Oliver _____ English by reading novels.

## 4 Listening 🔊

Listen to three short dialogues and answer the questions. Choose picture a, b or c.

**1.** What does Ian like about his new job?

**2.** What time is the break?

**3.** What would Dennis like to change about his job?

## 5 Speaking

**Talk in pairs.**

**Student A:** Imagine that you work for the ideal company. Student B is a new employee. Tell him/her about it. Use the ideas in the box.

| your boss | the facilities |
|---|---|
| your colleagues | the working hours/days |
| the salary | the days/time off you get |
| the benefits | the breaks you can have |

**Student B:** It's your first day at work. Talk to your new colleague (Student A) about the ideas in the box. Ask him/her about anything you'd like to know.

❝ *The boss is very easygoing. He doesn't mind when we come in late.*
*Really? And what about...?* ❞

## 1 Reading 🔊

**A. Discuss.**

- Which foreign languages are people in your country interested in learning?
- Do you think it is important to learn foreign languages? Why?/Why not?

**B. Listen and read. What is the main idea of the two texts? Choose a, b or c.**

**a.** The people are thinking of learning a different language.
**b.** The people tried to learn a language, but failed.
**c.** The people are satisfied with what they have achieved so far.

🔄 🏠 ✖ ➕  http://www.yourforum.com/languagelearningexperience/  🔍

# *your* FORUM

| About | Forum | Downloads | FAQs | Contact |

## Tell us your language learning experiences.

**Dan Booster**
28

*posted at 10:39*

Last year the company I work for moved offices to Doha, Qatar, so I had to move too. I couldn't speak a word of Arabic so daily communication was a very big obstacle, and my busy work schedule didn't allow me to attend an intensive language course. So for nearly a year now, I have been using an online method. Working online really suits me as I can study anywhere, anytime. This method has proved to be very useful, but I've made good progress only in the past few months. This is because I have been participating in a language exchange program with a local person. He has been studying English for 4 years and wants to improve his speaking skills, so we have been meeting twice a week ever since. We talk for an hour in English and then for an hour in Arabic, and we have both benefited enormously! We haven't been practicing grammar or anything like that, we just talk naturally about subjects that interest us. I'm slowly coming to grips with the language and I'm finally starting to feel confident about myself. I have been thinking of getting a novel in Arabic and starting to work on my reading skills, too. I'll just have to get used to reading from right to left!

**Lizzy Silver**
25

*posted at 12:43*

I have lots of Mexican friends, so over the years I've picked up Spanish words and expressions. However, I couldn't actually hold a conversation in Spanish, so I decided to learn it properly by going to a language school. In the past whenever I enrolled, I dropped out in a month or two. But this time I decided not to give up so easily. I've been attending for six months now and have completed a great deal of assignments. I have started understanding the language and using it correctly. I have also been chatting online with my friends in Spanish and they have been helping me with some of my grammar problems. It's great; I'm practicing and socializing at the same time! Recently, I have been watching movies in Spanish, too. I don't add English subtitles, of course, and I try to imitate the pronunciation and intonation. And everyone tells me that I've improved very much. Isn't that something to be proud of?

◄ 1 2 ►

**C. Read again and write D for Dan, L for Lizzy or B for Both.**

**1.** I'm learning from face-to-face meetings. ☐
**2.** The Internet has helped me learn. ☐
**3.** I had to learn fast. ☐
**4.** I use a variety of media to learn. ☐

**5.** I'm planning on trying a new idea. ☐
**6.** I'm getting help from someone. ☐
**7.** I'm learning just for the fun of it. ☐
**8.** I met someone through my learning experience. ☐

**D.** Match the words/phrases from the text with their meanings.

1. obstacle ☐
2. suit ☐
3. participate ☐
4. come to grips with ☐
5. get used to ☐
6. pick up ☐
7. enroll ☐
8. drop out ☐
9. imitate ☐

a. to take part in sth.

b. to learn sth. by chance, without trying

c. to copy the speech or behavior of sb.

d. sth. that makes it difficult for you to achieve sth.

e. to officially join a school, college, course, etc.

f. to begin to understand and deal with sth. that is difficult

g. to be convenient for sb.

h. to leave school, college, etc. before finishing your studies

i. to become familiar with sth.

**E.** Discuss.
- Do you like learning foreign languages?
- Do you think English is an important language? Why?/Why not?
- Is learning English easy for you?

ENGLISH
DEUTSCH
FRANÇAIS
ITALIANO
ESPAÑOL
PORTUGUÊS
NEDERLANDS

## 2 Grammar Present Perfect Progressive, Present Perfect Simple vs. Present Perfect Progressive → p. 147

**A.** Read the example and answer the questions. Then complete the rule.

Mario **has been learning** English since 2011.

1. When did Mario start learning English?
2. Is he still learning English?

**Present Perfect Progressive**

*have* or _____ + _____ + verb + _____

**Use:**

the Present Perfect Progressive for actions or situations that started in the _____ and continue up to the _____.

**B.** Read the sentences below. Which tenses are used? Which sentence emphasizes the result and which the duration of the action?

- Tina and Kelly **have been watching** TV for two hours.
- Tina and Kelly **have watched** three TV shows so far.

**C.** Complete with the Present Perfect Simple or the Present Perfect Progressive of the verbs in parentheses.

1. **A:** Bill! Long time no see!

   **B:** Ted! I 1 _____ (not see) you for ages. How's work?

   **A:** I can't stand it any longer. I 2 _____ (work) at that coffee shop for two years now. I need a change. I 3 _____ (try) to find a new job since last month, but I 4 _____ (not find) anything interesting yet.

   **B:** 5 _____ you _____ (think) of asking at the college? They might have something interesting.

   **A:** You're right, I will.

2. Sally Dale 6 _____ recently _____ (move) to Peru. She 7 _____ (live) there for six months and 8 _____ (enjoy) every minute of it. She 9 _____ (not decide) if she's going to come back yet, but at the moment she wants to stay there. She's an English teacher and 10 _____ (teach) English at a school in Lima ever since she got there.

## 3 Listening 🔊

Listen to a conversation between Jenna and Mike, who is learning Mandarin, and answer the questions. Choose a, b or c.

1. What does Mike think of Mandarin?
   a. That it's more difficult than he thought.
   b. That it's not as difficult as he thought.
   c. That it's too difficult for most people.

2. What can Mike do so far?
   a. Speak, read and write a little.
   b. Speak and read a little.
   c. Speak a little but not read or write.

3. How is Mike learning Mandarin?
   a. He is using an online method.
   b. He is taking a class.
   c. He is doing both of the above.

4. Which of the following does Mike do?
   a. watch movies in Mandarin
   b. read magazines and newspapers in Mandarin
   c. communicate with a Chinese person

5. What is Mike planning to do in the future?
   a. work abroad
   b. study abroad
   c. travel abroad

## 4 Speaking & Writing Survey

**A.** Talk in pairs. Go to page 136.

**B.** Use the survey on page 136 to write about your experiences in learning English. Write some general information about the ways you learn/practice English and the reasons why you are learning it.

# 1 Vocabulary

**A. Discuss.**
- Have you ever had a job? If yes, how did you get it?
- Where can you find job advertisements?
- How do people apply for a job they are interested in?

**B. Read the job advertisements and try to guess the meaning of the words in blue. Then match them with their definitions 1-8.**

## LIFEGUARDS WANTED
### Jacksonville Swimming Pool
- Lifeguard and first-aid training required
- Must be in shape
- Previous work experience
- Flexible working hours

**Apply in person or online**
**swjackson@zmail.com**

## CARL'S MOTORS
### We are looking for salespeople

**We offer:**
- full-time work in an excellent environment
- a good salary plus benefits

**Applicants must:**
- have a driver's license
- be fluent in English and Spanish
- be computer literate
- have experience in sales
- have excellent communication skills
- have a professional appearance

Call 555-432-7761 for an interview

## THE NATIONAL MUSEUM

### Position: Tour guide
- part or full time
- training and uniform provided

**We require:**
- good communication skills
- knowledge of at least one foreign language
- ability to work weekends

Send résumé
to Lucy Atkins at
a.lucy@nationalmuseum.net

1. able to speak a language very well: _____
2. a person who applies for a job: _____
3. needed, necessary: _____
4. a short written description of your education, qualifications, previous jobs, etc. that you send to an employer when you are applying for a job: _____
5. happening before the time you are talking about: _____
6. able to use a computer well: _____
7. able to change easily: _____
8. the special set of clothes which is worn by the members of a group or organization at work: _____

# 2 Listening 🔊

**A. Discuss.**
- Have you ever been to a job interview?
- What kind of questions are people asked?

**B. Listen to part of a job interview and answer the questions.**
- What position is the man applying for?
- Do you think he should get the job?

**C. Listen again and check the sentences that are true for Tim.**
1. He has created a website showing his work.
2. He has worked as a graphic designer.
3. He wants to work full time.
4. He has worked as part of a team.
5. He can work overtime during the week.
6. He can work on weekends.
7. He can speak French.

# 3 Speaking

**A. Read the table below and check what is true about you.**

| | YES | NO |
|---|---|---|
| Do you have a college/university degree? | | |
| Do you have previous work experience? | | |
| Do you want a full-time job? | | |
| Are you fluent in more than one language? | | |
| Are you computer literate? | | |
| Do you have a driver's license? | | |
| Do you have good communication skills? | | |
| Do you like working as part of a team? | | |
| Can you work flexible hours? | | |
| Are you able to work on weekends or overtime? | | |

**B. ROLE PLAY**
Choose one of the jobs from activity 1B or some other job and talk in pairs.

**Student A:** Imagine that you're applying for a job and Student B is interviewing you. Answer his/her questions.

**Student B:** Imagine that Student A is applying for a job in the company you work for. Interview him/her using ideas from the table above and your own.

❝ *So, do you have a college degree?*
*Yes, I studied...* ❞

# 4 Writing A cover letter

**A. Read the advertisement on the right and the cover letter below. Do you think that Emily is suitable for the job. Why?/ Why not?**

**Business Opps**

**WAITER/WAITRESS WANTED**
for airport coffee shop

• Foreign languages required
• Pleasant personality
• Flexible working hours
  and weekends

Apply to: coffee@airstop.com

Dear Sir/Madam,

I saw your advertisement in The Daily News on March 5th and I am interested in working as a waitress at the airport coffee shop.

I have been working at a small coffee shop for about a year now and I have picked up all the necessary skills and experience for working as a waitress. You can see from my résumé that I am fluent in Polish and I am currently learning Russian, too. I am a responsible, hard-working and outgoing person, and I enjoy meeting new people. I believe these qualities make me suitable for the job. What is more, I am available to work on any day of the week, including weekends.

I hope you will consider my résumé. I look forward to hearing from you.

Yours sincerely,
Emily Miles

**B. Read the following sentences. Check the ones that apply to the cover letter.**

The writer:

1. knows the person she is writing to. ☐
2. uses set phrases to begin and end. ☐
3. mentions where she saw the advertisement. ☐
4. uses short forms and abbreviations. ☐
5. describes her qualifications and experience. ☐
6. describes some bad qualities she has. ☐
7. explains why she is suitable for the job. ☐
8. refers to points mentioned in the advertisement. ☐

**C. What features make the cover letter formal?**

**D. Imagine you have decided to apply for one of the jobs in activity 1. Write your cover letter. Follow the plan and tip.**

> **TIP**
> When writing a cover letter,
> • use the appropriate layout (see page 139).
> • use formal language. Also, don't use short forms or abbreviations.
> • read the advertisement carefully. Identify the qualities/qualifications required for the job and explain why you think you are suitable.
> • write in a confident manner, describing your good qualities. Don't mention your bad qualities.
> • be brief and to the point. Don't include unnecessary details/information.

## Plan
### A cover letter

**GREETING**
**Use a formal greeting, not first names.**
• *Dear Sir/Madam,*
• *Dear Mr./Mrs./Ms./Miss + last name,*

**OPENING PARAGRAPH**
**Use set phrases to state the position you are applying for and say where/ when you saw the job advertised.**
• *I am interested in applying for the job of...*
• *I am writing to apply for the position of...*
• *I am interested in working as...*
• *I saw your advertisement in/on...*

**MAIN PART**
**Describe your qualifications and any experience that is relevant to the job. Include only important information, as the details are in your résumé. Explain why you think you are suitable for the job advertised. Use phrases like:**
• *I am fluent in... / able to... / good at...*
• *As you can see from my résumé, I...*
• *I have been working for/at/in...*
• *I am currently working/ learning...*
• *At present I am...*
• *I worked full time/part time for/at...*
• *I am available to work...*
• *I believe I am suitable for this job/ position because...*
• *I strongly believe these qualities/ qualifications make me suitable for the job.*
• *I am a responsible/hard-working... person.*

**CLOSING PARAGRAPH**
**Use set phrases like:**
• *I look forward to hearing from you.*
• *I hope you will consider my résumé.*
• *I am available for an interview whenever it is convenient for you.*
• *Please contact me if you have any questions about my résumé.*

**SIGNING OFF**
**Use a formal signature ending and write your full name underneath it.**
• *Yours sincerely,*
• *Yours truly,*

## Vocabulary

**A. Circle the correct words.**

1. My brother has always been good with numbers, so he's decided to become a(n) **plumber / accountant**.

2. Last month, I got a **bonus / salary** for my hard work.

3. I was surprised to hear that Mr. Jones gave Greg a **raise / benefit**.

4. Why did you have to work **time off / overtime** this month?

5. People **quit / retire** at the age of 65 in my country.

6. Are you computer **literate / fluent**?

7. No **previous / current** experience is required for this position.

8. The **surgeons / paramedics** arrived ten minutes after the accident happened.

**B. Complete the sentences with the words in the box.**

> hired   provided   fired   workplace
> enrolled   qualifications   industry

1. If you keep coming to work late, you'll get _____!

2. Tina was _____ by a successful law firm in Chicago.

3. Have you ever considered a job in the tourist _____?

4. We recently _____ in a language school. We hope to learn some basic French by June.

5. This applicant has excellent _____ and can work flexible hours.

6. Unfortunately, uniforms are not _____ by the company.

7. It's very important for one's _____ to be safe and pleasant.

## Grammar

**C. Circle the correct words.**

1. I'm sorry, but I can't help you. You have to do this by **myself / yourself**.

2. Amanda's sick, but don't worry about **her / herself**. She can take care of **her / herself**.

3. Ted and I learned how to cook all by **ourselves / themselves**.

4. Mr. Smith introduced **me / myself** to the other employees.

5. The boys enjoyed **them / themselves** at the park.

**D. Complete using the Present Perfect Simple or the Present Perfect Progressive of the verbs in parentheses.**

1. Where _____ (you / be)? We _____ (wait) for you since ten o'clock!

2. **A:** Ricky _____ (teach) first-aid for years.
   **B:** Really? I _____ (never / take) a course in first-aid. Maybe I should.

3. Diana _____ (try) to find a job that suits her for months. She _____ (send) her résumé to twelve companies.

4. Paul _____ (publish) three books so far and I think he might publish another one pretty soon. He _____ (work) on it for the past six months.

5. I _____ (always / want) to visit Australia but I _____ (not manage) to go there yet.

## Communication

**E. Complete the dialogues.**

1. **A:** I always feel nervous during interviews.
   **B:** _____ I.
   **C:** Well, I _____. I'm very confident about myself.

2. **A:** Sally hasn't graduated yet.
   **B:** I haven't _____.
   **A:** I _____, and now I'm looking for a job.

3. **A:** I didn't know Linda was Spanish.
   **B:** _____ I.
   **C:** Me _____. I thought she was Italian.

**F. Choose a or b.**

1. **A:** What do you do for a living?
   **B:** _____
   **a.** I live near the downtown area.
   **b.** I work for a computer company.

2. **A:** Do you speak French?
   **B:** _____
   **a.** Not a word.
   **b.** I don't pick up words.

3. **A:** How is John managing after losing his job?
   **B:** _____
   **a.** He still can't come to grips with it.
   **b.** He still can't figure it out.

## Self-assessment

**Read the following and check the appropriate boxes. For the points you are unsure of, refer back to the relevant sections in the module.**

### NOW I CAN...

| | |
|---|---|
| ‣ talk about my studies and/or my job | ☐ |
| ‣ express agreement and disagreement | ☐ |
| ‣ link the past with the present | ☐ |
| ‣ understand information in job advertisements | ☐ |
| ‣ describe my qualifications | ☐ |
| ‣ distinguish between formal and informal language | ☐ |
| ‣ write a cover letter | ☐ |

# 10 Facts and figures

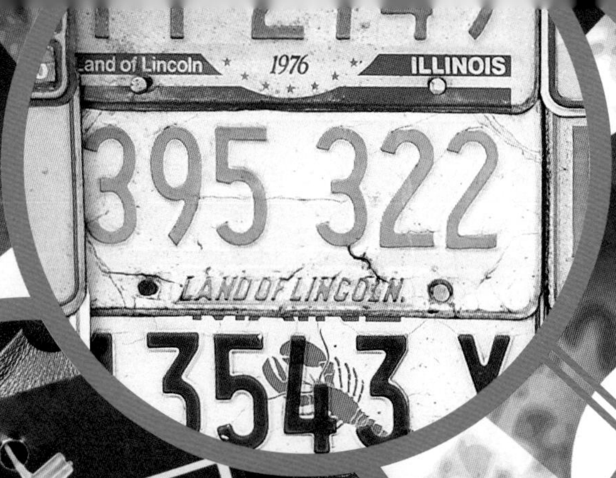
Land of Lincoln 1976 ILLINOIS
395 322
LAND OF LINCOLN
13543 Y

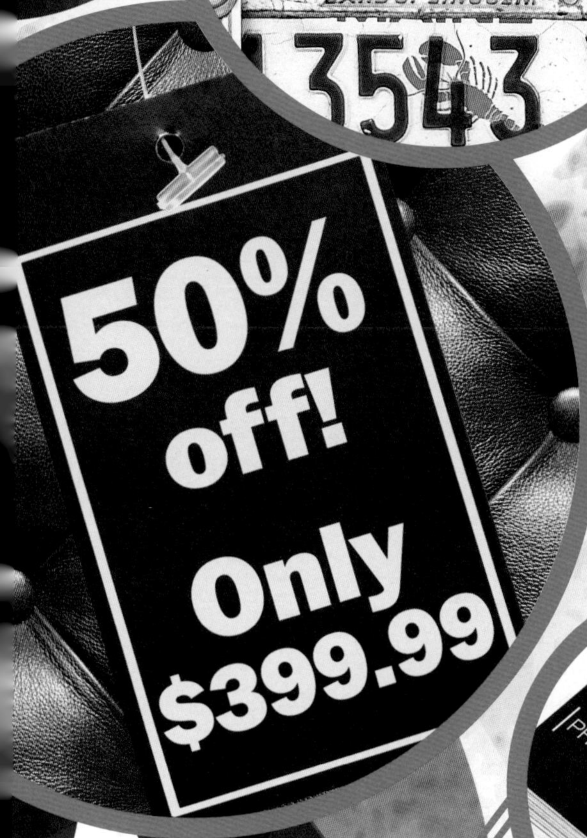
50% off!
Only $399.99

**Discuss:**

- How would you say the numbers in the pictures? Listen and check your answers.
- How good are you at remembering phone numbers?
- Do you have a lucky number?

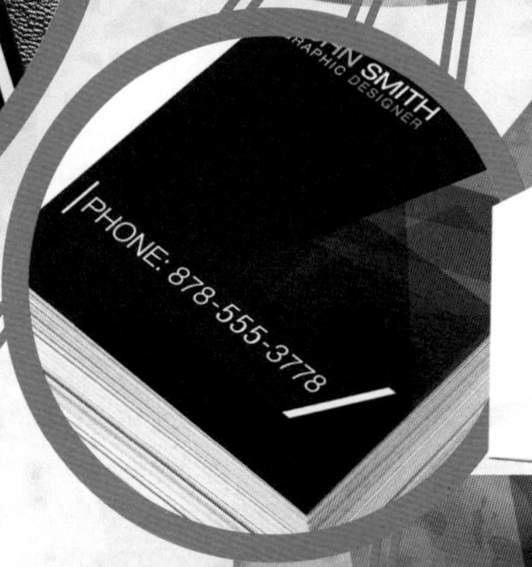
SMITH
GRAPHIC DESIGNER
PHONE: 878-555-3778

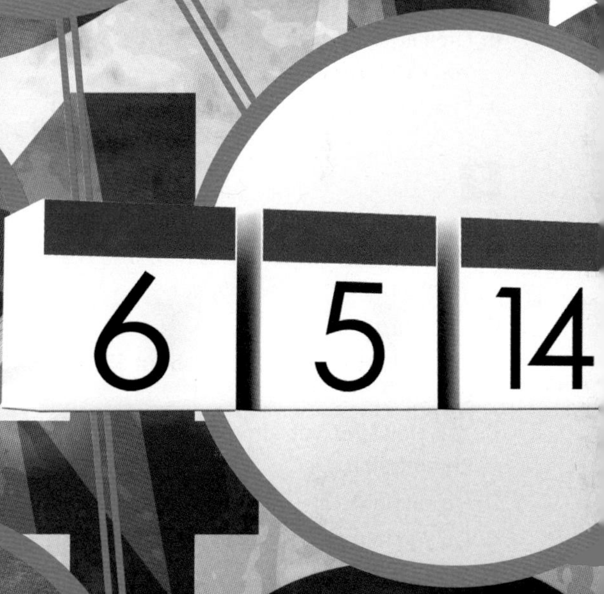
6
5
14

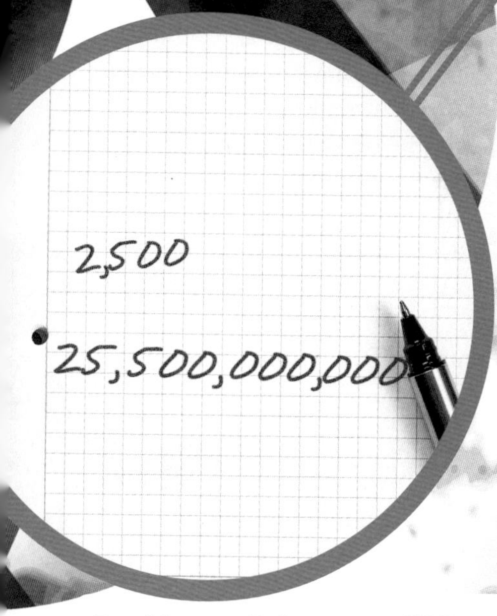
2,500
25,500,000,000

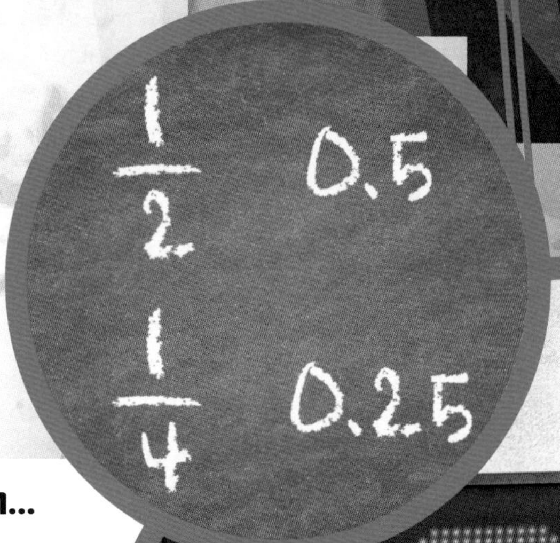
1/2 0.5
1/4 0.25

## In this module you will learn...

- to carry out money transactions
- to indicate degree and extent
- to give and understand different kinds of instructions
- common units of measurement
- ways to improve your memory
- to write an e-mail giving information and opinion

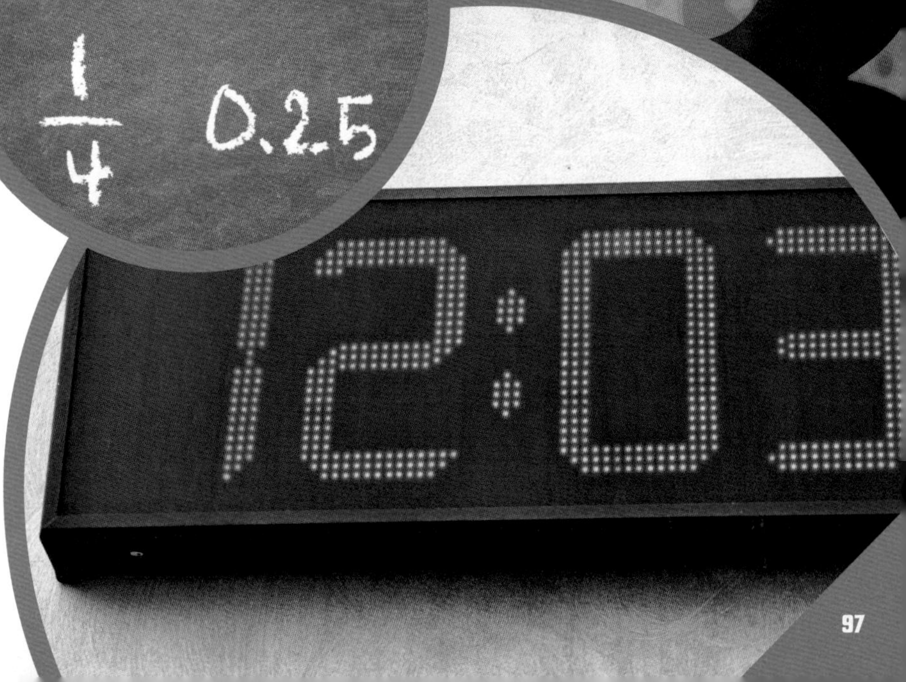
12:03

## 10a

### 1 Reading 🔊

**A. Listen and read. Where are the dialogues taking place?**

**a.** at a bank   **b.** at a currency exchange office
**c.** at an ATM

**1**

**A:** I won't be too long, Steve. I want to withdraw some money because I'm broke. Oh, no! It won't accept my PIN!

**B:** Maybe you entered it incorrectly. Try again.

**A:** I'm confused. I don't remember it.

**B:** It happens. Too many numbers to remember nowadays. I usually use my son's date of birth or something like that.

**A:** No, that's not it either.

**B:** Careful, that was your second time. If you enter another wrong PIN, it will swallow your card.

**A:** It's no use. Steve, I need a favor. I have to get something from the bookstore, so could I borrow...

**B:** I'm a little short of cash myself. I only have $20, but you can have it.

**A:** That's enough money to buy what I want. Thanks.

**2**

**C:** Good morning. How may I help you?

**D:** I'd like to exchange some euros into U.S. dollars. What's the exchange rate?

**C:** One euro is $1.30.

**D:** OK, well, I think I will need about $500. Is €400 enough?

**C:** Yes. However, you should also know we charge 1% commission.

**D:** Oh, all right.

**C:** Do you mind if I give you fifty-dollar bills?

**D:** No, that's fine.

> **ATM** stands for Automated Teller Machine.
> **PIN** stands for Personal Identification Number.
> **ID** is the abbreviation for Identity/Identification.

**3**

**E:** Excuse me. Am I old enough to open a savings account on my own? I'm eighteen.

**F:** Do you have your ID with you?

**E:** Yes.

**F:** Then there's no problem.

**E:** Do your savings accounts come with debit cards?

**F:** Yes, we give you a debit card free of charge.

**E:** Great. When I pay for things with a debit card, the amount is taken directly from my account, right?

**F:** Exactly. In addition, our new savings account has an interest rate of 5% and online banking is included.

**E:** That's useful.

**F:** You will have to make a deposit into your new account, though.

**E:** OK, no problem.

**F:** We'll take care of that right after you fill out this form.

**E:** OK. Thank you.

**B. Read again and match the two halves of the sentences.**

1. When you put your card in an ATM,
2. When you enter your PIN three times incorrectly,
3. When you exchange money,
4. When you want to open a savings account,
5. When you pay by debit card,

a. you usually have to fill out a form.
b. it asks for your PIN.
c. money is taken directly from your account.
d. you usually have to pay commission.
e. the ATM will swallow your card.

**C. Read again and answer the questions. Write A-F. You will not need to use all the letters.**

Which person...

1. is going to receive money?
2. is going to receive a card?
3. can't use a service?
4. has to give personal information?

**D. Discuss.**

• Do you have a bank account? If yes, how often do you make deposits?
• How do you feel about using ATMs?
• How do you feel about online banking?

98

## 2 Vocabulary

Complete the sentences with the words in the box. Use each word twice.

> **TIP** Keep in mind that some words can have more than one meaning. Also, some words can be both verbs and nouns.

| bill | change | check | charge |

1. How much did they _____ for the repairs to your car?

2. Here's your _____, $10.50. The receipt is in the bag.

3. **A:** That was a great meal. Would you like some dessert?

   **B:** No, I'm full. Let's ask for the _____.

4. Delivery is free of _____.

5. I got a huge telephone _____. How am I going to pay for it?

6. Could you break a twenty-dollar _____?

7. You can pay in cash, by credit card or by _____.

8. Do you have any _____? I want to buy a soda.

## 3 Grammar too / enough → p. 147

**A. Read the examples and complete the rules.**

1. I have **enough** money for the jacket, but I don't think I need another jacket.
2. I'm **too** short of money to go out tonight.
3. I'm not rich **enough** to buy a house by the beach.
4. I have **too much** money and I waste it on things I don't really need.

**Use:**

- _____ + adjective or adverb

- adjective or adverb + _____

- _____ and _____ + uncountable nouns

- *too many* and *enough* + plural countable nouns

**B. Read the examples again and match them with the meanings a-c below.**

a. I have as much as I need.  ☐

b. I have more than I need.  ☐

c. I don't have as much as I need.  ☐ ☐

**C. Rewrite the sentences using the words in parentheses.**

1. I'm too young to get a driver's license.  (enough)

   _____

2. Tina has more clothes than she needs in her closet.  (too)

   _____

3. I can't use the payphone because I have less change than I need.  (enough)

   _____

4. For some people, online banking isn't easy enough to use.  (too)

   _____

## 4 Pronunciation 🔊

**A. Listen and repeat. What do you notice about the *gh* sound in each word?**

flight     enough     spaghetti

**B. Read the words below. Circle the word in each group that contains a *gh* sound that is different from the rest. Then listen and check your answers.**

1. through      laugh       highway
2. cough        straight    daughter
3. weigh        neighbor    Ghana

## 5 Speaking Role Play

**Talk in pairs. Act out the following conversations.**

**Student A:** You're at a currency exchange office and you want to exchange some money. Talk to Student B who works there.

**Student B:** You work at a currency exchange office and Student A wants to exchange some money.

**Student A:** You see your friend (Student B) in a store and ask him to lend you some money.

**Student B:** You are in a store when you see your friend (Student A) who asks to borrow some money.

**Student A:** You are at a bank and you want to open a new account / withdraw some money / make a deposit. Talk to Student B who is a bank teller.

**Student B:** You are a bank teller and Student A is a customer. Help him/her.

**Student A:** You are passing by an ATM. Student B is there and needs some help. Tell him/her how to use it.

**Student B:** You are at an ATM but it's your first time using it. Ask Student A for help.

## 1 Reading 🔊

**A.** Look at the abbreviations below and discuss the questions.

- What do you think they stand for?
- What do they measure?
- Where would you see them?

**mi.   lb.   °F   min.   gal.**

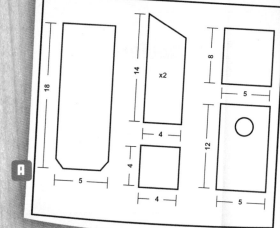

**A**

**B.** Read the instructions below quickly and match them with the pictures A-F. Don't pay attention to the gaps.

**1** Stir about ½ cup dry mix into 1 cup hot water. Cover and let it stand for 10 mins. _____

**2**
- It is best to take this medication on an empty stomach. (_____)
- Shake well before each use.
- Keep out of reach of children.

**3**
- Fill a large pot with 2 lbs. of soil.
- Make 1/2 inch holes in the soil.
- _____
- Plant two seeds in each hole.
- Water regularly.

**4**
1. Pour 1 pt. of cream into an electric mixer bowl and mix for a few minutes.
2. _____ Mix until the whipped cream is thick.
3. Serve immediately.

**Helpful hints**
- Make sure the cream is cold.
- If you plan to add any flavorings, such as vanilla or spices, remember to add them with the sugar.

**5**
- Mix dye with 4 fl.oz. (120 ml.) hot water and leave for 10 mins.
- Wear gloves to protect your hands.
- _____
- Leave for 60 mins.
- Shampoo hair.

**6**
Make your own birdhouse!
_____ Use a ruler to draw the shapes accurately (as shown in the diagram), before you cut them out.

**B** COOK BOOK

**C** Penicillin Solution 500mg

**D** New! 100% organic Tomato S·O·U·P packet of dried soup

**E** BASIL seed packet HUNTER AND GOULD

**F** Color Change 5.02 Red

**C.** Read again and complete the instructions 1-6 with the missing information a-f. Then listen and check your answers.

a. Apply with 2 in. brush. Make sure you cover hair completely.
b. Try to keep them 2 inches apart from each other.
c. You will need a thin piece of wood 2 ft. long and 1½ ft. wide.
d. 1 hr. before or 2 hrs. after meals.
e. Add about 2 oz. (7 tbsp.) powdered sugar.
f. Serve.

## 2 Vocabulary 🔊

**Look and listen. Then complete the sentences with the measurements in the box.**

### Units of measurement

| Length: | Weight: | Capacity: |
|---|---|---|
| 1 inch (in. or ") = 2.54 centimeters (cm.) | 1 ounce (oz.) = 28.35 grams (g.) | 1 fluid ounce (fl. oz.) = 29.5 milliliters (ml.) |
| 1 foot (ft. or ') = 30.48 centimeters (cm.) | 1 pound (lb.) = 0.45 kilograms (kg.) | 1 pint (pt.) = 473 milliliters (ml.) |
| 1 yard (yd.) = 0.91 meters (m.) | 1 ton (tn.) = 907 kilograms (kg.) | 1 quart (qt.) = 0.95 liters (l.) |
| 1 mile (mi.) = 1.6 kilometers (km.) | | 1 gallon (gal.) = 3.78 liters (l.) |

180 miles
7 tons
12 inches
29,029 feet
2 quarts
7 pounds
3 gallons

1. An adult elephant can weigh about _____.
2. A ruler is _____ long.
3. My family usually drinks about _____ of milk every day.
4. The distance between Liverpool and London is about _____.
5. A baby weighs about _____ when it is born.
6. The highest mountain in the world is _____ high.
7. I use about _____ of gas a day to get to and from work.

## 3 Grammar Infinitives → p. 147

**A. Read the examples and complete the rules.**

**A:** I want **to plant** these seeds. Is it difficult **to do**?

**B:** No. Let me **show** you how **to plant** them. Umm... that pot is too small **to fit** all of them in.

**A:** I'll go to the store **to get** another pot, then.

**B:** Don't forget **to ask** how often you should **water** them.

### Use the full infinitive (e.g. to do)

- to express purpose.
- after certain verbs (e.g. _____, _____, would like, decide, need, plan, try, offer).
- after *it + be + adjective*.
- after _____ and *enough*.
- after question words (e.g. *what, where,* _____ ).

### Use the bare infinitive (e.g. do)

- after modal verbs (e.g. *can, could,* _____, *must*).
- after the verbs *make* and _____.

**B. Complete with the full or the bare infinitive of the verbs in parentheses.**

1. **A:** I think we need _____ (cut) this piece of cardboard first. Can you _____ (give) me the scissors?

   **B:** I can't _____ (see) them anywhere. Let me _____ (check) in the kitchen.

2. **A:** I've decided _____ (prepare) something special for dessert. I'd like _____ (make) a chocolate cake!

   **B:** Do we have enough sugar _____ (make) a cake? I think you should _____ (check) in the cabinet first.

   **A:** Don't worry. I went to the store _____ (get) all the ingredients after work.

## 4 Listening 🔊

**Listen to three dialogues and answer the questions. Choose a, b or c.**

1. What should the woman do first?
   a. unplug the device
   b. turn the device off
   c. enter a password
2. How many cups of milk did they use?
   a. ½
   b. 1
   c. 1 ½
3. Which instructions are correct?
   a. Cut 3 pieces, 2 ft. long each.
   b. Cut 2 pieces, 2 ft. long each.
   c. Cut 2 pieces, 3 ft. long each.

## 5 Speaking

**Talk in pairs.**

**Student A:** Ask Student B for help with one of the following:
- how to use something (e.g. microwave, printer)
- how to make one of his/her favorite recipes

**Student B:** Give Student A instructions. Use some of the phrases in the box.

| | |
|---|---|
| First... / Then... / Next... / After that... / Lastly... The first/next/last thing you do / have to do is... When you finish that... Remember to... | Don't forget to... Make sure you... Be careful with... It is best to... Use... to... |

🞂🞂 *I'm not sure how to use this... / How does this... work? / How can I make...?*

   *Let me show you. First, put some...* 🞀🞀

## 6 Writing

**Imagine a friend is staying at your apartment/house. You have classes most of the day and get home late at night. Choose something in your home that you think your friend might need to use and write a note with the instructions on how to use it.**

*If you need to use the washing machine, here's what you have to do:*

# 1 Reading ◀))

**A. Discuss.**

**B. Listen, read and check your answers.**

- What do you know about how memory works?
- Do you know of any ways to improve your memory?

# Memory

How good are you at remembering names, dates, PIN and telephone numbers? It is not an easy process for all. Memory is one of the most interesting functions of the human brain, which is why scientists spend so much time studying how it works.

Studies have shown that when we learn something new, it stays in our memory for 20-30 seconds. This is our short-term memory and it can hold up to seven bits of information, for example a 7-digit phone number. If we repeat it and use it often, this information can move from short-term to long-term memory, which is the place where memories are stored for a long time. Scientists say that long-term memory will never fill up completely with memories in one lifetime!

Then why do we forget things? Forgetting things that are not important helps our brain to remember things that are. Our brain is always "cleaning out" useless information to make room for something more useful.

There is no limit to the possibilities of memory. There are many people throughout history who had incredible memories.

Winston Churchill, a former prime minister of the U.K., knew almost all of Shakespeare's works by heart. Wolfgang Amadeus Mozart, one of the best composers ever, wrote down Gregorio Allegri's composition *Miserere* after only hearing it once.

There are even competitions for memory. One of them is the annual World Memory Championship, which was first held in 1991. The winner that year was Dominic O'Brien and he went on to win seven more times. In 1993, he broke the record by memorizing 900 random numbers in an hour. However, the current record is 2,660 by Wang Feng from China. O'Brien has written several books on the techniques he uses to improve his memory.

If you are interested in improving your memory, apart from using memory techniques, there are lots of simple things you can do, like eating healthily, sleeping well and exercising daily. Challenging your brain also helps you keep it healthy and active. So, why not start doing puzzles and crosswords, playing mind games, learning a musical instrument or studying a new language?

**C. Read again and write T for True, F for False or NM for Not Mentioned.**

1. Our short-term memory can't hold information for more than half a minute.
2. Most phone numbers contain seven digits because people can't remember more than that.
3. There is a limit to how much information our long-term memory can hold.
4. Our brain remembers important things by "cleaning out" useless information.
5. Mozart composed *Miserere*.
6. Dominic O'Brien has won the World Memory Championship 8 times since 1991.
7. Dominic O'Brien isn't good at memorizing words.
8. Learning how to play the guitar can help improve your memory.

**D. Match the words/phrases below from the text with their meanings.**

1. store (v.) ☐
2. fill up ☐
3. room ☐
4. prime minister ☐
5. by heart ☐
6. composition ☐
7. annual ☐
8. memorize ☐
9. random ☐

a. learned in such a way that you can repeat it exactly from memory

b. without any particular plan or order

c. happening once a year

d. space

e. to learn sth. so that you remember it exactly as it is

f. a piece of music

g. to become full

h. the leader of the government (in some countries)

i. to save information on a computer or to keep it in your memory

**E. Discuss.**

• What is your earliest memory?
• Do you think you have a good memory?
• What kind of things do you usually forget?
• Do you know anyone who has an unusually good memory?

## 2 Grammar -ing form → p. 148

**A. Read the examples and match them with the uses of the -ing form.**

• I enjoy **learning** new things. ☐
• Lots of people try to improve their memory by **doing** crosswords. ☐
• **Exercising** is good for the body and mind. ☐

**Use the -ing form (e.g. doing)**

a. as a subject
b. after certain verbs (e.g. like, love, enjoy, hate, finish, start, spend) and expressions (e.g. how about, it's worth)
c. after prepositions

**B. Complete the dialogues with the -ing form or the bare or full infinitive of the verbs in parentheses.**

1. **A:** I want _____ (go) for a picnic. Would you like _____ (come) with me?
   **B:** Yes, but we need _____ (get) some food and something to drink before we leave.
   **A:** How about _____ (make) something?
   **B:** No, I'm too lazy _____ (cook) right now.
   **A:** OK, I can _____ (make) some sandwiches. I enjoy _____ (do) that.

2. **A:** Are you looking forward to _____ (see) your brother again?
   **B:** Yeah. _____ (have) him around is lots of fun.
   **A:** Is he staying long?
   **B:** Well, he's planning _____ (stay) for a month. But he might _____ (change) his mind and stay for the whole summer.
   **A:** Awesome!

**C. Make sentences using the following verbs/expressions.**

love  enjoy  can't stand  would like
look forward to  spend time  be interested in  hope

## 3 Listening & Speaking ◀))

**A.** Imagine you had to remember the telephone number below and the items on the shopping list. If you couldn't write them down, what would you do to remember them?

247-365-1879

oranges
cheese
yogurt
bananas
milk
strawberries
ice cream

**B. Listen to part of a radio show with an expert giving tips about memory and compare your answers.**

**C. Listen again and complete the blanks.**

1. The host isn't good at remembering _____ and _____.

2. The expert connected the number 24 to _____.

3. Albert Einstein was born in _____.

4. The radio host's mother is _____ years old.

5. "Chunking" means putting items into _____.

6. You should imagine someone _____ with another person with the same name, to help you remember their name.

**D. Talk in pairs. Discuss and find ways to remember the following information.**

205-555-2013
3493775108

onions
bread
cereal
shampoo
carrots
potatoes
toothpaste

FAE 1604

# 1 Listening 🔊

**A. Discuss.**

• Do you know of any charity events that take place in your city?
• What happens at these events?
• Where does the money they raise go?

**B. Listen to a radio announcement and complete the poster.**

**C. Listen to two people talking about the event and answer the questions.**

1. How much money did the boy give?
2. What time did he go?
3. How long did he stay?
4. What did he like?
5. What didn't he like?

## ALL-DAY CHARITY 1 _____

LOCAL BANDS
&
SURPRISE
GUEST STAR!

AT LINCOLN
COLLEGE

2 _____

ON JULY 3 ___ AND 4 ___
START: 5 _____      END: MIDNIGHT

Entrance fee: 6 _____ or make a donation!
All money raised goes to 7 _____
**Free refreshments!**

# 2 Speaking

**A. Think about a place you have been to (e.g. museum, restaurant, fitness center, place of entertainment) or an event you have attended (e.g. concert, performance). Complete the table below with information about it and give your opinion.**

**B. Talk in small groups. Discuss the place or event you have chosen using the ideas in the box.**

Talk about:
• where it is / takes place
• when it is best to go
• the age group it is for
• what it is like
• what you can do there
• the cost
• whether or not it is worth going

❝ *Last week I went to the new ice-skating rink.*
    ***Really? Where is it?***

...

*What's it like?* ❞

| PLACE NAME | |
| --- | --- |
| ADDRESS/VENUE | |
| DAYS/HOURS/DATE | |
| COST/FEE | |
| GOOD POINTS | |
| BAD POINTS | |

# 3 Writing An e-mail giving information and opinion

**A.** Read the two e-mails below and answer the questions.

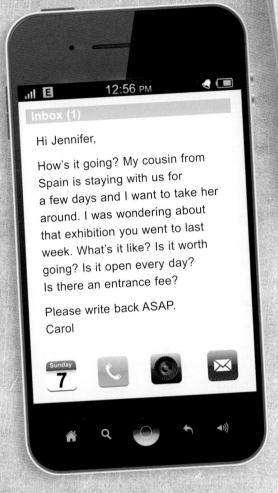

Hi Jennifer,

How's it going? My cousin from Spain is staying with us for a few days and I want to take her around. I was wondering about that exhibition you went to last week. What's it like? Is it worth going? Is it open every day? Is there an entrance fee?

Please write back ASAP.
Carol

**1.** What does Carol ask for in her e-mail to Jennifer?

**2.** Why is Jennifer writing to Carol?

**3.** Does Jennifer answer all her questions?

**4.** Does she give her any extra information?

**5.** What is the topic of each of the paragraphs in Jennifer's e-mail?

**B.** Imagine that you have received the following e-mail from a friend. Write a reply.

Hi there,

How's it going? A cousin of mine from abroad is staying with us for a few days and I want to take her around. You go out a lot and have been to lots of restaurants, museums and performances. Can you tell me about one place I could take her to? What's it like? Is it expensive? When should we go? E-mail me ASAP.

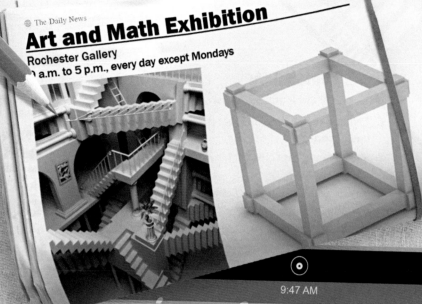

### The Daily News
## Art and Math Exhibition
**Rochester Gallery**
a.m. to 5 p.m., every day except Mondays

9:47 AM

Hello Carol,

I just got back from my yoga class and saw your e-mail. Taking your cousin to the Art and Math Exhibition is a great idea. I'll tell you all about it.

To begin with, the exhibition is organized by the National Science Museum, but it's held at a different building. It's just down the road at the Rochester Gallery. The exhibition is open from 9 a.m. to 5 p.m., every day except Mondays. As for the exhibition itself, it was fascinating! There are three main rooms and each one presents a different artist. My favorite was the Escher room. M. C. Escher was a graphic artist who was inspired by mathematics. He is known for his works of art featuring impossible constructions. Google him and you'll see what I mean. Anyway, at the exhibition there are guides who take groups around and explain everything. The entrance fee was 20 dollars but it was well worth it. Don't forget to go to the gallery store. It's full of amazing posters, postcards, mugs, etc.

You really should go if you have time. However, I recommend you go during the week, because I went on a Saturday and it was packed. If there's anything else you'd like to know, don't hesitate to ask.

Take care,
Jennifer

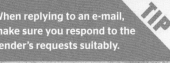

When replying to an e-mail, make sure you respond to the sender's requests suitably.

## Vocabulary

**A. Circle the correct words.**

1. Children under five can enter the museum free of **cash / charge**.

2. She gave me a receipt but forgot to give me my **change / check**.

3. Dan drew me a **diagram / shape** to help me understand how the machine worked.

4. Don't forget to take your **ingredients / medication** before you go to bed.

5. Roger Hill is going to try to **change / break** the national record later this evening.

6. There is a **rate / limit** to how many numbers I can remember.

7. What color did Lisa **dye / apply** her hair?

8. I think there's a **packet / cardboard** of sugar in the cabinet.

9. I can't lend you any money. I'm **packed / broke**.

**B. Complete the sentences with the words in the box.**

| pint room check withdraw venue |
| memorize inch repair |

1. After I finished my dessert, I asked the waiter for the _____.

2. Do you think your uncle can _____ my bike?

3. Did you _____ any cash from the ATM today?

4. We need about a(n) _____ of milk for this recipe.

5. Is there enough _____ in the car for my suitcase?

6. Try to _____ your PIN number, because it's dangerous to write it down.

7. We need to find a new _____ for the event.

8. Can you cut about a(n) _____ off the end of this piece of wood?

## Grammar

**C. Circle the correct words.**

1. This crossword puzzle is **too difficult / difficult enough** for me to solve.

2. I'm sorry but I'm not **too strong / strong enough** to lift this box.

3. Tony didn't have **cash enough / enough cash** so he paid by credit card.

4. The poem was **too long / long enough** for me to memorize, so I gave up.

5. We raised **money enough / enough money** to buy a new school bus.

6. The journey up the mountain was **too tiring / too much tiring** to complete in a day.

7. I didn't like the special effects. They weren't **enough realistic / realistic enough**.

8. I think you eat **too much / too many** chocolate.

**D. Complete the blanks with the correct form of the words in parentheses.**

1. Unfortunately, we couldn't afford _____ (go) skiing this winter.

2. Could you _____ (tell) me the way to the nearest bank, please?

3. I'm thinking about _____ (challenge) Danny to a Ping-Pong match.

4. My daughter makes me _____ (pick) her up from school every afternoon.

5. I was really surprised _____ (meet) Kyle at the supermarket.

6. I avoid _____ (pay) for things in cash. I prefer _____ (use) my debit card.

7. You should _____ (come) with us to the beach on Sunday.

8. We managed _____ (find) a pharmacy, but it was closed.

9. Linda doesn't mind _____ (go) to work by bus, but she can't stand _____ (get) stuck in traffic.

## Communication

**E. Put the dialogues in order.**

**1.**

☐ U.S. dollars. Do you charge commission?

☐ Yes, it's 1%. Is that OK?

☐ Good morning. How can I help you?

☐ Which currency would you like to change them into?

☐ That's fine.

☐ I'd like to exchange some euros.

**2.**

☐ OK. Next, you press this button here.

☐ Sure. It's very easy to use. First, you have to choose what you want.

☐ Yes, but be careful when it comes out. It's very hot.

☐ Is that it?

☐ Hey, Ricky. Do you know how to use this coffee machine?

☐ I want an espresso, without sugar.

## Self-assessment

**Read the following and check the appropriate boxes. For the points you are unsure of, refer back to the relevant sections in the module.**

### NOW I CAN...

▶ carry out money transactions ☐

▶ indicate degree and extent ☐

▶ give and understand different kinds of instructions ☐

▶ use common units of measurement ☐

▶ write an e-mail giving information and opinion ☐

Task 9 & 10 p. 131

experiencing
different ways
of life

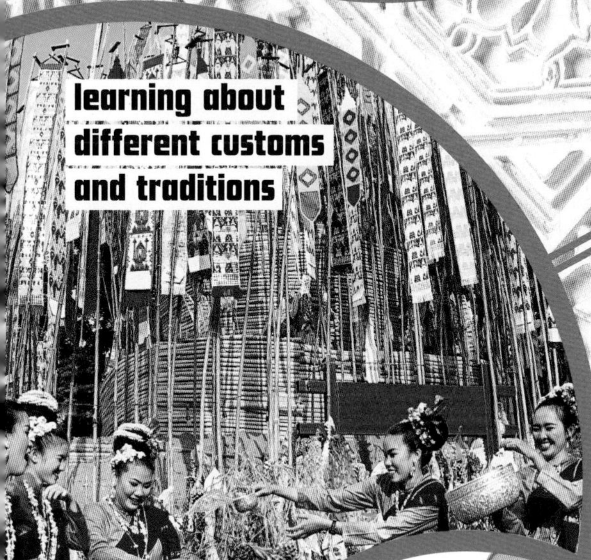

learning about
different customs
and traditions

**Discuss:**

• Look at the pictures.
Do you think traveling is
a good way to have these
experiences?

• Which of these do you
consider important? Why?

• Which countries would
you like to visit?
Why?

visiting
new places

learning
new languages

meeting people
from different cultures

## In this module you will learn...

• **to ask for information informally and formally**

• **to ask for clarification and repetition**

• **to give information**

• **differences between American and British English**

• **to talk about imaginary situations**

• **to make wishes and express regret**

• **about celebrations in different countries**

• **to write a formal e-mail asking for information**

# 1 Reading 🔊

## A. Discuss.

- Do you know any differences between American and British English?
- Is American or British English easier for you?

## B. Listen and read. What does the British man (B) think the American man (A) is asking for?

**A:** Excuse me, could you tell us where we can get some gas?

**B:** Did you say gas?

**A:** That's right.

**B:** You're American, right? I can tell by your accent.

**A:** Yes, we're from the States.

**B:** Are you here on holiday?

**A:** Well, I wouldn't exactly call our anniversary a holiday.

**B:** Sorry?

**A:** My wife and I have always wanted to take a vacation in England, so here we are!

**B:** Well, you've chosen the best season to go camping. The weather is beautiful. There's a shop around the corner that sells...

**A:** Who mentioned camping? We're staying at a hotel. I'm not sure I get what you mean. Anyway, where can we find some gas?

**B:** Well, why do you need gas if you aren't going camping?

**A:** I think you misunderstood me. We need gas for the car. Do you know if there's a gas station nearby?

**B:** Ah! You need a petrol station. Right, just go straight and after the bend, you'll see a zebra crossing. After that...

**A:** Excuse me? A zebra doing what?

**B:** A zebra crossing. You know, where people can cross from one pavement to the other?

**A:** Pavement? I'm not following you.

**B:** The thing I'm standing on now.

**A:** Oh, you mean the sidewalk and crosswalk. Now, I understand.

**B:** Great. After the crossing, you'll see a petrol station on the right. But at this time of day, you can expect a queue.

**A:** A what? Oh, never mind. Thank you so much!

**B:** No problem.

**A:** Betty, let's just find the gas station and we can deal with whatever a 'Q' is when we get there. Oh, and honey, I think we should buy a phrasebook.

---

Use *Excuse me:*
- to get someone's attention politely.
- to get past someone.
- to tell someone politely that you are leaving a place.
- to apologize for disturbing or interrupting someone.

Use *Excuse me?*
- to show that you didn't understand or hear what the other person said and need him/her to repeat it. ([BrE] Sorry?)
- to show that you disagree with what the other person has just said or that you are very surprised / upset.

## C. Read the dialogue again and find:

1. three questions the American man uses to ask for gas.
2. four phrases the American man uses to show he doesn't understand.
3. three questions the British man uses to show he doesn't understand.

## D. Read the dialogue again and find sentences to prove the following.

1. The British man realizes the other man isn't from the U.K.
2. The American man misunderstands the word "holiday."
3. The British man believes the American man is going camping.
4. The British man realizes what the American man is referring to when he says "gas."
5. The British man explains what "pavement" means.
6. The American man doesn't know what "queue" means.

## E. Discuss.

- Have you ever been in a situation similar to this? What happened? What did you do?

# 2 Vocabulary 🔊

**A. Complete the table with words from the dialogue in activity 1.**

| American English | British English |
|---|---|
| gas station | |
| | holiday |
| store | |
| crosswalk | |
| | pavement |
| line | |

**B. The words 1-12 below are British English. Do you know their American equivalents? Listen and check your answers.**

1. jumper _____
2. chips _____
3. CV _____
4. mobile phone _____
5. rubbish _____
6. cinema _____
7. trainers _____
8. underground _____
9. lift _____
10. flat _____
11. trousers _____
12. crisps _____

> **TIP**
> There are various differences between American and British English, but they do not often cause serious problems when communicating. Pay attention to the context to guess the meaning of a word you do not understand.

# 3 Grammar Indirect questions → p. 148

**A. Read the dialogues, notice the phrases in blue and answer the questions that follow.**

**DIRECT QUESTIONS**

**A:** Where's the information desk?
**B:** It's down there, next to the coffee shop.
**A:** Do they have a map of the city?
**B:** I don't know.

**INDIRECT QUESTIONS**

**A:** Excuse me, could you tell me where the information desk is?
**B:** Certainly. It's down there, next to the coffee shop.
**A:** Do you know if/whether they have a map of the city?
**B:** I don't know.

1. Which of the dialogues is more formal?
2. What is the difference in word order in direct and indirect questions?

**B. Read the direct questions and form indirect questions.**

1. When does the train leave?

   Excuse me, could you tell me _____?

2. Do I need a ticket to enter?

   Do you know _____?

3. What time is it?

   Do _____?

4. What does "queue" mean?

   Could _____?

5. Is there a subway station nearby?

   Can _____?

# 4 Intonation 🔊

**A. Listen and repeat. What's the difference in intonation between the two questions?**

a. Where is the gas station?
b. Could you tell me where the gas station is?

**B. Listen and repeat. Is the intonation rising ↗ or falling ↘?**

1. Can you tell us what time the stores close?
2. How far is the post office?
3. Who is the manager?
4. Do you know where I can get a phrasebook?
5. Could you tell me how much it costs?
6. Where can I buy camping equipment?

# 5 Speaking
## Information gap activity

Talk in pairs. Student A go to page 135. Student B go to page 137.

# 1 Reading

**A. Discuss.**

- Do you enjoy traveling to other countries?
- Is there anything that scares you when traveling?
- What do you think the benefits of traveling are?

**B. Read the quiz. Answer the questions, add up your score and find out what kind of traveler you are.**

# What kind of traveler are you?

**1** Which of the following would be your ideal trip abroad?
  a. Staying with friends or family abroad.
  b. Going on a package tour abroad.
  c. Going to the airport and getting on the first plane out of the country.

**2** What would you do if you lost your passport while in a foreign country?
  a. I'd stay calm and go to the nearest embassy. I always carry photocopies of my passport with me.
  b. I'd enjoy the rest of my trip and worry about it later.
  c. I'd panic, be terrified of what would happen, and wish I could wake up and be safely back home.

**3** What would you do if you got sick while in a foreign country?
  a. I'd ignore my symptoms and keep traveling. Getting sick abroad is an adventure and I'd be happy to lose some weight anyway.
  b. I'd take the necessary medicine from my well-prepared medicine bag, and wait to get better.
  c. I'd book the next flight home. Getting sick abroad is too risky.

**4** What would you do if a waiter suggested an exotic dish without telling you what was in it?
  a. I'd say, "Thanks, but I'm not very hungry."
  b. I'd ask what's in the dish and then make up my mind.
  c. I'd definitely taste it. I always enjoy trying new dishes.

**5** What would you do if you got lost while in a foreign city?
  a. I'd go to the nearest police station and ask them to drive me to my hotel.
  b. I'd celebrate the experience. When you get lost, you discover the best places in a city.
  c. I wouldn't get lost in the first place! I always carry a map and a GPS with me and have a good sense of direction.

**6** What would totally ruin your trip abroad?
  a. Losing a suitcase at the airport.
  b. Realizing that hardly anyone speaks my language.
  c. Realizing that the place is very similar to my home country.

**Score:**

|   | a. | b. | c. |
|---|----|----|----|
| 1 | a. 0 | b. 1 | c. 2 |
| 2 | a. 1 | b. 2 | c. 0 |
| 3 | a. 2 | b. 1 | c. 0 |
| 4 | a. 0 | b. 1 | c. 2 |
| 5 | a. 0 | b. 2 | c. 1 |
| 6 | a. 1 | b. 0 | c. 2 |

## Results:

**9-12:** You're a confident and adventurous traveler who is very curious about the world. You want to live life to the fullest and do things that are out of the ordinary. You feel that life isn't worth living otherwise. However, you sometimes take risks which could have negative consequences.

**5-8:** You're a very organized and practical traveler. You always plan ahead, you prepare to the last detail and are usually ready for unexpected events. You enjoy traveling when it is safe and no risks are involved. You always consider the results of your actions.

**0-4:** You're a nervous traveler who is afraid of trying new things and of being in unfamiliar environments. You can't cope with unexpected events and refuse to take risks or try anything out of the ordinary. You might enjoy traveling in groups more than traveling independently.

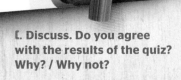

**C. Discuss. Do you agree with the results of the quiz? Why? / Why not?**

## 2 Vocabulary

**A.** Look at the adjectives below. Which prepositions are they followed by? Find the adjectives in the quiz and check your answers.

terrified    similar    curious    ready    afraid

**B.** Complete the table with the adjectives in the box. Then make sentences using some of these adjectives.

nervous    popular    allergic    scared    proud    satisfied    excited    responsible    worried    full
suitable    addicted    disappointed    famous    married

| + about | + for | + to | + of | + with |
|---------|-------|------|------|--------|
| nervous |       |      |      |        |
|         |       |      |      |        |
|         |       |      |      |        |

## 3 Grammar Conditional Sentences Type 2, Wishes → p. 148

**A.** Read the example, answer the questions and complete the rule.

> If I **had** lots of money, I **would travel** around the world.

1. Does the sentence refer to the present/future or past?
2. Does the speaker have lots of money?

**CONDITIONAL SENTENCES TYPE 2**

They express imaginary situations or things that are unlikely to happen in the present or future.

**If + Past Simple →** _____, **could + base form**

**B.** Read the example, answer the questions and complete the rule.

> I **wish** I **were** home.

1. Does the sentence refer to the present/future or past?
2. Is the speaker at home?
3. How does he/she feel about that?

**WISHES**

We use **wish +** _____ **Simple** to make a wish and express regret about a present situation which we would like to be different.

In Conditional Sentences Type 2 and after *wish* we usually use **were** for all persons.

**C.** Complete the dialogue with the correct form of the verbs in parentheses.

**A:** I don't know where to go on vacation this summer.

**B:** If I **1** _____ (be) you, I **2** _____ (visit) a foreign country.

**A:** I'd like that. I wish I **3** _____ (can) visit Australia, but it's very far and very expensive to get there.

**B:** That's a nice idea, out of the ordinary. If I **4** _____ (have) the money, I **5** _____ (lend) it to you.

**A:** Really? Thanks. It's the thought that counts. Anyway, where are you going?

**B:** I'm not sure yet. I wish I **6** _____ (speak) Russian. If I **7** _____ (do), I **8** _____ (go) to Moscow. I've always wanted to go there.

**A:** Why do you need to speak Russian? Just buy a phrasebook and you'll be fine.

**B:** You think so?

**A:** Of course. When are you taking your vacation?

**B:** In June.

**A:** I wish I **9** _____ (can) take time off in June and come with you.

## 4 Listening 🔊

Listen to a conversation between two colleagues and answer the questions. Write M for Man, W for Woman or B for Both.

1. Who would go abroad if they were offered a job?  ☐
2. Who can speak a foreign language?  ☐
3. Who would go abroad even if the salary was bad?  ☐
4. Who has family abroad?  ☐
5. Who has traveled abroad many times?  ☐

## 5 Speaking

Talk in pairs. Imagine that you are in a foreign country. What would you do if the following things happened to you?

- You go to a restaurant and you don't understand the menu/waiter.
- Someone offers you something to eat but you can't eat it.
- You need to communicate but can't speak the language.
- You get lost while exploring the downtown area.
- Someone steals your wallet on the subway.

66 *What would you do if you...?*
   *I would...* 99

## 1 Reading 🔊
**A. Discuss.**
- Have you ever attended a street festival?
- If yes, what sort of activities did you do there?
- If not, have you heard of any famous street festivals?

**B. Listen, read and choose the best subheading for the text.**

# Notting Hill Carnival

*a. A chance to remember the past*
*b. Where a festival atmosphere comes to life*
*c. A special day of music and culture*

The Notting Hill Carnival is the largest street festival in Europe and one of the largest in the world. The first carnival was a small event which was held in 1964 as a way for Afro-Caribbean and West Indian communities to celebrate their cultures and traditions. This annual festival fills the streets of Notting Hill in West London with amazing displays of music, costumes and colorful sights. In recent years, this spectacular event has become multi-ethnic and has attracted more than one million people.

The earliest form of this festival goes all the way back to the early 19th century. The first Caribbean-themed carnivals were mainly a way for the steel band musicians who played their drums in Earls Court to demonstrate their skills. When the parades passed through the streets of Notting Hill, residents gathered in the streets. The festivities reminded them of the homes they had left behind.

In the past, steel band, soca and calypso music were the main styles featured at the carnival. However, in recent years you can hear anything from reggae to R&B, funk, house, dub and more. Sound systems are set up, but also live stages. Local bands as well as international artists take part, so it is an opportunity for everyone to enjoy sounds from around the world.

The Notting Hill Carnival takes place every August and lasts for three days. On Saturday, you can follow the event known as the "Panorama," a drumming competition between steel bands, which now takes place in Hyde Park. Sunday is Children's Day and there is a short parade for children in costumes. The main parade is on Monday, and the route is about 3 miles long. Expect to see colorful floats and people in Caribbean-style costumes dancing to loud music. It is the day most people attend and everyone is welcome.

There's nothing like the inviting smell of traditional Caribbean food, which is characteristic of the Notting Hill Carnival. There are more than 300 street stalls where you will get the chance to taste jerk chicken, fried fish, curry goat, rice and peas as well as other exotic dishes.

**C.** **Read again and answer the questions. Choose a, b or c.**

TIP
- Read each question carefully to get an idea of what you are looking for and underline the section in the text where the answer is found.
- Make sure you have chosen the correct answer by eliminating the wrong options.

1. What is true about the Notting Hill Carnival?
   a. It is the oldest street festival in Europe.
   b. People from different ethnic communities take part in it.
   c. It is a traditional celebration that started in the Caribbean.

2. How did the first Caribbean-themed carnival start?
   a. As a way for people from the Caribbean to socialize.
   b. As a way to help people who felt homesick.
   c. As a way for musicians to perform and express themselves.

3. What kind of music could you listen to at the original carnivals?
   a. Calypso, reggae and funk.
   b. Music from around the world.
   c. Soca and calypso.

4. What is true about the drumming competition?
   a. It takes place at a different venue.
   b. It takes place during the main parade.
   c. It takes place on the same day as the children's parade.

5. Apart from the music and the parade, what is another main attraction at the Notting Hill Carnival?
   a. traditional arts and crafts
   b. street stalls with a great variety of food
   c. traditional dance competitions

6. What is the purpose of this text?
   a. to describe a popular carnival
   b. to explain how the carnival is organized
   c. to provide information about Caribbean traditions

**D. Look at the highlighted words in the text and match them with the meanings below.**

1. to show something
2. a large vehicle which is decorated and used to carry people dressed in costumes in festivals, parades, etc.
3. a show or an exhibition of something
4. to prepare a piece of equipment or a machine for use
5. very typical
6. a raised area which actors, dancers, singers stand on when they perform
7. to help or make somebody remember
8. people who are considered a group because of their common interests, social group or nationality
9. a table where you sell things outdoors, e.g. at a market
10. a musical instrument which you play by hitting it with your hands or with sticks

**E. Discuss.**

- Would you like to go to the Notting Hill Carnival? Why? / Why not?

# 2 Listening 🔊

**Listen to three short dialogues and answer the questions. Choose the correct picture a, b or c.**

1. What didn't the man see at the winter festival in Quebec, Canada?

2. What is the woman not interested in experiencing on her trip to China?

3. How many grapes did Pablo manage to eat last New Year?

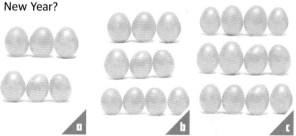

# 3 Speaking & Writing

**A. Talk in pairs or small groups about a celebration/festival/event that takes place in your city/country. Think about the ideas in the box.**

- when and where it takes place
- how long it lasts
- when it first started and why
- who takes part
- what preparations people make
- what happens
- what people wear/do/eat
- how many people attend

**B. Write a short description of the celebration/festival/event you discussed above.**

# 1 Vocabulary

**Complete the sentences with the phrases in the box.**

| in addition | in advance | in general | in a hurry |
|---|---|---|---|
| in mind | in particular | in common | |

1. It's cheaper to book the tickets _____.
   I booked mine a month earlier.

2. I really like Spanish food. I love "paella" _____.

3. Keep _____ that buses don't run after midnight.

4. This book contains information about different sights in the city. _____, there's a map at the back showing you their exact location.

5. We are not very different from other cultures. In fact, people around the world have a lot of things _____.

6. We left the house _____ and forgot to take our passports with us.

7. _____, people learn more about a country when visiting it than when reading books about it.

# 2 Listening 🔊

**A. Listen to a conversation taking place at a travel agency. What is the main reason the man is at the travel agency?**

a. He's booking a trip.

b. He's asking for information.

c. He's changing a booking arrangement.

**B. Listen again and write T for True or F for False.**

1. The man is going to Japan for less than a week. ☐

2. The man wants to rent a car. ☐

3. The man has an International Driver's License. ☐

4. Visitors to Japan find driving difficult because of parking problems. ☐

5. The man had a hard time driving in the U.K. ☐

6. The travel agent advises the man not to rent a car. ☐

7. The man is arriving during the day. ☐

8. The man decides to take a taxi from the airport to his hotel. ☐

# 3 Speaking Role play

**Talk in pairs.**

**Student A:** Imagine you are a visitor to your town/city. Ask the information desk clerk (Student B) for information about some of the topics below. Use a combination of direct and indirect questions and some of the phrases in the box.

> Excuse me, can/could you tell/inform me...?
> Do you know...?
> Where can I...?
> Do you have any maps/brochures?
> Thank you so much.

**Student B:** Imagine you are an information desk clerk. You are responsible for giving visitors to your town/city information on the topics below. Use some of the phrases in the box.

> May I help you?
> What can I do for you?
> Which... are you interested in?
> Do you have anything in particular in mind?
> You can/could...
> How about...?
> Is there anything else I can help you with?
> Would you like any more information?
> Enjoy your stay.

TOPICS
accommodations
places to eat
attractions/sights
transportation
cultural events
places to shop
currency

# 4 Writing A formal e-mail asking for information

**A.** On the right is an e-mail Wendy Kent sent to the Peruvian Tourism Board. She wants to visit Cuzco and would like some information about it. What do you think Wendy is going to ask about? Read and compare your answers.

**B.** Read the e-mail again and answer the following questions.

1. What features make this e-mail formal?

2. What is the topic of each paragraph?

3. How many questions does Wendy ask?

4. What kind of questions has she used?

5. Which words/phrases has she used to list the questions?

Dear Sir/Madam,

I am writing to ask for some information about Peru as I am interested in visiting the city of Cuzco next month. I tried searching on the Internet, however, I could not find answers to all my questions.

Firstly, could you please tell me if I need a visa to enter the country? I am a Canadian citizen and I am planning on staying in Cuzco for about a week. Furthermore, could you tell me what currency is used in Peru? This is my first time traveling abroad so I am not an experienced traveler. Will I be able to use Canadian dollars? If not, where is it safe to exchange money? Lastly, could you inform me about the opening and closing hours of stores and restaurants during the weekend and public holidays?

I would like to thank you in advance for your time and assistance. I look forward to hearing from you.

Yours truly,
Wendy Kent

**C.** Imagine you want to visit a city abroad and need some information. Write an e-mail to the Tourism Board asking about the following:

- if you can enter the country on an ID card instead of a passport
- if English is widely spoken
- which is the best area to stay in
- how you can get to the downtown area from the airport

**Follow the plan below.**

## Plan

**A formal e-mail asking for information**

### GREETING

**Use a formal greeting, not first names.**
- *Dear Sir/Madam,*
- *Dear Mr./Mrs./Ms./Miss + last name,*

### OPENING PARAGRAPH

**Begin by saying why you are writing. Use phrases like:**
- *I am writing to ask for some information about...*
- *I am writing to request information about...*
- *I am interested in... and would like some information about...*

### MAIN PART

**Ask for information in a formal and polite way. Use a combination of direct and indirect questions and remember to use linking words/phrases to list your questions:**

> *firstly, first of all, to begin with*
> *secondly, also, what is more, furthermore, in addition, apart from that*
> *finally, lastly*

### CLOSING PARAGRAPH

**End by thanking and saying that you'd like a reply as soon as possible. Use phrases like:**
- *I would like to thank you in advance.*
- *Thank you for your time and assistance.*
- *I look forward to hearing from you.*
- *Please send me a reply with any information as soon as possible.*

### SIGNING OFF

**Use a formal signature ending and write your full name underneath it.**
- *Yours sincerely,*
- *Yours truly,*

Travel Guide
PERU

Photographs by Frank Tiller

WIND publications

## Vocabulary

**A. Choose a, b or c.**

1. It's John and Freda's 50th wedding ____ next month.
   **a.** carnival        **b.** anniversary        **c.** tradition

2. I'm having a hard ____ trying to open this bottle.
   **a.** time        **b.** mind        **c.** way

3. Let's do something out of the ____ this weekend.
   **a.** unfamiliar        **b.** organized        **c.** ordinary

4. ____ me to go to the post office tomorrow morning.
   **a.** Remind        **b.** Ignore        **c.** Mention

5. A ____ day in Antarctica is very cold.
   **a.** typical        **b.** particular        **c.** custom

6. Keep in ____ that you have to finish this project by the end of the month.
   **a.** particular        **b.** advance        **c.** mind

7. You're not from around here, right? I can tell by your ____ .
   **a.** accent        **b.** visa        **c.** community

**B. Complete the sentences with the words in the box.**

> photocopy   parade   citizen   sidewalk
> exact   agent   hurry   curious

1. Last winter, I slipped on some ice on the _____ and sprained my ankle.

2. The travel _____ recommended three hotels and we chose the one that was in the downtown area.

3. Sandra, can you make a(n) _____ of this document, please?

4. Julia was _____ to know who was sending the e-mails.

5. Roberto is Italian, but he is now an American _____.

6. The whole family went out on the street to watch the _____ go by.

7. Can we walk faster? I'm in a(n) _____.

8. I don't know the _____ time, but it's about seven o'clock.

## Grammar

**C. Complete with the correct form of the verbs in parentheses.**

**A:** I'm going to Korea next month.

**B:** Really? That's great. If I **1** _____ (be) you, I **2** _____ (get) a phrasebook before I left.

**A:** Good idea. If I **3** _____ (have) more time, I **4** _____ (take) a Korean language course. I'd love to learn Korean.

**B:** Me too. How long are you staying?

**A:** Just a week. I wish I **5** _____ (have) more time off to stay longer.

**B:** Yeah. If I **6** _____ (visit) Korea, I **7** _____ (stay) for a month. There's so much to see and do.

**A:** I know. I wish you **8** _____ (can) come with me.

**B:** Yes, that would be great. I wish I **9** _____ (not have) so much work to do.

**D. Read the direct questions and form indirect questions.**

1. Where is the embassy?
   Do you know _____?

2. Is the carnival today?
   Can you tell me _____?

3. What does "CV" mean?
   Could you _____?

4. Do I need to have my passport with me?
   Could _____?

5. Is it a public holiday tomorrow?
   Do _____?

6. How much does this cost?
   Can _____?

## Communication

**E. Complete the dialogue with a-e.**

> **a.** I'm not following you.
> **b.** Can you say that again?
> **c.** Could you tell me where I can catch a bus?
> **d.** Never mind.
> **e.** Why didn't you say so in the first place?

**A:** Excuse me. **1** ____

**B:** I'm sorry, I didn't hear you. **2** ____

**A:** Yes, I need to catch the 452. Can you help me?

**B:** **3** ____ Do you want a bus stop, or the bus station?

**A:** Umm, just a bus stop. I need to get downtown.

**B:** I'm sorry. I don't know where the bus stop is, or the bus station. I'm not from around here, you see.

**A:** Huh? **4** ____

**B:** OK, calm down. I just didn't know where you wanted to go. Now, I think there's a subway station somewhere near here.

**A:** **5** ____ I'll get a taxi.

## Self-assessment

Read the following and check the appropriate boxes. For the points you are unsure of, refer back to the relevant sections in the module.

### NOW I CAN...

- ask for information informally and formally ☐
- ask for clarification and repetition ☐
- differentiate between American and British English words ☐
- talk about imaginary situations ☐
- make wishes and express regret ☐
- write a formal e-mail asking for information ☐

I fell in front of friends.

**Discuss:**

Look at the situations shown. How do the people feel? What do you think they should do?

I'm homeless.

I won a competition.

I saw a huge bug in my bedroom.

I found somebody's wallet.

## In this module you will learn...

- to express uncertainty and ask for confirmation
- to express emotions like surprise, anger, annoyance
- language needed in different medical situations
- idioms describing feelings
- to give an account of a true event
- to report statements, questions, commands and requests
- to ask for and give advice
- to describe a problem
- useful phrases that help you when you need more time to think
- to write an e-mail asking for or giving advice

I'm sick in bed.

# 1 Reading

## A. Discuss.

- When was the last time you went to the doctor's?
- Do you go to the dentist's regularly? Do you mind it?

## B. Listen and read. Where is each dialogue taking place?

| a. at a pharmacy | b. at a dentist's | c. at a doctor's |

**1**

**A:** So, what exactly are your symptoms?

**B:** I have a terrible rash. My skin is red and really itchy.

**A:** Do you feel like you're coming down with something?

**B:** No, I just got over a stomach bug last week, but I'm feeling fine now.

**A:** How about allergies? Do you suffer from any?

**B:** I'm allergic to bee stings, but I wasn't stung by one.

**A:** So, you aren't allergic to nuts or anything else, are you?

**B:** No, I don't think so.

**A:** What did you eat yesterday?

**B:** Well, I had lunch at a restaurant and had a spicy dish. You don't think it's those spices, do you?

**A:** They're probably responsible for your condition. Nothing to worry about. First, I'll examine you. Then I'll give you a prescription for some cream and medication. I'm sure it will go away in a few days.

**B:** Thank you.

**2**

**A:** I'm sorry, ma'am, but we've run out of these pills so I cannot fill your prescription.

**B:** Oh, no! What am I supposed to do now? I am in a lot of pain!

**A:** Well, we will have these pills tomorrow morning, so until then you can always take a regular pain reliever.

**B:** I've already taken some but they didn't relieve the pain at all. Don't you have anything else that might help?

**A:** I can't give you medication that your doctor has not prescribed, can I?

**B:** No, I guess not. I'll just have to put up with the pain for one more night.

**3**

**A:** Hello, Mr. Jameson. Weren't you here for a check-up a couple of weeks ago?

**B:** Yes, but one of my fillings came out. I couldn't come and see you yesterday because you were all booked up.

**A:** That's right, it was a very busy day. Let's take a look. Yes, the whole filling has gone. Doesn't it hurt?

**B:** No, not very much. Isn't that one of my old fillings?

**A:** Yes, don't worry, it shouldn't be too difficult to fix. You were chewing on something hard when it came out, weren't you?

**B:** No, I was eating pizza.

**A:** That's strange. Well, this won't take long. Open wide, please.

## C. Read again and find sentences to prove the following.

### Dialogue 1

1. The patient was recently sick.
2. The doctor is not sure about something and wants to confirm it.
3. The patient makes a guess about what the problem might be.

### Dialogue 2

4. The pharmacist can't help the customer.
5. The pharmacist suggests the customer should take a different kind of medication.
6. The customer has tried something that didn't really work.
7. The customer doesn't find her condition easy to deal with.

### Dialogue 3

8. The dentist is surprised to see the patient.
9. The patient tried to make an appointment but couldn't.
10. The patient is not sure about something and wants to confirm it.

## D. Look at the phrasal verbs below from the dialogues and match them with their meanings a-e.

1. come down with ☐
2. get over ☐
3. go away ☐
4. put up with ☐
5. come out ☐

a. to accept an unpleasant situation without complaining

b. to become better, e.g. after an illness

c. to get an illness

d. to disappear

e. to be removed from a place

# 2 Grammar Negative questions, Tag questions → *p. 148*

**A. Read the rule and the examples. Then circle the correct words for sentences 1-4 to show the meaning of the negative questions.**

Negative questions are used to express emotions (e.g. surprise, anger, annoyance), to ask for confirmation, to express opinion politely, when a positive answer is expected, etc.

> **1. Aren't you** Dr. Davis?
> **2. Shouldn't you** lie down when you're dizzy?
> **3. Can't he** drive?
> **4. Haven't you** seen a doctor yet?

1. I think you **are / aren't** Dr. Davis, but I want to be sure.

2. I think you **should / shouldn't** lie down when you're dizzy. What do you think?

3. I thought he **could / couldn't** drive, but he **can / can't**.

4. You **were / weren't** supposed to see a doctor, but you **have / haven't**, right?

**B. Imagine a friend of yours is sick. Think of as many negative questions as you can to ask him/her.**

> *Didn't you take your medicine?*

**C. Read the examples, notice the words in blue and then complete the rules by circling the correct words.**

> • You don't have any allergies, **do you**?
> • Pharmacies close at 10 p.m., **don't they**?
> • You'll come with me to the dentist, **won't you**?

- Tag questions are short questions which we put at the **beginning / end** of a sentence.
- They are formed with **an auxiliary / a main** verb (*am, is, are, was, were, do, does, did, have, has, can, could, will, etc.*) and a subject personal pronoun (*I, you, he, she, etc.*)
- We use a **positive / negative** tag question with a negative sentence and a **positive / negative** tag question with a positive sentence.

**D. Complete the dialogues with the correct tag questions.**

1. **A:** Susan, you don't have Dr. Brown's number, _____?

   **B:** You left it on the refrigerator, _____? Yes, here it is.

   **A:** Thanks. I want to make an appointment for tomorrow.

   **B:** You know that his office is on Park Avenue, _____?

   **A:** No, I didn't know. So, I can take the subway there, _____?

   **B:** Yep, it's very easy.

2. **A:** There aren't any pain relievers left, _____?

   **B:** I don't think so.

   **A:** The pharmacy is open at this time, _____?

   **B:** Yes. You aren't feeling well again, _____?

   **A:** No, I have a terrible headache and I can't put up with it any longer. Charlie, you'll go to the pharmacy for me, _____?

   **B:** Of course.

# 3 Intonation 🔊

**A. Listen and repeat. In which sentence is the speaker not sure about something and wants to confirm it? In which sentence is the speaker sure and expects the listener to agree?**

You know the way to the hospital, don't you? ↗

You know the way to the hospital, don't you? ↘

**B. Listen and repeat. Is the intonation rising ↗ or falling ↘?**

1. You'll help me out, won't you?
2. Your cousin is a dentist, isn't he?
3. We aren't going there by bus, are we?
4. She took her medicine, didn't she?
5. Jill hasn't broken her leg, has she?
6. You brush your teeth twice a day, don't you?

# 4 Speaking Role play

**Talk in pairs using some of the words in the boxes and your own ideas.**

**1.**
**Student A:** You are a doctor.
**Student B:** You have a health problem and are visiting your doctor.

> come down with    stomach bug
> runny nose    cough    fever    the flu
> headache/earache, etc.    itchy skin
> rash    allergy    bee sting
> symptoms    examine    prescribe
> get over    go away    take vitamins
> drink fluids    rest

**2.**
**Student A:** You are a pharmacist.
**Student B:** You want to buy some medicine.

> prescription    pills
> medicine    cream

**3.**
**Student A:** You are a dentist.
**Student B:** You are visiting your dentist.

> check-up    filling    come out
> toothache    in pain    chew
> pain relievers

119

# 1 Vocabulary

Read the sentences below and decide what the idioms in bold express.
Do the people feel shocked, embarrassed or annoyed?

1. When I realized I had introduced my boss with a wrong name, I **went red as a beet**.
2. Linda **couldn't believe her eyes** when she waved at the famous actor and he waved back.
3. My neighbor keeps throwing trash in my yard and it's **driving me up the wall**.
4. I didn't enter the competition because I knew I would **make a fool of myself**.
5. When the phone rang in the middle of the night, I **nearly jumped out of my skin**.
6. I fell flat on my face in the middle of the square. **I wanted the ground to open up and swallow me**.

# 2 Reading 🔊

**A. Look at the pictures. What do you think happened? Listen, read and check your answers.**

# NOW, THAT'S EMBARRASSING!

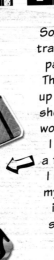

So, there I was, sitting at the station waiting for my train. I was doing a crossword puzzle and wasn't really paying attention to what was going on around me. The train approached and when it stopped, I picked up my bag and quickly got on. Then I heard a woman shouting, "Stop, thief!" I looked around and saw the woman get on the train and walk straight up to me. I couldn't believe my ears! She kept saying that I was a thief and that I had stolen her bag. That's when I realized I had my bag on my shoulder, and her bag in my hand. I apologized and told her that I hadn't done it on purpose, but I don't think she believed me. Luckily, she didn't call the police.

Linda Jameson

I was sitting on the bus the other day, and I hadn't noticed an old lady standing near me. Someone eventually gave up their seat and as she sat, she looked at me angrily. I felt really bad. A little later, a large lady got on the bus. She was carrying lots of shopping bags and I wanted to do something to help her. I offered her my seat and told her she shouldn't carry heavy bags in her condition. "What do you mean?" she asked. I told her it wasn't good for the baby. "What baby? You think I'm pregnant?" she replied and refused to sit in my seat. When I realized my mistake, I went red as a beet.

Amy Winters

This happened during one of my lunch breaks from work. I was eating a sandwich in the park, and some kids were playing soccer nearby. They were kicking the ball in my direction and almost hit me a couple of times. I tried to ignore them but they were really driving me up the wall. I told them I wanted some peace and quiet, but they didn't go away. Finally, the ball hit me right on the head. I was furious. So, I took the ball and kicked it in the opposite direction. Unfortunately, it smashed into a store window. It was a ridiculous reaction, I know. I just wanted the ground to open up and swallow me!

Henry Walker

**B. Read the texts again and write L for Linda, A for Amy or H for Henry for the statements below.**

1. I reacted without thinking. ☐
2. I misunderstood a situation. ☐
3. Someone said I had done something I hadn't. ☐

4. I did something by accident. ☐ ☐
5. I was angry with what had happened to me. ☐
6. I was just trying to help someone out, but it didn't work out. ☐

**C. Discuss.**

• Which of the situations in activity A do you think is the most embarrassing? Why?

# 3 Grammar Reported Speech: Statements → p. 149

**A. Read the examples, answer the questions and complete the rules.**

| DIRECT SPEECH | REPORTED SPEECH |
|---|---|
| • "You are a thief!" the woman said. | • The woman said that I was a thief. |
| • "I didn't do it on purpose," I said to the woman. | • I told the woman that I hadn't done it on purpose. |
| • "You shouldn't carry heavy bags in your condition," I said to the woman. | • I told the woman that she shouldn't carry heavy bags in her condition. |

• When do we use Reported Speech?
• In the examples above, which words have changed in Reported Speech?

• *Say* and *tell* are reporting verbs. Use _____ before an indirect object (person) and _____ when there is no indirect object.
• Pronouns and possessive adjectives change according to the meaning of the sentence.
• Tenses, modal verbs and time expressions usually change as follows:

| DIRECT SPEECH | | REPORTED SPEECH | DIRECT SPEECH | | REPORTED SPEECH |
|---|---|---|---|---|---|
| Present | → | _____ | this | → | that |
| Past | → | _____ | today | → | that day |
| Present Perfect | → | Past Perfect | yesterday | → | the previous day / the day before |
| will | → | would | last week | → | the previous week / the week before |
| can | → | could | tomorrow | → | the next day / the following day |
| should | → | _____ | next year | → | the following year |

**B. Complete the sentences using Reported Speech.**

1. "I felt so embarrassed yesterday," Lisa said to me.

   Lisa told me _____ .

2. "I can give you a ride to the airport tomorrow," Fred said to Mike.

   Fred told _____ .

3. "We've never been to this restaurant before," the girls said.

   The girls said _____ .

4. "We'll go skiing together next year," Thomas said to Paul.

   Thomas told _____ .

# 4 Listening 🔊

**Listen to three people describing experiences they have had. Write T for True or F for False.**

1. Emily's friend woke up late and missed the interview. ☐
2. Emily's friend called her during a meeting. ☐
3. Emily got locked out of her apartment. ☐
4. The man at the airport needed help so George went over to him. ☐
5. George didn't know the man who was waving. ☐
6. George was embarrassed by what he had done. ☐
7. One of the clients told Melanie that there was something wrong with her appearance. ☐
8. Melanie's presentation was a success in the end. ☐

# 5 Speaking & Writing

**A. Talk in pairs. Think of a funny, embarrassing or annoying experience that you have had and describe it to your partner. Answer any questions he/she may have. Think about:**

• what happened
• how you reacted
• how you felt

**B. Write about your experience.**

**12c**

# 1 Reading 🔊

## A. Discuss.

- Have you read Charles Dickens' *Oliver Twist*? If so, did you like it?
- What do you know or can you guess about life in England in the 19th century? How do you think poor / rich people lived?

**B. Below is an extract from an adapted version of the novel *Oliver Twist*. Look at the picture. Can you guess what's happening? What was life like for an orphan at the workhouse? Listen, read and check your answers.**

CHARLES DICKENS

OLIVER TWIST

At last, it was evening. The large stone hall of the workhouse filled with hungry, skinny, young orphans dressed in filthy rags. Perhaps the word *hungry* doesn't accurately describe their grumbling, empty little stomachs. *Starving* would probably be more suitable. They had three meals a day, which consisted of only one bowl, and no more, of watery, tasteless soup; except on special occasions when they enjoyed a tiny piece of bread, too.

Moments after the food was served, it disappeared. The boys licked bowls, spoons and fingers and searched busily for a splash that they hadn't noticed. Because of this, the bowls never needed cleaning. Then they stared, as they always did, at the huge copper pot that held the soup. It appeared that that evening was no different from any other. It was, though.

Before dinner, all the boys had held a meeting and had made a decision. They couldn't suffer any longer. They had to act and it was Oliver Twist who was chosen to perform the task. First, the boys whispered to each other, then they winked at Oliver. The boy next to him nudged him and told him to go and ask for more food. It was time. Perhaps it was the hunger, or the misery that comes with it that gave him courage. He rose from the table and walked up to the master, bowl and spoon in hand, and said:

"Please, sir, I want some more."

The whole room fell silent. The master's face turned white, not believing what he was hearing. He stared at Oliver for a few long seconds, speechless. All eyes were on the master, half fear, half hope.

"What?" he said angrily. Without hesitating, again Oliver asked if he could have some more soup. The master was furious and did not reply. He raised his ladle high, not to serve more soup, but to hit poor Oliver violently on the head.

The men in charge of the workhouse were shocked when the master rushed into their room.

"I beg your pardon, sir! Oliver Twist asked if he could have some more!"

They quickly decided that they had to do something at once. The next morning, there was a poster at the gate of the workhouse offering five pounds to anyone who would take Oliver Twist off their hands.

## C. Read again and answer the questions.

1. Why does the writer prefer the word *starving* to *hungry*?
2. What did the orphans eat on special occasions?
3. Why did the boys' bowls never need cleaning?
4. What did the boys decide at the meeting?
5. Why did the boys wink at Oliver?
6. What did Oliver do?
7. What were the other boys doing while Oliver was performing his task?
8. How did the master react the second time Oliver asked for more soup?
9. What did the men in charge of the workhouse decide to do with Oliver?

**D. Match the words below from the text with their meanings.**

1. orphan ☐        6. nudge ☐
2. rags ☐          7. courage ☐
3. stare ☐         8. rise ☐
4. whisper ☐       9. speechless ☐
5. wink ☐          10. ladle ☐

a. to quickly close and open one eye as a signal to sb.

b. a large deep spoon used for serving soup

c. old, torn clothes

d. not able to speak because you are very angry, surprised, etc.

e. to give a little push to sb. especially with your elbow

f. the ability to do sth. difficult or dangerous without showing fear

g. a child whose parents have died

h. to speak very quietly so that other people cannot hear you

i. to get up

j. to look at something/someone for a long time without moving your eyes

**E. Discuss.**

• Would you have done what Oliver did?

• Why do you think the master hit Oliver?

• Oliver and the other boys had to work hard at the workhouse. Do children have to work nowadays? If yes, under what circumstances?

# 2 Vocabulary

**A. Read the first paragraph of the text in activity 1 again and find adjectives which mean:**

| very thin | very dirty | very hungry | very small |

**B. Think of "strong" adjectives which mean:**

1. very big        4. very tired
2. very angry      5. very tasty
3. very scared     6. very funny

# 3 Grammar Reported Speech: Questions-Commands-Requests → p. 149

**A. Read the examples and answer the questions.**

| DIRECT SPEECH |
| --- |
| **Oliver:** Can I have some more?<br>**Master:** Why do you want some more? |

| REPORTED SPEECH |
| --- |
| Oliver asked if/whether he could have some more.<br>The master asked why he wanted some more. |

• What comes after *asked* when the question begins with a question word?

• What comes after *asked* when we report a Yes/No question?

• Are the verbs in reported questions in the affirmative or in the question form?

**B. Read the examples and complete the rule.**

| DIRECT SPEECH |
| --- |
| **Oliver:** Please, give me some more.<br>**Master:** Don't ask for more! |

| REPORTED SPEECH |
| --- |
| Oliver asked the master to give him some more.<br>The master told him not to ask for more. |

The imperative changes to: _____ **+ base form** and the negative imperative (**don't**) changes to: _____ **+ base form**.

> When the request is in the question form, in Reported Speech it usually changes to *to + base form*.
> *"Will you lend me that book, please?" Kate asked me.*
> *Kate asked me if/whether I would lend her that book.*
> *Kate asked me to lend her that book.*

**C. Complete the sentences using Reported Speech.**

1. "Where have you put the keys?" Mario asked me.
   Mario asked me _____.

2. "Please show me the way to the station," Andy said to the woman.
   Andy asked the woman _____.

3. "Don't eat the cake!" Kim said to Gary.
   Kim told Gary _____.

4. "Do you want some coffee?" Dave asked me.
   Dave asked me _____.

5. "Sit down at once!" Mrs. Humphrey said to the student.
   Mrs. Humphrey told the student _____.

6. "Why are you whispering?" Fred asked Tony.
   Fred asked Tony _____.

# 4 Speaking
**Discuss the following:**

• Do you like reading books? What kind?

• Who is your favorite author?

• What was the title of the last book you read? What was it about?

• Can you describe a scene from your favorite book?

# 1 Listening 🔊

### A. Discuss.

- What do you usually fight about with family and friends?
- How do you solve these problems?
- Who do you turn to when you need advice?

**B. Listen to the first part of a conversation. Tanya is describing a problem she has to some friends. What is Tanya's main problem?**

a. Tanya wasn't accepted to a college.

b. Tanya's cousin is jealous of her because she was accepted to a college.

c. Tanya is having difficulty persuading her cousin to apply to a different college.

**C. Now listen to the second part of the conversation. Three of Tanya's friends are giving her advice. Match each person with the statements below. There is one extra statement which you do not need to use.**

MARIA      a. Be nice to your cousin and she will get over it.

KELLY      b. Explain to your cousin that she shouldn't behave like that.

JILL       c. Wait for your cousin to make the first move.

           d. Help your cousin to build her confidence.

# 2 Speaking

### Talk in pairs.

**Student A:** Choose one of the situations, explain the problem to Student B and ask him/her for advice. Use the words/phrases given.

> I have a problem with... and I'd like your advice.
> I feel helpless and don't know what to do.
> Can you give me some good advice?
> What should I do? Any ideas?
> What would you do if you were me?

**Student B:** Listen to Student A's problem, symphathize and give him/her advice. Use the words/phrases given.

> I'm sorry to hear that you are having problems with...
> Don't worry, we'll think of something.
> I understand what you're going through.
> I think you should / had better...
> If I were you, I'd...
> If I were in your shoes, I'd...
> It would be a good idea to...
> One/Another thing you can do is...
> Why don't you...?

**1 SA:** Your best friend has become addicted to playing video games. He/She never wants to do anything else and he/she has stopped hanging out with you. His/Her addiction is starting to affect his/her studies as well. You are worried about him/her.

**SB:**
- stand by
- support
- get professional help

**TIP**
- When you need more time to think about what to say, use phrases like:
  "Well, let's see now...", "Well, let me think...", "Umm, give me a minute...".
- If one of you gets stuck, help each other by asking a question, for instance.

**2 SA:** Your boss has asked you to give a presentation to some colleagues of yours on something you've been working on. You feel too nervous and insecure, but can't refuse because your boss is insisting.

**SB:**
- try to get over fear
- practice in front of mirror
- feel confident

**3 SA:** You feel stressed and tired all the time. You have difficulty sleeping at night and when you finally get to sleep, you keep waking up thinking about your problems. You can't concentrate on your work or have fun with your friends.

**SB:**
- take it easy
- discuss the problem with sb. you trust
- take a break

# 3 Writing An e-mail asking for or giving advice

**A. Below is an e-mail Greg sent to his friend Mike asking for advice. Read the e-mail and say what advice you would give him.**

Hey Mike,

I hope you're well. My new apartment is great, but I need some advice about something. I've been having problems with my roommate, Brian, and I don't know what to do.

I know I'm not the neatest person in the world, but Brian is something else! He never does his share of the chores and the apartment is constantly a mess. It's annoying and it's impossible to concentrate in there with so many things lying around. Also, he wastes a lot of money on clothes and DVDs, and then he doesn't have enough to pay the bills. Yesterday, we got into an argument because he was broke again, and I had to pay the whole electricity bill, instead of splitting it in half. I feel helpless. What would you do if you were me?

I hope I'm not troubling you too much, but I really need some advice. I'm counting on you.

Greg

**B. Read Mike's reply to Greg and compare it to the advice you would give him. Do you think Mike's advice is helpful? Why? / Why not?**

Dear Greg,

I'm sorry to hear that you aren't getting along with your new roommate. I thought about your problem and I've come up with a few solutions.

First of all, I think you should sit down and talk with him. Make sure he understands that what he is doing is annoying you. If I were you, I'd try to remain calm, and discuss the situation in detail, explaining how unfair it is. Nobody likes housework, so perhaps it would be a good idea to create a chores schedule where you can note down who does what and when. As for the bills, how about suggesting that he should get a part-time job so he can pay his share? He might listen to you, or at least he will understand there is a problem. The main thing is to talk about the problem. Otherwise, it's only going to get worse.

That's all I have to say. I hope everything turns out OK. Let me know what happens.

Take care,
Mike

**C. Read the plan below. Can you think of a few more phrases for each part?**

## Plan
**An e-mail asking for or giving advice**
**GREETING**
**OPENING PARAGRAPH**
**Begin your e-mail and say why you're writing. Use phrases like:**

| ASKING FOR ADVICE | GIVING ADVICE |
|---|---|
| • I've been having problems with... and I'd like your advice.<br>• I hope you can help me with a problem.<br>• I need your advice about something that is troubling me. | • I'm sorry to hear that you are having problems with...<br>• I hope my advice will help you.<br>• I've thought about your problem and I've come up with the following solution. |

**MAIN PART**

| ASKING FOR ADVICE | GIVING ADVICE |
|---|---|
| **Explain the problem and how you feel and ask for advice. Use phrases like:**<br>• What should I do?<br>• I feel terrible/down/helpless and don't know what to do.<br>• What would you do if you were me?<br>• What would you do if you were in my shoes?<br>• What do you suggest?<br>• Do you think I should...? | **Give your advice and make various suggestions. Use phrases like:**<br>• First of all, I think you should(n't)...<br>• You'd better (not)...<br>• If I were you, I'd...<br>• If I were in your shoes, I'd...<br>• Perhaps it would be a good idea to...<br>• How/What about...?<br>• Why don't you...?<br>• Something else you can try is... |

**CLOSING PARAGRAPH**
**State anything you want to emphasize and end your e-mail. Use phrases like:**

| ASKING FOR ADVICE | GIVING ADVICE |
|---|---|
| • I hope I haven't troubled you too much.<br>• Let me know what you think ASAP. I'm counting on you.<br>• I look forward to hearing from you. | • I hope everything goes well.<br>• Let me know what happens.<br>• Don't worry. You'll get over it.<br>• There's no need to panic. |

**SIGNING OFF**

**D. Write an e-mail to a friend asking for advice on a problem you have. Then swap with another student and write an e-mail giving him/her advice. Follow the plans above.**

## Vocabulary

### A. Choose a, b or c.

1. Ralph was sick last week. He had a stomach ____.
   **a.** rash      **b.** pain      **c.** bug

2. The dentist was booked ____ all week so I got an appointment for next Monday.
   **a.** up      **b.** away      **c.** down

3. Try not to make a ____ of yourself out there on the soccer field today.
   **a.** beet      **b.** face      **c.** fool

4. It takes a lot of ____ to stand up and speak in front of hundreds of people.
   **a.** courage      **b.** hope      **c.** fear

5. There's no need to ____. We have lots of time.
   **a.** stare      **b.** rush      **c.** nudge

6. It's nice to know that your friends are there to ____ you.
   **a.** turn      **b.** support      **c.** stand

7. I'm ____. What's for dinner?
   **a.** starving      **b.** filthy      **c.** jealous

8. What did the doctor ____ for your illness?
   **a.** examine      **b.** relieve      **c.** prescribe

## Grammar

### B. Complete the dialogue with tag questions.

**A:** Emma, you haven't seen my hand cream anywhere, 1 _____?

**B:** No. It's in your purse, 2 _____?

**A:** I can't find it. You don't have any, 3 _____?

**B:** Sorry. I've run out.

**A:** But you're going to the mall later, 4 _____?

**B:** Yes.

**A:** You'll get me some, 5 _____?

**B:** Of course, I will. You can't come along, 6 _____?

**A:** No, I have a lot of studying to do.

**B:** I thought so.

### C. Rewrite using Reported Speech.

1. "Do you like mountain biking?" my brother asked me.

   _____

2. "I bought two pounds of apples yesterday," said Oliver.

   _____

3. "I'll do the chores this weekend," said Fiona.

   _____

4. "Don't play soccer in the house," John's mother told him.

   _____

5. "Why can't you come to the museum tomorrow?" Brian asked Tiffany.

   _____

6. "Take these vitamins for a month," the doctor told me.

   _____

7. "Delia hasn't returned my DVD yet," said Norma.

   _____

### D. Read the situations and make negative questions.

1. You're surprised that your friend doesn't have a cell phone. What do you say?

   _____

2. You see a car outside your house and you think it's Kelly's. What do you say?

   _____

3. You see your grandfather taking medication, but you think he's already taken it. What do you say?

   _____

## Communication

### E. Read and choose a or b.

1. **A:** How did you feel when the bird smashed into the window?
   **B:** ____

   | a. | I fell flat on my face. |
   |----|--------------------------|
   | b. | I nearly jumped out of my skin. |

2. **A:** I need to go to the pharmacy.
   **B:** ____

   | a. | It's not open at this hour, is it? |
   |----|-------------------------------------|
   | b. | Isn't it open at this hour? |

3. **A:** I bet you were embarrassed!
   **B:** ____

   | a. | Yes, I couldn't believe my eyes. |
   |----|-----------------------------------|
   | b. | Yes, I wanted the ground to open up and swallow me. |

4. **A:** What would you do if you were in my shoes?
   **B:** ____

   | a. | I understand what you're going through. |
   |----|------------------------------------------|
   | b. | I'd take it easy. |

5. **A:** The food here is horrible!
   **B:** ____

   | a. | Can't you stop complaining about everything? |
   |----|-----------------------------------------------|
   | b. | You can stop complaining about everything, can't you? |

## Self-assessment

Read the following and check the appropriate boxes. For the points you are unsure of, refer back to the relevant sections in the module.

### NOW I CAN...

- express uncertainty and ask for confirmation ☐
- express emotions like surprise, anger, annoyance ☐
- use language needed in different medical situations ☐
- use idioms describing feelings ☐
- give an account of a true event ☐
- report statements, questions, commands and requests ☐
- ask for and give advice ☐
- describe a problem ☐
- use different phrases to take more time to think ☐
- write an e-mail asking for or giving advice ☐

Task 11&12 p. 132

**A. Below are some pictures of Robert Rogers. Look at the pictures and try to guess as many facts about his life as you can. Discuss information such as:**

**what he does**

**what his interests are**

**what he is like**

**B. Read the magazine Mini Bio of Robert and compare your answers. What have you guessed correctly about him? What other information did you learn about him?**

**C. Work in pairs. Read the Mini Bio again and decide what questions the magazine interviewer asked Robert to get all the information.**

**D. Role play**
Work in pairs. Don't forget to swap roles.

**Student A:** Imagine you work for a magazine and want to interview Student B. Use the questions from activity C. You can also add your own questions (e.g. about music, movies, books, sports) to add more topics to your interview. Note down Student B's answers.

**Student B:** Imagine Student A works for a magazine and wants to interview you. Answer his/her questions.

**E. Use the information you have gathered to create a Mini Bio of your partner like the one on the right.**

**F. Present your Mini Bio and tell the class two interesting facts that you have learned about your partner.**

> **MINI BIO**

# Meet Robert Rogers
Up-and-coming but not famous yet!

**Name:** Robert John Rogers

**Nickname:** R.J.

**Occupation:** Writer

**Nationality:** American

**Date of birth:** July 6th, 1980

**Place of birth:** Chicago, Illinois, U.S.A.

**Family:** Two older sisters, Sally and Fay. Father and mother, Robert and Wendy (also writers).

**Education:** Northwestern University

**Interests:** Crazy about photography, basketball, poetry and comic books. Enjoys cooking for friends.

**Dislikes:** Can't stand football and moody people. (friends say)

**Positive qualities:** Easygoing, trustworthy.

**Negative qualities:** Extremely forgetful.

**Most interesting experience:** He's swum with dolphins in the Caribbean!

**Worst experience:** When he didn't have a cell phone for 3 days!

**Greatest fear:** Snakes, planes and losing touch with old friends.

**At the moment:** He's writing his first children's book.

**Done so far:** Written 2 science-fiction novels.

**Future dreams:** Wants to travel around the world and write graphic novels.

**Message to others:** Don't use your car or public transportation. Ride a bike!

**A.** Listen to a conversation between a police officer and a driver involved in a car accident and choose the correct picture a, b or c.

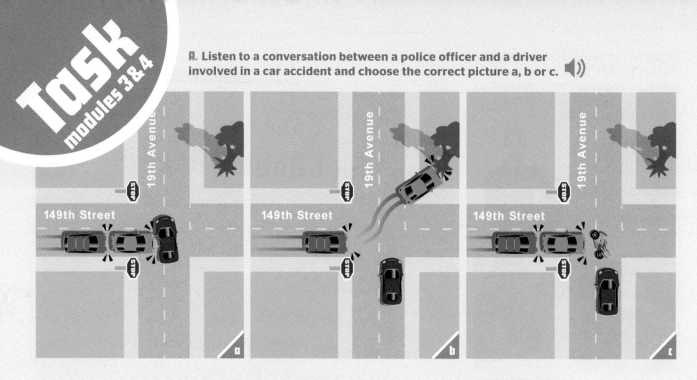

**B.** Look at the pictures above again. What did the green car crash into in each accident? Can you describe what happened in each accident? Use some of the words/phrases in the box.

| | | | | | |
|---|---|---|---|---|---|
| stop at a stop sign | speed | slam on the brakes | crash into | push | hit |

**C.** Listen to two eyewitnesses describing what they saw and take notes of any new information they give about the accident and the people involved.

1st eyewitness:

2nd eyewitness:

**D.** Work in pairs. Discuss the information you have each collected.

**E.** Work in pairs. Imagine you are reporters who want to write about the accident. Write your news article describing what exactly happened. Then present it to the class.

**A.** How much do you know about pie charts? Look at the pie chart below and read the statements. One of the statements is false. Do you know which one?

**Tourists' opinion on the most beautiful city in Europe**

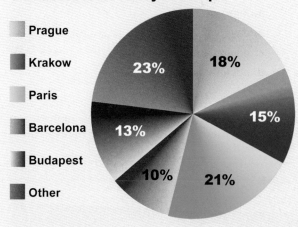

- Prague
- Krakow
- Paris
- Barcelona
- Budapest
- Other

1. A pie chart presents data and percentages visually.
2. A pie chart has different parts which are called slices.
3. The slices in a pie chart add up to 100%.
4. "Other" can be used to make the pie chart complete.
5. You have to write the names/categories on the slices so that the pie chart makes sense.
6. Color-coding helps make the pie chart easier to read.

**B.** Read the text below and complete the gaps in the pie chart.

These days tourism is big business and travel agencies try hard to offer the best to their customers. To improve its services a travel agency for young travelers in Miami asked a hundred first-year college students about their favorite types of vacation.

Half of the students said that they preferred *active vacations*. They like taking part in exciting activities such as skiing or water sports, or spending time in the countryside, camping or hiking, for example.

A quarter of the students chose *educational vacations*, visiting historic sites or learning about local culture. Only 5% of the students chose *peaceful vacations* at quiet resorts on the beach or in the mountains.

The survey also showed that some young people think about the environment when choosing their vacations. 12% of the students chose *volunteer vacations*, which give them the opportunity to see new places and also do something for the environment.

The rest of the students chose other types of vacations such as visiting family or friends or going to health resorts.

**First-year college students' vacation choices**

Number of students: _____

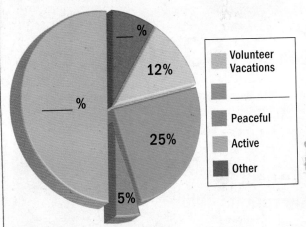

- Volunteer Vacations
- _____
- Peaceful
- Active
- Other

**C.** Talk in pairs. Discuss the percentages in the pie chart in B. Now think about people of your age in your country. What kind of vacations do they like? Do you think the percentages would be the same or different? Discuss, using some of the phrases in the box.

| | |
|---|---|
| This pie chart shows that... | People our age prefer.... |
| Fewer/More students like... than... | I believe... vacation is not very popular |
| Not many students... | because... |
| Half / A quarter of the students chose... | I think... vacation is more popular |
| A high/low percentage of students... | because... |
| The most common vacation choice is... | |

**D.** Discuss.

- Do you think the pie chart is a good way to show the results of a survey? Why?/Why not?
- Where have you seen a pie chart before?
- Do you think pie charts are useful for project work or presentations? Why?/ Why not?

**A. Listen to two friends trying to decide which activity to take up together and answer the questions.** 🔊

1. Which activity did they decide to take up?

   a. scuba diving

   b. astronomy

2. Why didn't they choose to take up the other activity? Choose two reasons.

   a. time

   b. days

   c. equipment

   d. not interesting enough

**B. Talk in pairs.** Imagine that you and your partner have decided to take up a new activity together. Read the four flyers below and discuss which activity you think is the most suitable for both of you. Talk about the ideas in the box. Make sure you give reasons why you think each activity is or isn't suitable.

| time | days | equipment needed | how interesting it is | cost |
|------|------|------------------|----------------------|------|

LEARN TO COOK JAPANESE FOOD WITH YOGO RESTAURANT CHEF YU SHIMURA!

Every Monday 6 p.m.–8 p.m. or Thursday 5 p.m.–7 p.m.

No experience necessary
10 students per class

**Book now! $300**

From July 5th – August 28th
Towervale City Hall

Yogo Restaurant provides all food and equipment

**Russian, Arabic Hindi**
**Language Matters Institute**
**25 Crowndale Road**

Choose from beginners, intermediate and advanced levels.

Classes every day, except for Friday and Sunday, 6 p.m. – 7 p.m.

Courses run
**September 5th – May 15th $650**

10% discount for students and unemployed

With over 500 students already learning at our school, it's a great way to meet people!

**Make your own smartphone applications!**
An exciting course for all true technology fans!

Wednesdays and Fridays
**7 p.m. – 9:30 p.m.**

Courses start the first Wednesday of every month and last for 4 weeks

A good understanding of cell phone technology is necessary

Learn with the best teachers with only 4 students per class

$200 (5% discount if you book more than one month before course starts)

**Hendersons Sports Center**

**SPECIAL OFFER!**

Become a full member for only $30 per month (12 months minimum)

Running club – Mondays 6:30 p.m. – 8 p.m.
Karate – Tuesdays, Thursdays 7 p.m. – 8:30 p.m.
Aerobics – every day 7 p.m. – 9:30 p.m.
Swimming pool - open 8 a.m. – 10 p.m.

❝ *So, what do you think of...? It might be interesting.*

*I'd rather...*

*If we take up..., we will/won't...*

*OK, I agree. Which days are you free?*

*... What about you?*

*... is more convenient for me because...*

*...* ❞

**C. Tell the class about your decision, giving reasons.**

❝ *We both like... so...*

*We are both interested in...*

*We are both free on... so...*

*We'd like to take up... because...* ❞

**A. Read Ken Fielding's résumé and the three job advertisements. Which of the three jobs is he most suitable for? Why?**

## Ken Fielding

1320 Maple Street, Denver, Colorado 80215
Home: 303-521-2400 | Cell: 212-555-0123
ken@fielding.com

### Work Experience

**2009 – present**   Sales Manager at "City Cellphones"
- manage relations with customers
- organize company's online marketing

**2006 – 2009**   Personal Assistant to Sales Manager at "Top Travel"
- assisted Sales Manager with sales calls
- organized schedule of Sales Manager

### Education

**2001 – 2005**   Denver University, BA in Business and Marketing, including 6-month Erasmus program in Salamanca, Spain.

### Personal Skills

- Fluent in Spanish and French, good knowledge of Japanese
- Advanced user of MS Word, Excel and Outlook programs
- Excellent communication skills
- Fast learner

### Interests

Traveling, exploring new places, learning about different cultures, rock climbing and mountain biking

### References

Available upon request

---

**Adventure Tours**
is looking for a
## Sales Manager

Applicants must:
- have a degree in Business
- have at least 10 years' work experience
- speak Spanish fluently
- be computer literate
- be available to work weekends
- have excellent communication skills

*An interest in outdoor activities is an advantage*

---

**Sunshine Travel**
## Position: Sales Manager

We offer:
- full-time work in an excellent working environment
- excellent salary
- flexible working hours

We require:
- a degree in Business
- knowledge of at least 2 foreign languages (one must be Japanese)
- previous work experience (at least 4 years)
- good knowledge of computers
- excellent communication skills, especially over the phone
- driver's license

---

**Sales Manager** needed for
**Goldstar Luxury Travel**

Applicants must:
- have a degree in Business
- have previous work experience in sales
- speak fluent Spanish, and very good Japanese
- be computer literate
- be able to work weekends
- be confident talking to customers over the phone and face-to-face

---

**B. Work in pairs. Read the résumé above again and the advice below. Which of the statements are false?**

1. You should write full sentences.
2. Don't write information that is unnecessary (e.g. appearance).
3. Do not use informal language (e.g. short forms, abbreviations).
4. Focus on your qualifications which are required for the job you are applying for.
5. In the "Work Experience" section, start by describing your first job.
6. You should describe your positive and negative qualities in the "Personal Skills" section.
7. It is a good idea to highlight headings in bold, or underline them.
8. Be brief and to the point.
9. Sign off with *Yours sincerely*.

**C. Think about your educational background, your qualifications, any work experience you have had, etc. and create your own résumé.**

**D. Work in pairs. Swap résumés with your partner. Read each other's résumé and point out any mistakes your partner has made. Then give him/her advice about how he/she could make it better.**

66 *You don't need to…*

*You have a point.*

*You shouldn't… I think you should…*

*Perhaps you're right.*

*You could… Don't forget to…*

*OK. I will.*

*It might be a good idea to…* 99

**E. After you have corrected your résumés, show them to your teacher and ask for feedback.**

**A.** Look at the statement below. Do you agree or disagree?

## "Traveling in a group is better than traveling alone."

**B.** Listen to four monologues and decide which speaker is FOR (F) and which speaker is AGAINST (A) the above statement.

Speaker 1: ☐    Speaker 3: ☐

Speaker 2: ☐    Speaker 4: ☐

**C.** Listen again and answer the questions.

**Which speaker...**

**a.** thinks you learn more by traveling alone? ☐

**b.** thinks traveling alone is more expensive? ☐

**c.** thinks it's less stressful to travel alone? ☐

**d.** thinks it's safer to travel as part of a group? ☐

**D.** Work in groups. Read the statement below. Group A should think of arguments FOR the statement and Group B should think of arguments AGAINST it. Think about the ideas given and also add your own. Make sure you support your arguments by giving persuasive reasons. Discuss your ideas with your group, keeping any necessary notes.

## "It's better to travel by car than by plane when traveling within a country."

> **Think about:**
> • how convenient it is
> • the time required
> • the cost
> • safety
> • how bad it is for the environment

**E.** Debate with the other group and try to persuade them that your view is the correct one. Use some of the phrases in the box.

| | | |
|---|---|---|
| First of all,... | In our opinion/view,... is better/worse than... | We agree, but think about... |
| To begin with,... | We believe/think... because... | You have a point, but... |
| Secondly,... | The way we see it,... | We don't agree because... |
| In addition,... | The main advantage/disadvantage of... is... | We don't think so because... |
| Furthermore,... | As for... | |
| What is more,... | One of the best/worst things about traveling by... is that... | |
| Finally,... | | |

## 2b Pair work

Talk in pairs. Choose a situation from the ones below. Don't forget to use phrases/expressions you have learned and to be friendly.

**1. Student A:** You are in a dentist's waiting room. There is only one seat left, next to Student B. Ask if you can sit there, and start a conversation.

**Student B:** You are in a dentist's waiting room and Student A asks to sit next to you. Reply "yes" politely, and have a conversation with him/her.

**2. Students A + B:** You are walking around a mall when you suddenly see each other. You are old friends from elementary school. You haven't seen each other for years and are very happy. Greet each other and ask questions to find out about each other's lives so far.

**3. Student A:** You are walking down the street when you see Student B. He/She looks familiar so you decide to go and talk to him/her. You think you've met at the gym.

**Student B:** You are walking down the street when Student A stops you and asks you if he/she knows you from the gym. However, Student A is a complete stranger to you. Try to explain politely that you don't go to that gym and you don't recognize him/her.

## 3a Pair work

Talk in pairs. Act out one or two of the conversations. Don't forget to use phrases/expressions you have learned.

**1. Student A:** You want to go to a vegetarian restaurant and decide to invite Student B to come with you. He/She is a meat eater. Try to persuade him/her to come along.

**Student B:** Student A invites you to a vegetarian restaurant but you don't really want to go because you are a meat eater. Discuss with Student A.

**2. Student A:** You have invited Student B to your house and have cooked a meal for him/her. Ask him/her what he/she thought of the meal.

**Student B:** Student A has invited you to his/her house and has cooked for you. Give him/her your opinion about the meal. Don't forget to be polite.

**3. Student A:** You want to make a reservation at a Mexican restaurant. Call and give all the necessary information.

**Student B:** You are a host/hostess at a Mexican restaurant. Student A wants to make a reservation. Answer the phone and help him/her.

**4. Student A:** You are at a restaurant and are looking at the menu. You don't like spicy food and don't know what the dishes contain. Ask the waiter/waitress (Student B) to help you decide what to order.

**Student B:** You are a waiter/waitress at a restaurant. Student A is a customer but is confused by the menu. Help him/her decide what to order by making recommendations.

# 4d Group work

**A.** Work in groups of three. Look at the pictures a-f which show what happened to Steve. The pictures are mixed up. Put them in order and make up a story using the prompts given. Then think of an interesting ending.

- Last Saturday morning, Steve...
- As soon as...
- While he was...
- However, ...
- When he arrived, ...
- Luckily, ...
- So, he...
- Fortunately/Unfortunately, ...

| | |
|---|---|
| wake up / late | not panic |
| business trip | get off / bus |
| catch / flight | ask / farmer |
| get ready | farmer / agree |
| run / bus stop | sit / back of / |
| suitcase | truck |
| catch bus | arrive / airport |
| fall asleep | forget / suitcase |
| countryside | |

**a** ☐

**b** ☐

**c** ☐

**d** ☐

**e** ☐

**f** ☐

?

**B.** Tell your story to the class and listen to the other groups' stories. Decide on the most interesting story.

# 5a Student A

**A.** Read the text about the explorer Robert Falcon Scott and answer Student B's questions.

**Robert Falcon Scott** was an English explorer who tried to become the first man to reach the South Pole. In November 1911, Scott led a group of men across the Antarctic. It was an extremely difficult journey, and on January 17th, 1912, he finally reached his destination. However, when he arrived, he found a Norwegian flag and realized that another explorer, Amundsen, had reached the pole before him. Scott was very disappointed and decided to return home. However, he and all his men died on the journey home.

**B.** Student B has information about the explorer David Livingstone. Use the prompts below to ask him/her questions and complete the table.

| | David Livingstone |
|---|---|
| • Where / Livingstone / be / from? | |
| • Which continent / he / explore? | |
| • What / he / decide / do / 1866? | |
| • What / happen / during / expedition? | |
| • Why / newspaper / send / Stanley / to find him? | |
| • Stanley / find / him? | |
| • When / Livingstone / die? | |

# 8c Pair work

Talk in pairs. Form questions using the prompts below and the Present or Past Simple Passive, and try to guess the answers. Then check the answers with your teacher.

- What / Beijing National Stadium / also call?

- Where / elephant polo / play?

- Which sport / play / in the French Open?

- How many points / score / by Wilt Chamberlain / NBA basketball game / 1962?

- Where / bicycle polo / invent?

- Which sport / invent / Massachusetts, U.S.A. / 1895?

- Which stadium / build / Rio de Janeiro / 1950?

- When / first modern Olympics / hold?

- How many goals / score / 2012 / by Lionel Messi?

- When / yellow tennis balls / use / first time / at Wimbledon?

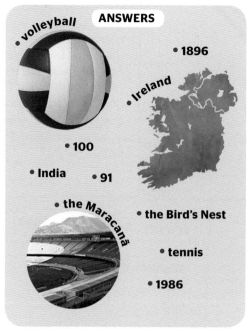

**ANSWERS**

volleyball

- 1896
- Ireland
- 100
- India
- 91
- the Bird's Nest
- tennis
- 1986

the Maracanã

**❝** *What is the Beijing National Stadium also called?*
*I think it's also called...* **❞**

# 11a Student A

**A.** Imagine that you work at Springfield Language Institute. Look at the information below and answer Student B's questions.

Springfield Language Institute
2525 Main Street

We teach – You learn!

4-month courses
for all levels of English
Courses start October
and February

ONLY $1,200!
&
FREE BOOKS

**B.** Imagine that you want to attend a language course at Langstone Language Institute. Student B works there. Use the prompts to ask for information, and the phrases in the box.

- how long / courses / last?
- have / evening classes?
- what else / course / offer?
- how much / course / cost / per month?
- where / be / institute?

**TIP**

When having a conversation with somebody, listen carefully. If you don't understand something, ask him/her to repeat or clarify what they are saying.

**Asking for clarification and repetition**
Excuse me?
Did you say...?
Sorry, I don't understand. What does... mean?
What do you mean by that?
I'm not following you.
I'm not sure I get what you mean.
Sorry, I didn't get that.
Could you say/explain that (again)?
Could you repeat that, please?

**❝** *Hello. How can I help you?*
*I'd like some information about your English courses.*
*Certainly.*
*First of all, could you tell me...?*
*...*
*Did you say...?* **❞**

# 9c Pair work

**Student A:** Imagine you are a reporter for a local magazine. Interview Student B using the prompts below and complete the survey sheet.

- What / name?
- How old / be?
- How long / learn English?
- How old / when start?
- Where / learn English?
- How often / have lessons?
- How many hours / study?
......................................
- Do you watch...?
......................................
- Why / learn / English?

## Survey: Learning English

### GENERAL INFORMATION

name: _____

age: _____

learning English for/since: _____

age when started: _____

place where you learn: _____

frequency of lessons: _____

hours of studying: _____

### OTHER WAYS YOU LEARN/PRACTICE

- watch TV or movies in English without subtitles:  yes ☐  no ☐
- read English books/magazines/newspapers:  yes ☐  no ☐
- listen to English songs:  yes ☐  no ☐
- use English websites:  yes ☐  no ☐
- play video games that are in English:  yes ☐  no ☐
- communicate with people who speak English:  yes ☐  no ☐
- visit English-speaking countries:  yes ☐  no ☐
- take (summer) classes in English-speaking countries:  yes ☐  no ☐

### REASONS WHY YOU ARE LEARNING

- meet people:  yes ☐  no ☐
- travel:  yes ☐  no ☐
- study abroad:  yes ☐  no ☐
- work abroad:  yes ☐  no ☐
- other: _____

**Student B:** Student A is a reporter for a local magazine and wants to interview you. Answer his/her questions.

# 5a Student B

**A.** Student A has information about the explorer Robert Falcon Scott. Use the prompts below to ask him/her questions and complete the table.

|  | Robert Falcon Scott |
|---|---|
| • Where / Scott / be / from? | |
| • What / he / want / do? | |
| • When / he / begin / expedition? | |
| • When / he / reach / destination? | |
| • What / he / find / there? | |
| • What / Amundsen / do? | |
| • What / happen / on / journey home? | |

**B.** Read the text about the explorer David Livingstone and answer Student A's questions.

**David Livingstone** was a Scottish explorer who spent most of his life exploring Africa. In 1866, Livingstone decided to go on an expedition to find the source* of the River Nile. Livingstone spent six years doing so and during this expedition, became sick. He lost contact with the outside world and there were many stories that he had died. In 1869, the *New York Herald* newspaper sent Henry Stanley to find Livingstone. When the two met in November 1871, Livingstone was very sick and confused. However, he didn't want to leave Africa until he found the source of the Nile. Unfortunately, Livingstone died in 1873.

* source= the place where a river starts

# 11a Student B

**A.** Imagine that you want to attend a language course at Springfield Language Institute. Student A works there. Use the prompts to ask for information, and the phrases in the box.

**B.** Imagine that you work at Langstone Language Institute. Look at the information below and answer Student A's questions.

- how long / courses / last?
- when / courses / start?
- how much / course / cost?
- need / buy / books?
- where / be / institute?

> **TIP**
> When having a conversation with somebody, listen carefully. If you don't understand something, ask him/her to repeat or clarify what they are saying.

**Asking for clarification and repetition**
Excuse me?
Did you say...?
Sorry, I don't understand. What does... mean?
What do you mean by that?
I'm not following you.
I'm not sure I get what you mean.
Sorry, I didn't get that.
Could you say/explain that (again)?
Could you repeat that, please?

**66** *Hello. How can I help you?*
    **I'd like some information about your English courses.**
*Certainly.*
    **First of all, could you tell me...?**
...
    **Did you say...? 99**

**LANGSTONE LANGUAGE INSTITUTE**
305 Park Avenue
**The BEST place to learn English!**

We offer:
• intensive 3-month courses
• morning or evening classes
• trips to places of cultural interest

**TUITION FEES: $400 per month**

# 3d An informal e-mail

**An informal e-mail is usually sent to a friend, a relative or an acquaintance.**
**Note the layout below:**

Subject: a brief phrase that indicates what the content of the e-mail is.

Greeting: on the left-hand side of the page. Put a comma after the name.

Paragraphing: write in blocked paragraphs leaving a blank line in between the paragraphs.

Signing off: on the left-hand side of the page. Use your first name.

To... eileen728@mymail.com
From... karen341@freenet.com
Subject... Awesome news

Dear Eileen,

_____
_____
_____

_____
_____
_____

_____
_____

Hope to see you soon,
Karen

# An informal letter

**An informal letter is a personal letter usually written to a friend, a relative or an acquaintance.**
**Note the layout below:**

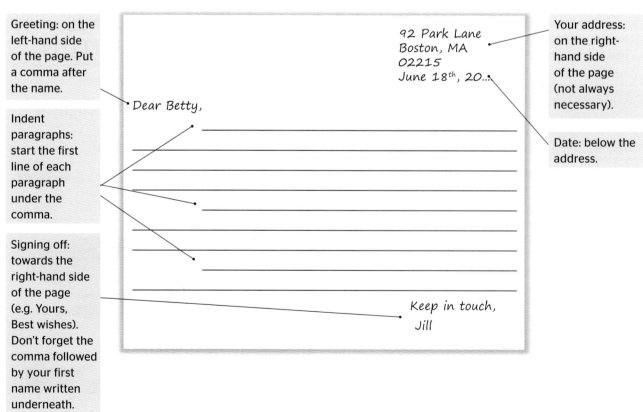

Greeting: on the left-hand side of the page. Put a comma after the name.

Indent paragraphs: start the first line of each paragraph under the comma.

Signing off: towards the right-hand side of the page (e.g. Yours, Best wishes). Don't forget the comma followed by your first name written underneath.

92 Park Lane
Boston, MA
02215
June 18th, 20...

Dear Betty,

Keep in touch,
Jill

Your address: on the right-hand side of the page (not always necessary).

Date: below the address.

# 9d A formal letter

A formal letter is written to someone you don't know personally and it is usually of a business nature. Note the layout below:

Position of the person you are writing to and/or name of company (start one line below the date).

Address of the person or company you are writing to.

Greeting: on the left-hand side of the page (leave a blank line before and after the greeting).

Signing off: on the left-hand side of the page, followed by a comma.

Your signature and your full name clearly written underneath.

92 Park Lane
Boston, MA
02215

June 18th, 20....

Human Resources Manager
Jacksonville Swimming Pool
72 Albany Ave.
Chicago, IL 60616

Dear Sir or Madam, / Dear Mr. Jones,

_____
_____
_____
_____
_____
_____
_____
_____

Yours truly, / Yours sincerely,

Jill Thomas (Ms.)

Your address: on the right-hand side of the page (without your name).

Date: below the address, leaving a blank line in between.

Paragraphing: You can indent or write in blocked paragraphs leaving a blank line in between the paragraphs. Note that when using blocked paragraphs, everything begins on the left-hand side of the page, except your address and the date.

**TIP**

In a formal letter/e-mail, when you don't know the name of the person you are writing to, begin with Dear Sir/Madam. When you are writing to a woman and are unsure of her marital status, begin with Dear Ms. + last name.

# Phonetic symbols

| Vowel sounds | | | |
|---|---|---|---|
| /iː/ read | /ɪ/ did | /ɛ/ next | /æ/ back |
| /ɑː/ bottle | /ɔː/ boring | /ʊ/ good | /uː/ food |
| /ʌ/ butter | /ɜː/ bird | /ə/ father | /eɪ/ player |
| /oʊ/ boat | /aɪ/ nine | /aʊ/ about | /ɔɪ/ point |

| Consonant sounds | | | | | |
|---|---|---|---|---|---|
| /p/ pet | /b/ book | /d/ doctor | /k/ kid | /g/ grandson | /tʃ/ chair |
| /dʒ/ large | /f/ first | /v/ vet | /θ/ theater | /ð/ that | /s/ space |
| /z/ has | /t/ take | /ʃ/ shop | /ʒ/ usually | /h/ whole | /m/ man |
| /n/ neat | /ŋ/ thing | /w/ wear | /l/ lips | /r/ room | /j/ yellow |

# Module 1

## ▶ Present Simple vs. Present Progressive

| Present Simple | | | | |
|---|---|---|---|---|
| **Affirmative** | | **Negative** | | |
| I | work | I | don't | work |
| He/She/It | works | He/She/It | doesn't | work |
| We/You/They | work | We/You/They | don't | work |

| Questions | | |
|---|---|---|
| Do | I | work? |
| Does | he/she/it | work? |
| Do | we/you/they | work? |

| Present Progressive | | | | |
|---|---|---|---|---|
| **Affirmative** | | **Negative** | | |
| I | am working | I | 'm not working | |
| He/She/It | is working | He/She/It | isn't | working |
| We/You/They | are working | We/You/They | aren't | working |

| Questions | | |
|---|---|---|
| Am | I | working? |
| Is | he/she/it | working? |
| Are | we/you/they | working? |

| We use the Present Simple: | We use the Present Progressive: |
|---|---|
| • for permanent states. *Ben lives in Boston.* | • for temporary states. *I'm taking driving lessons this month.* |
| • for habits or actions that happen regularly. *We always have breakfast at eight.* | • for actions happening at the moment of speaking. *Lucy is sleeping now.* |
| • for general truths. *The earth goes around the sun.* | • for future arrangements. *We're flying to Acapulco tonight.* |

| Time Expressions | |
|---|---|
| **Present Simple** | **Present Progressive** |
| usually, always, often, etc. every day/week, etc. in the morning/spring, etc. on Mondays/Monday morning, etc. on the weekend, etc. once/twice/three times, etc. a week/day, etc. | now, right now, at the moment, today, these days, this week/year, etc. tonight, tomorrow, etc. next week/year, etc. |

## ▶ Stative Verbs

The following verbs are usually **not** used in progressive tenses:

- **Verbs of the senses:**
  see, feel, hear, smell, taste, seem, look (=seem), appear, etc.

- **Verbs of emotion:**
  like, dislike, love, hate, want, need, prefer, etc.

- **Verbs of perception and opinions:**
  know, mean, think, understand, remember, forget, imagine, hope, believe, etc.

- **Other verbs:**
  be, have, own, belong, cost, etc.

## ▶ Past Simple

| Affirmative | |
|---|---|
| I/He/She/It We/You/They | worked/went |

| Negative | |
|---|---|
| I/He/She/It We/You/They | didn't work/go |

| Questions | | |
|---|---|---|
| Did | I/he/she/it we/you/they | work/go? |

> Irregular verbs in the Past Simple don't take -ed.
> For a list of irregular verbs go to page 150.

We use the **Past Simple** for:

- actions that started and were completed at a specific time in the past.
  *We bought our house five years ago.*

- habitual or repeated actions in the past.
  *I always went to bed early when I lived with my parents.*

- completed actions that happened one after the other in the past.
  *I made a sandwich, turned on the TV and watched the game.*

> The Past Simple of the verb *can* is **could**.
> The Past Simple of the verb *be* is **was/were**.

| TIME EXPRESSIONS |
|---|
| yesterday / yesterday morning, etc. in + years / centuries last night / month / Friday / summer, etc. two days / a week ago |

## ▶ Prepositions of Time

- **at:** at six o'clock / at two-thirty
  at noon / at night / at midnight
  at breakfast/lunch/dinner
  at fifteen / at the age of twenty
  at the moment, etc.

- **in:** in the morning/afternoon, etc.
  in April / in spring, etc.
  in 2026 / in the 20th century
  in two hours
  in my spare time, etc.

- **on:**           on Friday
                    on Friday morning/afternoon, etc.
                    on weekdays /
                    on the weekend
                    on May 15th, etc.
- **till/until:**   9p.m. / midnight / Friday, etc.
- **during:**       the week / the night / the winter /
                    my trip, etc.
- **before/after:** lunch / school / work / midnight, etc.
- **from... to/till/until:** ...Monday... Friday / ...8... 4 /
                    ...January... May, etc.

## ) The verb *used to*

| Affirmative | |
| --- | --- |
| I/He/She/It
We/You/They | used to play |

| Negative | |
| --- | --- |
| I/He/She/It
We/You/They | didn't use to play |

| Questions | | |
| --- | --- | --- |
| Did | I/he/she/it
we/you/they | use to play? |

- We use **used to** to talk about something that happened regularly in the past, but no longer does.
  *We used to go skateboarding every afternoon when we were young.*

# Module 2
## ) Present Perfect Simple

| Affirmative | | |
| --- | --- | --- |
| I | have | |
| He/She/It | has | worked / brought |
| We/You/They | have | |

| Negative | | |
| --- | --- | --- |
| I | haven't | |
| He/She/It | hasn't | worked / brought |
| We/You/They | haven't | |

| Questions | | |
| --- | --- | --- |
| Have | I | |
| Has | he/she/it | worked / brought? |
| Have | we/you/they | |

We use the **Present Perfect Simple**:

- for actions which happened in the past, but we don't mention when exactly.
  *I've traveled to Colombia twice.*

- for actions which happened in the past and finished, but their results are obvious in the present.
  *I'm tired. I've just finished studying.*
  *Look! Jerry has broken his leg!*

> For a list of irregular verbs go to page 150.

| TIME EXPRESSIONS |
| --- |
| always, ever, never, before, once, twice, many times, so far, just, recently, lately, for, since, already, yet, etc. |

## ) Present Perfect Simple vs. Past Simple

- We use the **Present Perfect Simple** for actions that happened at some time in the past, but the exact time is not mentioned.
  *I have visited Rome.*

- We use the **Past Simple** for actions that happened at a definite time in the past and the time is mentioned.
  *I visited Rome last year.*

## ) have/has gone, have/has been

- **have/has gone** means that someone has gone somewhere and is still there.
  *Beth has gone to the mall. (= She's still there.)*

- **have/has been** means that someone has visited a place but has come back.
  *Ian has been to the new mall. (He visited the new mall at some point in the past but he's not there anymore.)*

## ) since/for

We use the **Present Perfect** with **for** and **since** for actions that started in the past and continue up to the present.

| | |
| --- | --- |
| **since + a point in time**
It refers to the time when the action started. | *I've had this car since 2010.* |
| **for + a period of time**
It refers to the duration of the action. | *I've had this car for six years.* |
| **Present Perfect Simple + since + Past Simple**
To indicate when an action which started in the past and continues up to the present started. | *Anna has worked here since she moved to this city.* |

## ) yet/already

| | |
|---|---|
| **yet** is used only with the question and negative form of verbs. It is placed at the end of the sentence. It is used to talk about something that has not happened but will probably happen soon. | *Have you finished yet? He hasn't arrived yet.* |
| **already** is used with the affirmative and question form of verbs. It is placed between the auxiliary and the main verb, or at the end of the sentence for emphasis. It is used to emphasize that something has happened before now. | *I've already seen that movie.* *You've finished eating already!* |

# Module 3

## ) Quantifiers

**some / any / no**

- **some + uncountable / plural countable nouns** in affirmative sentences and in questions when we offer something or ask for something politely.
  *There is some orange juice in the refrigerator.*
  *Would you like some fries?*
  *Could I have some coffee?*

- **any + uncountable / plural countable nouns** in questions and negative sentences.
  *Is there any orange juice in the refrigerator?*
  *There aren't any fries on the table.*

- **no (= not any) + uncountable / plural countable nouns** in affirmative sentences to give a negative meaning.
  *There is no cheese in the refrigerator. = There isn't any cheese in the refrigerator.*

**many / much / a lot (of) / lots (of)**

- **many + plural countable nouns** mainly in questions and in negative sentences.
  *How many people were at the meeting yesterday?*
  *I didn't see many people from work there.*

- **much + uncountable nouns** mainly in questions and in negative sentences.
  *How much sugar do you need?*
  *I didn't manage to learn much information from him.*

- **a lot (of) / lots (of) + uncountable / plural countable nouns** mainly in affirmative sentences.
  *There were a lot of people at the meeting.*
  *Have some more food. There's lots of pasta left.*

**(a) few / (a) little**

- **(a) few + plural countable nouns: a few** has a **positive** meaning whereas **few** has a **negative** meaning.
  *I need a few more things from the supermarket.*
  *Very few people agreed with him.*

- **(a) little + uncountable nouns: a little** has a **positive** meaning whereas **little** has a **negative** meaning.
  *There's still a little cake left. Have some.*
  *There's very little time left. Hurry!*

---

- For emphasis we can use:
  - **very, so, too + little / few**
    *There's very little milk in my coffee.*
  - **only + a little / a few**
    *He has only a few friends.*
- **Some, any, much, many, a little, a few, a lot, lots** can also be used without nouns, as pronouns.
  *Do you have any money? No, I don't have any.*
  *We didn't buy any bread. We have a lot.*

---

## ) Relative pronouns (who, which, that)
## Relative adverb (where)

The relative pronouns *who, which, that* and the adverb *where* introduce relative clauses.

| | Pronouns | Examples |
|---|---|---|
| **PEOPLE** | who/that | *The woman who/that is driving that sports car is my aunt.* *The teacher (who/that) I like the most is Mrs. Robbins.* |
| **THINGS ANIMALS IDEAS** | which/that | *The bag which/that is on the table is mine.* *The movie (which/that) I watched last night was terrible.* |

| | Adverb | |
|---|---|---|
| **PLACE** | where | *The place where I live is beautiful.* |

---

- **Who**, **which** and **that** can be omitted when they are the object of the verb in the relative clause.
- **Where** can never be omitted or replaced by **that**.

---

# Module 4

## ) Past Progressive

| Affirmative | | |
|---|---|---|
| I/He/She/It | was working | |
| We/You/They | were working | |

| Negative | | |
|---|---|---|
| I/He/She/It | wasn't working | |
| We/You/They | weren't working | |

| Questions | | |
|---|---|---|
| Was | I/he/she/it | working? |
| Were | we/you/they | working? |

We use the **Past Progressive**:

- for actions that were happening at a specific point of time in the past.
  *I was watching TV at 7 o'clock yesterday evening.*

- to set the scene in a story.
  *Jill was walking in the forest and it was raining.*

- for actions that were happening at the same time in the past. In this case, we usually use **while**.
  *While I was watching TV, my father was cooking.*

### ) Past Simple vs. Past Progressive
### Time clauses (when, while, as, as soon as)

- We use the **Past Progressive** and the **Past Simple** in the same sentence when one action interrupted another in the past. We use the **Past Progressive** for the longer action and the **Past Simple** for the shorter action. In this case we usually use **while, when** or **as**.
  *As/While I was driving, I saw a cat in the street.*
  *I was sleeping when the telephone rang.*

> We use **as soon as** with the **Past Simple**.
> *As soon as they left, we started cleaning up the house.*

# Module 5
### ) Past Perfect Simple

| Affirmative | |
|---|---|
| I He/She/It We/You/They | had worked/written |

| Negative | |
|---|---|
| I He/She/It We/You/They | hadn't worked/written |

| Questions | | |
|---|---|---|
| Had | I he/she/it we/you/they | worked/written? |

> For a list of irregular verbs go to page 150.

We use the **Past Perfect Simple** for an action which took place before a specific point of time or another action in the past. The second action is in the Past Simple.
*She had finished her homework by 8 o'clock.*
*The train had left by the time we arrived at the station.*

| TIME EXPRESSIONS |
|---|
| before + point in time |
| by + point in time |
| before, after, when, by the time |

### ) can / could / may / will / would

- We use **Can I..?, Could I..?, May I..?** to ask for permission.
  *Can/Could/May I go out tonight?*
  *Yes, you can/may.*
  *No, you can't.*

- We use **Can I..?, Could I..?, May I..?** to offer help and make requests.
  *Can/Could/May I help you?*
  *Can/Could/May I have some more cake?*

- We use **Can / Could / Will / Would you..?** to make polite requests and ask for a favor. **Could** and **Would** are more polite.
  *Can/Could/Will/Would you lend me your laptop?*

### ) Should / Shouldn't

We use **should/shouldn't + base form of the verb** to:

- ask for and give advice.
  *What should I do? Should I see a doctor?*

- express an opinion.
  *I think she should tell her mom about it.*

- make a suggestion.
  *We should go to the park. It's a beautiful day.*

> **Should/shouldn't + base form of the verb**
> refers to the present or future.

### ) Had better

We use **had better + base form of the verb** to give strong advice. It often expresses **threat** or **warning** and it's stronger than *should*. It refers to the present or future, not the past. Its negative form is **had better not**. In spoken English the short form is commonly used (I'd better, you'd better, etc.).
*You'd better ask a doctor about it.*
*You'd better not lie to me again.*

# Module 6
### ) Future *will*

| Affirmative | | Negative | |
|---|---|---|---|
| I He/She/It We/You/They | will work | I He/She/It We/You/They | will not / won't work |

| Questions | | |
|---|---|---|
| Will | I he/she/it we/you/they | work? |

| Short answers | | | | | |
|---|---|---|---|---|---|
| Yes, | I he/she/it we/you/they | will. | No, | I he/she/it we/you/they | won't. |

We use the **Future *will*** for:

- offers.
  *I'll help you with everything.*

- promises.
  *I promise, I'll be there for you.*

- requests.
  *Will you do me a favor?*

- on-the-spot decisions.
  *Fine, I'll meet you in an hour.*

- predictions, usually with the verbs **think** and **believe**.
  *I think he will be a great businessman one day.*

| TIME EXPRESSIONS |
| --- |
| tomorrow, tonight, soon, next week/month, in an hour / a week, etc. |

## Time Clauses

- Time clauses begin with **when**, **after**, **before**, **as soon as**, **until**, etc.
- When the sentence refers to the future, we usually use the Present Simple in the time clause and the Future *will* in the main clause.

| Time clause | Main clause |
| --- | --- |
| As soon as I know, Before I leave, | I'll tell you. I'll help you with the housework. |

When the **time clause** comes before the **main clause**, the two clauses are separated by a **comma**.

## be able to

- We usually use **can** to express ability in the present.
  *The baby can speak.*

- We usually use **could** to express ability in the past.
  *I could climb trees when I was young.*

- **Be able to** expresses ability and forms all tenses. It is mainly used in tenses where we cannot use can.
  *Jack will be able to play football on Saturday. He's feeling better.*

**Could** expresses general ability in the past.
**Was/were able to** expresses ability in a particular situation in the past.
*I could draw well at the age of five.*
*I was able to draw well at the age of five.*

*The firefighters were able to put out the fire after two hours.*
~~*The firefighters could put out the fire after two hours.*~~

# Module 7

## may / might / could

The verbs *may, might* and *could*
- are followed by the base form of the verb.
- are the same in all persons in the singular and plural.
- do not form the questions and negative forms with *do*.
- express possibility in the present/future.

  *We may/might/could go to the Fun Park next week.*

We use **may not/might not** to express improbability in the present or future.
*Henry may not / might not be able to join us.*

## Conditional Sentences Type 1

We use Conditional Sentences Type 1 for something which is likely to happen in the present or future.

Conditional Sentences consist of the if-clause and the main clause.

| if-clause | main clause |
| --- | --- |
| if + Present Simple | • Future *will* |
| | • Modal Verbs (may, might, can, should) |
| | • Imperative |

*If I find the book, I'll buy it for you.*
*If you go to the gym early, you might see him there.*
*If you see her, ask her about the meeting.*

When the **if-clause** comes before the **main clause**, the two clauses are separated by a **comma**.

## If vs. When

*When* is used to refer to the time something is going to happen, while *if* refers to the possibility of something happening.
*I'll tell him when I see him. (= I will definitely see him.)*
*I'll tell him if I see him. (= I may not see him.)*

## Comparative and Superlative forms

- We use the **comparative** of adjectives when we compare two people, animals or things.
- We use the **superlative** of adjectives when we compare one person, animal or thing with several of the same kind.

| Formation |
| --- |

| **Comparative:** | adjective + -er<br>more + adjective } + than |
| --- | --- |
| *John is older than Peter.*<br>*My watch is more expensive than yours.* | |
| **Superlative:** the + | adjective + -est<br>most + adjective } + of / in |
| *John is the oldest boy in his class.*<br>*This watch is the most expensive of all.* | |

| | |
|---|---|
| All one-syllable and most two-syllable adjectives take -er / -est. | short - shorter - shortest |
| One-syllable adjectives ending in -e take -r / -st. | safe - safer - safest |
| One-syllable adjectives ending in one vowel + one consonant, double the consonant before the -er / -est. | big - bigger - biggest |
| Adjectives ending in a consonant + -y, drop the -y and take -ier /-iest. | easy - easier - easiest |
| Adjectives with three or more syllables and some two-syllable adjectives take more + adjective / most + adjective. | dangerous - more dangerous - most dangerous |

| Irregular forms | | |
|---|---|---|
| **Positive Form** | **Comparative form** | **Superlative form** |
| good | better | the best |
| bad | worse | the worst |
| far | farther<br>further | the farthest<br>the furthest |
| many / much | more | the most |
| little | less | the least |

### ❭ Other Forms of Comparison

- **as + adjective + as**
  *My car is as fast as yours. (= My car and your car are equally fast.)*

- **not as + adjective + as**
  *He's not as smart as you are. (=You are smarter than he is.)*

- **less + adjective + than**
  *Ted is less active than Harry. (= Harry is more active than Ted.)*

- **the least + adjective + of/in**
  *I am the least active of all my friends. (=All my friends are more active than I am.)*

# Module 8
## ❭ Exclamatory Sentences

We use **exclamatory sentences** to give emphasis to the meaning of the adjective/adverb or noun. They are used to express enthusiasm, surprise, admiration, disappointment, anger, annoyance, etc.

- **how + adjective / adverb**
  *How wonderful!    How beautifully she sings!*

- **what + (a/an) + (adjective) + noun**
  *What a beautiful day!*

- **so + adjective/adverb**
  *It was so funny!    He plays the piano so well!*
- **such + (a/an) + adjective + noun**
  *He's such an unusual man!*

### ❭ Clauses of Result

We use Clauses of Result to express the result of an action or a conclusion:

- **so + adjective/adverb + (that)**
  *He was so bored (that) he left before the end of the movie.*
- **such + (a/an) + (adjective) + noun + (that)**
  *It was such a hot day that we all went swimming.*

---

- We say **so + much/many**, but **such a lot of**.
- *That* can be omitted, especially in spoken English.

---

### ❭ have to / don't have to / must / mustn't / need to / don't need to / needn't

- We use **must** and **have to** to express obligation in the present/future.
  *I must buy Sam a present.*
  *You have to wear a helmet when you go skydiving.*

---

We use **have to** to form all the other tenses.
*We had to work overtime yesterday.*

---

- We use **need to** when it is necessary for us to do something. (We have no other choice.)
  *I need to talk to you.*

- We use **don't have to**, **don't need to** and **needn't** when it isn't necessary for us to do something (to express lack of necessity/obligation).
  *You don't have to go out with her if you don't like her.*
  *You don't need to give me back the money.*
  *She needn't buy me a present.*

- We use **mustn't** and **can't** when we are not allowed to do something.
  *You mustn't / can't smoke inside the building.*

---

**Need** is used:

- as a **main verb** in all tenses, in the affirmative, negative and question form. It is followed by **to + base form** and forms the negative and question form with auxiliary verbs.
- as a **modal verb** only in the negative and question form of the **Present Simple**. It is followed by a **base form** and forms the negative and question form without auxiliary verbs.

---

| Affirmative | |
|---|---|
| I | need to go |
| He/She/It | needs to go |
| We/You/They | need to go |

### Negative

| I | don't need to go | | I | |
|---|---|---|---|---|
| He/She/It | doesn't need to go | | He/She/It | needn't go |
| We/You/They | don't need to go | | We/You/They | |

### Questions

| Do | I | | | I | |
|---|---|---|---|---|---|
| Does | he/she/it | need to go? | Need | he/she/it | go? |
| Do | we/you/they | | | we/you/they | |

## ❯ Passive Voice

### Use

We use the **Passive Voice** to emphasize the action rather than who or what is responsible for it.

### Formation

The Passive Voice is formed with the verb **be** in the appropriate form and the **past participle** of the verb of the sentence.

### Present Simple Passive

#### Affirmative

| I | am | |
|---|---|---|
| He/She/It | is | called / given |
| We/You/They | are | |

#### Negative

| I | am not | |
|---|---|---|
| He/She/It | isn't | called / given |
| We/You/They | aren't | |

#### Questions

| Am | I | |
|---|---|---|
| Is | he/she/it | called/given? |
| Are | we/you/they | |

### Past Simple Passive

#### Affirmative

| I/He/She/It | was | called / given |
|---|---|---|
| We/You/They | were | |

#### Negative

| I/He/She/It | wasn't | called / given |
|---|---|---|
| We/You/They | weren't | |

#### Questions

| Was | I/he/she/it | called / given? |
|---|---|---|
| Were | we/you/they | |

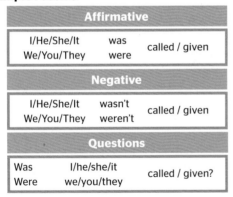

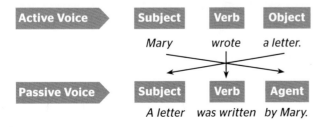

| Active Voice | Subject | Verb | Object |
|---|---|---|---|
| | *Mary* | *wrote* | *a letter.* |

| Passive Voice | Subject | Verb | Agent |
|---|---|---|---|
| | *A letter* | *was written* | *by Mary.* |

---

> The person who causes or carries out the action is called an **agent** and is preceded by the preposition **by**. We usually omit the agent:
> • when the action interests us more than the agent.
> • when we don't know the agent.
> • when it is easy to figure out who the agent is.
> *My bag was stolen! (by someone who we do not know)*
> *BMW cars are made in Germany. (by factory workers)*

# Module 9

## ❯ so / neither / too / either

### To express agreement

> • We use **so + affirmative auxiliary verb + subject** or **subject + affirmative auxiliary verb + too** when we agree with an affirmative statement, but we don't want to repeat it.
> *A: I play the guitar.*
> *B: So do I. / I do too.*
>
> *A: Sandra has seen this movie.*
> *B: So have I. / I have too.*
>
> • We use **neither + affirmative auxiliary verb + subject** or **subject + negative auxiliary verb + either** when we agree with a negative statement, but we don't want to repeat it.
> *A: Paul can't swim.*
> *B: Neither can I. / I can't either.*
>
> *A: Macy won't go to the meeting.*
> *B: Neither will I. / I won't either.*

> To express agreement we can also use *Me too* and *Me neither*.
> *A: I like pasta.*
> *B: Me too.*
> *A: I don't like yogurt.*
> *B: Me neither.*

### To express disagreement

> • We use **subject + affirmative auxiliary verb** when we disagree with a negative statement, but we don't want to repeat it.
> *A: I can't play tennis.*
> *B: I can.*
> • We use **subject + negative auxiliary verb** when we disagree with an affirmative statement, but we don't want to repeat it.
> *A: I've been to Peru twice.*
> *B: I haven't.*

## ❯ Reflexive Pronouns

| Personal Pronouns | | Reflexive Pronouns |
|---|---|---|
| **Subject** | **Object** | |
| I | me | myself |
| you | you | yourself |
| he | him | himself |
| she | her | herself |
| it | it | itself |
| we | us | ourselves |
| you | you | yourselves |
| they | them | themselves |

We use reflexive pronouns:

• as objects of verbs when the subject and the object of the verb are the same.
*I bought myself an expensive pair of shoes.*

• as objects of prepositions when the object of the preposition is the same as the subject of the verb.
*He never talks about himself.*

> We use **by + reflexive pronoun** to show that someone does something alone, without any help from anyone else.
> *I always pack my suitcases by myself.*

## Present Perfect Progressive

| Affirmative | |
|---|---|
| I | have been working |
| He/She/It | has been working |
| We/You/They | have been working |

| Negative | |
|---|---|
| I | haven't been working |
| He/She/It | hasn't been working |
| We/You/They | haven't been working |

| Questions | | |
|---|---|---|
| Have | I | |
| Has | he/she/it | been working? |
| Have | we/you/they | |

We use the **Present Perfect Progressive** for:

• a repeated action or situation which started in the past and continues up to the present.
*They have been using the Internet for more than two hours now.*

• an action which was happening over a period of time in the past and may have finished, but its results are obvious in the present.
*He's very tired. He's been studying all night.*

| TIME EXPRESSIONS |
|---|
| for, since, how long, all day/week, etc. |

## Present Perfect Simple vs. Present Perfect Progressive

| We use the Present Perfect Simple: | We use the Present Perfect Progressive: |
|---|---|
| • to emphasize the result of an action. *Lucy has typed eight letters since 10:30.* | • to emphasize the duration of an action. *Lucy has been typing letters since 10:30.* |

# Module 10

## too / enough

• We use **too** before adjectives and adverbs. *Too* has a negative meaning and it means "more than necessary."
*This coffee is too hot. I can't drink it.*

• We use **enough** after adjectives and adverbs. *Enough* has a positive meaning.
*The weather is warm enough for a picnic.*

• We use **too many** with plural countable nouns.
*We have too many eggs. What are we going to do with them?*

• We use **too much** with uncountable nouns.
*There's too much salt in this soup. I can't eat it.*

• We use **enough** before plural countable nouns and uncountable nouns.
*Are your friends hungry? There are enough sandwiches for everyone.*
*I can't buy those boots. I don't have enough money on me.*

> **Too** and **enough** can be followed by **to + base form of the verb**:
> *He's too young to travel by himself.*
> *He isn't old enough to go out alone.*

## Infinitives

We use the **full infinitive** (**to** + base form of the **verb**):

• to express purpose.
*I'm going to the supermarket to get some fruit.*

• after certain verbs: *want, would like, would love, hope, decide, manage, plan, arrange, advise, choose, learn, offer, promise, afford, agree, expect, seem, forget, teach, need, try, tell, refuse, remember,* etc.
*I haven't managed to find it yet.*

• after *it + be + adjective* (it's nice, it was stupid, etc.)
*It's difficult to explain.*

• after certain adjectives: *afraid, surprised, free, happy, ready, sorry, pleased,* etc.
*Are you afraid to ask him?*

• after *too* and *enough*
*You're too young to stay out late.*
*I'm strong enough to carry the box.*

• after question words (*who, how, what,* etc.) in indirect questions
*Do you know how to get there?*

We use the **bare infinitive** (base form of the verb **without to**):

• after modal verbs (*can, could, will, would, should, may, might, must*).
*Could you give me a glass of water?*
*You must visit the doctor today.*

• after the verbs *let* and *make* (in the active voice).
*She makes me study all the time.*

> We can use the verb **help** with a bare or full infinitive.
> *I always help my brother **do** his homework.*
> *I always help my brother **to do** his homework.*

## ❭ -ing form

We use the **-ing form**:

• after certain verbs: *like, love, hate, enjoy, prefer, suggest, start, finish, continue, keep, stop, begin, avoid, imagine, spend (time), etc.*
*I like listening to music, but I hate dancing.*

• after certain expressions: *don't mind, can't stand, be interested in, it's worth, How/What about...?, I look forward to, be good at, etc.*
*I look forward to seeing you.*

• after prepositions
*I'm so excited about going on this trip.*

• as a subject of a verb.
*Smoking is a bad habit.*

# Module 11
## ❭ Indirect questions

We use indirect questions when we ask for information. Indirect questions begin with phrases like:
*Can/Could you tell me...?*
*Do you know...?*
*I'd like to know...*

> **Direct Question**
> **Where** is the post office?
>
> **Indirect Question**
> Can you tell me **where** the post office is?

> **Direct Question**
> Is the museum open today?
>
> **Indirect Question**
> Do you know **if/whether** the museum is open today?

> • If the direct question begins with a question word, the indirect question also begins with **the same question word**.
> • If the direct question does not begin with a question word, the indirect question begins with **if/whether**.
> • In indirect questions, the word order is the same as in affirmative sentences and the tenses do not change.

## ❭ Conditional Sentences Type 2

We use Conditional Sentences Type 2 for unreal or imaginary situations which are unlikely to happen in the present or the future.

| If-clause | Main clause |
|---|---|
| if + Past Simple | would/could + base form |

*If I had enough money, I would buy a bigger apartment.*
*You could get that job if you took my advice.*

> • In Conditional Sentences Type 2 **were** is often used instead of **was** in the if-clause for all persons.
> *If Mary were older, she could take driving lessons.*
> • We use **if I were you** to express an opinion or give advice.
> *If I were you, I'd take it easy.*

## ❭ Wishes

We use:

• **wish + Past Simple:**
to make a **wish** about a **present situation** which we would like to be different.
*I wish I didn't have to take any more exams.*

• **wish + could + base form:**
to express **regret** about something we cannot do at **present**.
*I wish I could help you!*

> We usually use **were** for all persons in wishes.
> *I wish this course were easier.*

# Module 12
## ❭ Negative Questions

• Negative questions are formed with: **Auxiliary Verb + n't (= short form of *not*) + Subject + Main Verb**.

• We use negative questions to express emotions (e.g. surprise, anger, annoyance), to ask for confirmation, to express our opinion politely, when we expect the listener to agree with us.

• We reply to negative questions the same way we reply to regular questions.

*Haven't you been downtown before?*
*Don't you want to come with us?*
*Can't you do anything right?*

## ❭ Tag questions

**Tag questions** are short questions at the end of statements. We use them:

• when we are not sure about something and want to confirm it.

• when we want the other person to agree with us.

We form tag questions with the **auxiliary** or **modal verb** of the sentence and a **personal pronoun** in the same person as the subject.
*You couldn't see her, could you?*
*Tom believed him, didn't he?*

• When the statement is affirmative, we use a negative tag question.
*The boys are at school, aren't they?*

• When the statement is negative, we use a positive tag question.
*She hasn't seen the doctor yet, has she?*

> Be careful with the following tag questions:
> **I am** a very good actor, **aren't I?**
> **Let's** go to the movies, **shall we?**
> **Open** that door, **will you?**

## ▶ Reported Speech (Statements)

In **Direct Speech**, we repeat the exact words that someone said. We usually use the verb **say** and the words of the speaker are put in quotation marks.
*Irina said, "Tina is on the phone."*

In **Reported Speech**, we report the meaning of what someone said, without using their exact words. We use a reporting verb, usually **say** or **tell**, followed by **that** (which can be omitted) and the reported statement.
*Irina said that Tina was on the phone.*

> • We use **say** when there is no indirect object.
> *"I'll be there," he said.*
> **He said** that he would be there.*
>
> • We use **tell** when there is an indirect object.
> *"I'll call you, Mark," she said.*
> **She told Mark** she would call him.*

• When we change a sentence from Direct to Reported Speech, pronouns and possessive adjectives change according to the meaning of the sentence. Also, the verb **come** changes to **go**.

  *"**You** look great in **your** new dress," said David.*
  *David said that **I** looked great in **my** new dress.*

  *Kelly said, "I'll **come** to the mall with you."*
  *Kelly said she would **go** to the mall with me.*

• When the reporting verb (say or tell) is in the Past Tense, we usually make the following changes:

**Present Simple → Past Simple**
*Sue said, "I want to go bowling."*
*Sue said (that) she wanted to go bowling.*

**Present Progressive → Past Progressive**
*Beth said, "I'm reading a novel."*
*Beth said she was reading a novel.*

**Past Simple → Past Perfect Simple**
*Pete said, "Mom made some sandwiches."*
*Pete said his mom had made some sandwiches.*

**Present Perfect Simple → Past Perfect Simple**
*Jo said, "I've worked hard today."*
*Jo said she had worked hard that day.*

**will → would**
*Sean said, "I'll be there soon."*
*Sean said he would be there soon.*

**can → could**
*Jane said, "I can help you with your homework."*
*Jane said she could help me with my homework.*

**may → might**
*Frank said, "I may buy her a pair of shoes."*
*Frank said he might buy her a pair of shoes.*

**must → had to**
*Mom said, "You must be home early."*
*Mom said I had to be home early.*

**now → then**
*Tina said, "I'll call him now."*
*Tina said she would call him then.*

**here → there**
*Eric said, "I saw it here."*
*Eric said he had seen it there.*

**ago → before**
*Ben said, "I bought this house two years ago."*
*Ben said he had bought that house two years before.*

**today, tonight → that day, that night**
*Martha said, "We're having pizza for lunch today."*
*Martha said they were having pizza for lunch that day.*

**yesterday → the previous day / the day before**
*Dad said, "I visited the doctor yesterday."*
*Dad said he had visited the doctor the previous day.*

**this morning/year, etc. → that morning/year, etc.**
*Beth said, "I haven't bought anything this year."*
*Beth said she hadn't bought anything that year.*

**tomorrow → the next day / the following day**
*Lynn said, "I'm flying to Mexico tomorrow."*
*Lynn said she was flying to Mexico the following day.*

**last week/month, etc. → the previous week/month etc.**
                        **/ the week/month, etc. before**
*Colin said, "I met her last year."*
*Colin said he had met her the previous year.*

**next week / month, etc. → the following week/month, etc.**
*Bob said, "I'll finish the report next week."*
*Bob said he would finish the report the following week.*

> • The Past Perfect and the verbs *could, might, should, would* and *used to* do not change in Reported Speech.
>
> • The Past Progressive usually doesn't change in Reported Speech.

## ▶ Reported Speech (Questions)

• We usually introduce reported questions with the reporting verb **ask**.

• Reported questions follow the word order of affirmative sentences.
  *"Why did he come back?" he asked.*
  *He asked me why he had come back.*

• If the direct question begins with a question word, the reported question also begins with the same question word.
  *"**What** are you doing?" she asked.*
  *She asked me **what** I was doing.*

• If the direct question does not begin with a question word, the reported question begins with if/whether.
  *"Did you enjoy the concert?" he asked.*
  *He asked me **if/whether** I had enjoyed the concert.*

• When we change questions from Direct to Reported Speech, pronouns, tenses, adverbs, etc. change in the same way as when we report statements.

## ▶ Reported Speech (Commands - Requests)

• We commonly use **tell** when we report commands and **ask** when we report requests.

• The Imperative changes to **to + base form** or **not + to + base form**.
  *"Stay there," said the man.*
  *The man told me to stay there.*

  *"Don't take this away, please," she said.*
  *She asked me not to take that away.*

> When the request is in question form, in Reported Speech it usually changes to *to + base form*.
> *"Will you lend me that book, please?" Kate asked me.*
> *Kate asked me if/whether I would lend her that book.*
> *Kate asked me to lend her that book.*

| Base form | Past Simple | Past Participle | Base form | Past Simple | Past Participle |
|---|---|---|---|---|---|
| be | was/were | been | let | let | let |
| beat | beat | beaten | lie | lay | lain |
| become | became | become | light | lit | lit |
| begin | began | begun | lose | lost | lost |
| bite | bit | bitten | make | made | made |
| bleed | bled | bled | mean | meant | meant |
| blow | blew | blown | meet | met | met |
| break | broke | broken | mow | mowed | mowed/mown |
| bring | brought | brought | pay | paid | paid |
| build | built | built | put | put | put |
| burn | burned/burnt | burned/burnt | read | read | read |
| buy | bought | bought | ride | rode | ridden |
| catch | caught | caught | ring | rang | rung |
| choose | chose | chosen | rise | rose | risen |
| come | came | come | run | ran | run |
| cost | cost | cost | say | said | said |
| cut | cut | cut | see | saw | seen |
| deal | dealt | dealt | sell | sold | sold |
| do | did | done | send | sent | sent |
| draw | drew | drawn | set | set | set |
| drink | drank | drunk | shake | shook | shaken |
| drive | drove | driven | shine | shone | shone |
| eat | ate | eaten | shoot | shot | shot |
| fall | fell | fallen | show | showed | shown |
| feed | fed | fed | sing | sang | sung |
| feel | felt | felt | sit | sat | sat |
| fight | fought | fought | sleep | slept | slept |
| find | found | found | smell | smelled/smelt | smelled/smelt |
| fly | flew | flown | speak | spoke | spoken |
| forget | forgot | forgotten | spell | spelled/spelt | spelled/spelt |
| freeze | froze | frozen | spend | spent | spent |
| get | got | gotten/got | spill | spilled/spilt | spilled/spilt |
| give | gave | given | stand | stood | stood |
| go | went | gone | steal | stole | stolen |
| grow | grew | grown | sting | stung | stung |
| hang | hung | hung | swim | swam | swum |
| have | had | had | take | took | taken |
| hear | heard | heard | teach | taught | taught |
| hide | hid | hidden | tell | told | told |
| hit | hit | hit | think | thought | thought |
| hold | held | held | throw | threw | thrown |
| hurt | hurt | hurt | understand | understood | understood |
| keep | kept | kept | wake | woke | woken |
| know | knew | known | wear | wore | worn |
| lead | led | led | win | won | won |
| learn | learned/learnt | learned/learnt | withdraw | withdrew | withdrawn |
| leave | left | left | write | wrote | written |
| lend | lent | lent | | | |

## spelling

| American English | British English |
| --- | --- |
| airplane | aeroplane |
| apologize | apologise |
| behavior | behaviour |
| canceled | cancelled |
| center | centre |
| check | cheque |
| chili pepper | chilli pepper |
| civilization | civilisation |
| color | colour |
| cozy | cosy |
| favor | favour |
| favorite | favourite |
| gray | grey |
| humor | humour |
| jewelry | jewellery |
| lasagna | lasagne |
| license | licence |
| liter | litre |
| memorize | memorise |
| meter | metre |
| mustache | moustache |
| neighborhood | neighbourhood |
| omelet | omelette |
| organization | organisation |
| organize | organise |
| percent | per cent |
| practice (v) | practise |
| realize | realise |
| recognize | recognise |
| skillful | skilful |
| socialize | socialise |
| sympathize | sympathise |
| theater | theatre |
| tire | tyre |
| traveler | traveller |

## grammar and usage

| American English | British English |
| --- | --- |
| January 16th | 16th January |
| do well on | do well in |
| on the team | in the team |
| on the weekend | at the weekend |
| Turn right/left onto a street. | Turn right/left into a street. |
| It's ten after six. | It's ten past six. |
| learned | learnt, learned |
| spelled | spelt, spelled |

## words and phrases

| American English | British English |
| --- | --- |
| across from | opposite |
| aluminum | aluminium |
| anchorman | newsreader |
| apartment | flat |
| apartment building | block of flats |
| appetizers | starters |
| bill | note |
| blond (hair) | fair (hair) |
| candy | sweets |
| carry-on | hand luggage |
| cell | mobile |
| check | tick |
| coffee shop | café |
| cookie | biscuit |
| couch | sofa |
| crosswalk | zebra crossing |
| do/wash the dishes | do the washing-up |
| do the laundry | do the washing |
| doctor's office | doctor's surgery |
| downtown (area) | city centre |
| eggplant | aubergine |
| elementary school | primary school |
| elevator | lift |
| faucet | tap |
| flashlight | torch |
| (French) fries | chips |
| gas | petrol |
| give sb. a ride | give sb. a lift |
| go to the movies | go to the cinema |
| grade | mark |
| have a fever | have a temperature |
| high school | secondary school |
| highway | motorway |
| horseback riding | horse riding |
| last name | surname |
| license plate | number plate |
| line | queue |
| mad | angry |
| Math | Maths |
| mom | mum |
| motorcycle | motorbike |
| movie | film |
| movie theater | cinema |
| neat | tidy |
| newsstand | newsagent's |
| pants | trousers |
| parentheses | brackets |
| period | full stop |
| pharmacy, drugstore | chemist's |
| ping-pong | table tennis |
| potato chips | crisps |
| principal | head teacher |
| purse | handbag |
| refrigerator | fridge |
| register | till |
| résumé | CV |
| roommate | flatmate |
| RV (Recreational vehicle) | camper |
| salesperson | shop assistant |
| Science major | Science student |
| sick | ill |
| sidewalk | pavement |
| sneakers | trainers |
| soccer | football |
| stay in shape | stay fit |
| store | shop |
| stove, oven | cooker |
| subway | underground |
| sweater | jumper |
| talk show | chat show |
| the check | the bill |
| track and field | athletics |
| trash, garbage | rubbish |
| truck | lorry |
| trunk | boot |
| vacation | holiday |
| windshield | windscreen |
| yard | garden |
| zip code | post code |

**LEARNING TIPS**

## In class: How to learn better in class

- Look at the board and take notes.
- Listen carefully to your teacher and the CD.
- Ask your teacher when you don't understand.
- Speak in English as much as possible.
- Take part in pair and group work activities.

## Outside the class: How to learn better outside the class

- Read the dialogues and texts from your book and listen to them.
- Read the dialogues and texts aloud and sometimes record yourself.
- Study the vocabulary and grammar and then do your homework.
- Read selected texts from magazines and newspapers in English.
- Read websites in English.
- Listen to songs in English.
- Watch TV shows and DVDs in English.

## Vocabulary: How to learn vocabulary better

- Write down new words in a notebook. Together with the English word:
  - write the translation in your language
  - write an example sentence.
- Put words in groups or use diagrams.
- Learn whole phrases (e.g. verb+noun) not just isolated words.
- Learn new words in context (in sentences describing situations). This way, it is easier to remember them.
- When you learn new words, you must remember if they are verbs, nouns, adjectives, etc.
- When you learn new words, it's a good idea to learn any synonyms and/or opposites.
- Some words are very similar in meaning and can easily be confused. Try to remember the context where they are usually used.

- Pay attention to cognates and false friends. Cognates are English words which are similar in form and meaning to words in your language. False friends are English words which have a similar form to words in your language, but they have a different meaning.
- Refer to the Word List.
- Practice the spelling and pronunciation of new words.
- Look up unknown words in a dictionary. There, you can find a lot of useful information about a word: pronunciation, word class (noun, verb, etc.), meaning and example sentences.
- Regularly revise words you have learned.
- Try to use words you have recently learned when you speak or write.

## Grammar: How to learn grammar better

- Refer to the Grammar Reference.
- Use grammar tables.
- Have a grammar notebook. In it write:
  - tips and/or rules in your language
  - example sentences
  - important grammatical points  e.g. irregular verbs.
- Make a note of grammatical errors that you often make.

## Speak: How to do better when doing speaking tasks

- Before you speak, make sure you understand the task and how you should use the prompts.
- Look at the example and use the prompts given.
- Use the language you have learned.
- Speak only in English.
- Speak clearly.
- Don't worry if you make a mistake. Correct yourself if you can, otherwise continue speaking.
- If you can't remember a word, don't stop. Try to use other words.
- When talking to another person, listen carefully to what he/she is saying so that you can respond appropriately. Also, remember that a good way to maintain the conversation is by asking Wh-questions to find out about certain details. Avoid asking Yes/No questions.

- When expressing your opinion, always try to give reasons. Don't worry if you disagree with someone else. Remember, no answer is right or wrong as long as it is justified.
- Keep in mind that your tone of voice can help enhance what you are saying. You can show concern, surprise, admiration, enthusiasm, anger, disappointment, etc.
- When discussing with someone, listen carefully. If you haven't understood something, ask them to repeat or clarify what they are saying (*Could you please repeat that?, What do you mean?*).
- When you need more time to think about what to say, use phrases like: "Well, let's see now" or "Well, let me think".
- When talking in pairs or groups, help each other if one of you gets stuck, by asking a question, for instance.

## Read: How to do better when doing reading tasks

- Before you read, try to predict what the text is about with the help of the title and the pictures.
- Look for key words in the text to understand the main ideas.
- Try to understand which of the words in the text are really important. Try to guess the meaning of as many of these words as possible from the context. Use the following strategies:
  - Read the words before and after the unknown word and think of the context.
  - Try to figure out what part of speech the unknown word is.
  - See if the unknown word is similar to other words in English or in your language.
- Read the text quickly to understand the main idea.
- Read the text carefully to understand specific details.
- Read the whole text before you do an exercise. Sometimes the answers require overall understanding.
- Decide in which part of the text you can find the information you need.
- Make sure you understand who or what the pronouns (he, it, this, them, etc.) and the adverbs (here, there, etc.) refer to in the text.
- Don't rely on your general knowledge to answer questions. Check your answers with the information given in the text.
- When answering multiple choice questions, read each question carefully to get an idea of what you are looking for and underline the section in the text where the answer is found. Also, make sure you have chosen the correct answer by eliminating the wrong options.

## Listen: How to do better when doing listening tasks

- Before you listen, read the rubric carefully and look at the pictures. Try to predict what the speakers are going to talk about.
- Before you listen, read the statements or questions carefully. This will give you an idea of what to listen for.
- While listening for gist, try to understand the general idea, not every single word.
- Listen for key words to understand the main ideas.
- While listening, don't assume that an answer is correct just because the speakers mention a word that is in the activity. Listen carefully before you answer.
- When completing sentences, make sure that your answers make sense with the rest of the sentence.
- Don't be in a hurry to answer a multiple choice question. Listen carefully till the end and check all the options before your final decision.
- Pay attention to the speakers' tone of voice to understand how they are feeling.

## Write: How to do better when doing writing tasks

- Make sure you write what the rubric asks you to. Don't include irrelevant information.
- Before you start writing, think about the topic carefully and try to come up with ideas which are relevant to it. Make notes of the information you want to include. You can also make a mind map to come up with ideas as well as organize them.
- Plan your paragraphs. Before you start, think of the ideas you are going to include in each paragraph.
- Group relevant information together and put it in the same paragraph.
- Use linking words/phrases (and, but, so, because, also, What's more, etc.) to join your ideas and make your writing flow.
- Use time linkers (first, then, after that, when, while, as soon as, etc.) to show the order in which events happen.
- Use a variety of adjectives (e.g. fantastic, wonderful, terrible, awful) and adverbs/adverbial phrases (e.g. luckily, all of a sudden) in your writing to make it more interesting for the reader.
- Use words like he, she, it, them, there, etc. to avoid repeating the same words.
- When you are asked to write a letter or an e-mail, try to understand why you are writing (to give news, to invite, etc.). Also, think carefully about your relationship with the person you are writing to (is he/she a friend, a stranger, etc.?) and write in an appropriate style (formal or informal). Remember to use set phrases in the opening and closing paragraph.
- Write neatly.
- Write your first draft and correct it. Then write your final draft.
- Edit your writing. Check punctuation, capital letters, word order, spelling, grammar, vocabulary and linking words.

# Module 1

## 1b

**1.**

**A:** Hey, Jack. When did you get back from Florida?

**B:** Last week. It's beautiful at this time of year.

**A:** Did you fly down there?

**B:** I drove there.

**A:** Really? Is that because you want to help the environment?

**B:** Well, that too. But about a year ago, I was on a plane and there was a big storm. It was a terrible flight and I was really scared. I haven't been on a plane since.

**A:** I see.

**2.**

**A:** Morning, Linda. That's a nice bike. Is it new?

**B:** Yes, I got it last week.

**A:** I wanted to get one last year, but they were really expensive. I think the cheapest was $500.

**B:** That's pretty cheap. I think the cheapest I found cost $600. This one cost $900. It's a really good one, though.

**A:** Yes, I can see that. But still, it's just a bike.

**B:** I remember my first bike cost me $100.

**A:** Those were the days.

**3.**

**A:** So, do you have everything for the trip?

**B:** Yes.

**A:** So, you're not taking your tablet?

**B:** Well, I want to but I have no space. I guess I'll have to manage with my cell phone only.

**A:** What about that GPS device we got you last year? Do you use it?

**B:** Well, I use my cell phone for that, so I don't really need it.

**A:** Well, that was a waste of money, then.

**B:** Yeah, I suppose.

**4.**

**A:** This transportation museum is really interesting.

**B:** I told you.

**A:** Are those traffic lights?

**B:** Yes, they're from Salt Lake City and they're 100 years old.

**A:** Wow! Did they have colored lights like today?

**B:** Yes, look. But they only had red for "stop" and green for "go."

**A:** They haven't changed much in a century.

**B:** That's true.

## 1d

**A:** Hey, Roger. What's up?

**B:** I need some help with something, actually.

**A:** What's that?

**B:** Well, I'm staying with my friends Dan and Tina at their cabin up in the mountains this summer, and I'd like to get them a little something.

**A:** Of course. You can't go empty-handed. Hey, isn't Dan crazy about basketball? Get him a basketball shirt.

**B:** Hmmm, I don't know. He has so many, already. I had an idea for a watch for him. You know, because he...

**A:** Because he's late all the time! I know. You always tell me that. By the way, that's a perfect gift for him. So, what about Tina? What does she like?

**B:** Well, she listens to music a lot. I guess I can get her some headphones or some CDs.

**A:** Do you know what she's into at the moment?

**B:** No, I don't. That's a problem. Umm... She also enjoys cooking.

**A:** There's a great cookbook with Mexican recipes at the bookstore. I saw it yesterday and I'm thinking of buying it for myself.

**B:** So, it's either headphones or the cookbook. I like your idea more. Now, what about the kids?

**A:** Do they have children?

**B:** Yeah, two teenagers. Maya and Ollie. Ollie is a big basketball fan, too.

**A:** Why don't you get him a couple of basketball tickets?

**B:** Great idea. And he can go to the game with his father, too.

**A:** Or he can go with a friend.

**B:** Yeah, maybe you're right. That just leaves Maya. And I think I know what she'd like.

**A:** Something to do with fashion, maybe? A nice scarf or perhaps a watch?

**B:** Maya isn't interested in fashion. She's crazy about thrillers.

**A:** Really? I can't stand them.

**B:** I know. I don't understand why people like them. Anyway, I'll ask at the store about a movie that's popular at the moment. Thanks for your help, Vicky.

# Module 2

## 2b

**A:** Excuse me. Do I know you from somewhere?

**B:** I don't think so.

**A:** You look pretty familiar. Are you sure?

**B:** Pretty sure.

**A:** I'm Pamela. What's your name?

**B:** James.

**A:** James, James... Umm, are you from around here?

**B:** Well, I grew up here but I haven't lived here since 2005. I'm just visiting.

**A:** I was born in Waterville and I've lived here all my life. So, you went to school here?

**B:** Yes, I went to Chamberly High School. And you?

**A:** No, I don't think I know you from school. I went to Langford High. No, I think I remember you from somewhere else.

Let me see, did you work at a gas station?

**B:** Yes, I did.

**A:** I knew it! The gas station on 8th Avenue, right? I haven't been there for ages but I used to go there every other day.

**B:** No, the gas station was on Bentley Street. And I was there only for a few months.

**A:** No, that can't be it, then. I can't believe this. I'm sure I know you from somewhere.

**B:** Maybe you know my brother, Ken? He lives here.

**A:** Ken? Kenny! That's it! I took a Spanish class with Kenny two years ago.

**B:** I don't think so. Ken was never into languages. I took both a Spanish and a French class, but that was in London, not here.

**A:** Oh. Well, this is really embarrassing.

**B:** Sorry, I couldn't help much.

**A:** That's OK. It was nice talking to you.

## 2c

**Lucy**

I used to use instant messaging a lot when I was at college. It was really useful for keeping in touch with people. And it was really easy, too, because I used to spend a lot of time on my laptop. I don't think it was better than communicating face-to-face, though. Now, I use my smartphone more, and I send e-mail, or text people or just call them. For me, these are more convenient ways to communicate with people.

**Jerry**

I don't mind calling people, but I prefer instant messaging. I'm not sure why. I think it's because you can take your time to reply to someone. Also, you can send funny videos, or links to websites at the same time. You have to be careful, though. I sometimes spend all day chatting away and then don't have enough time to finish assignments. Next year is my last year at college, so I'm going to start using instant messaging less.

**Heather**

Well, a few years ago, I didn't use instant messaging at all. I spent all my time chatting on the phone with friends. As you can imagine, my phone bills were huge, so I tried to cut down a little. I also tried to meet up with people face-to-face more, but it was hard work. I just didn't have the time to go out so much. Then a group of friends found a great social media website and that was it. Now, all my friends are on there and we chat, make plans, help each other out with assignments, and all through instant messaging. It changed my life completely, and now I don't need to call my friends anymore.

## 2d

**A:** Here you go, Jason.

**B:** What's that?

**A:** Remember when you told me that you were worried about finding the right roommate at college? Well, it wasn't easy for me last year, either. But the college gave me this questionnaire, and it really helped.

**B:** Oh, thanks.

**A:** Come on, let's complete it together. The first section has just basic things. For example, do you want to live with a male or a female?

**B:** OK. Well, I think I'd prefer to live with another boy.

**A:** And not a smoker, I expect.

**B:** No way, and I don't want someone older or younger than me.

**A:** So, the same age.

**B:** Yeah, maybe someone who is in his first year, too.

**A:** OK. Do you mind pets?

**B:** No way! I don't want a cat or a hamster or anything creeping around the place.

**A:** OK, OK, calm down. No pets. Now let's look at the next section. This is important.

**B:** "What do you definitely want your new roommate to be like?" Umm...

**A:** Trustworthy? Cheerful? Neat?

**B:** I definitely want the first two, but I don't care about "neat."

**A:** OK, then. What else?

**B:** Let's see. I'd like him to be easygoing so that we can get along well. That's it. I don't care about the rest.

**A:** OK, next part. What don't you want him to be like? You said you don't mind him being messy, right?

**B:** Right. There are more important things. For example, I don't want to live with a bossy or noisy person, that's for sure.

**A:** OK, so I'm checking the boxes "bossy" and "noisy." Anything else? How about "moody"?

**B:** Being moody can create problems, so check that box, too. That's it. Let's read the next section.

**A:** "Which of the following do you consider important?"

**B:** OK, well sleeping and study habits aren't really important to me.

**A:** Do you care about housework?

**B:** Umm... Not really, no. But we have to share all the bills.

**A:** You're right about that. Also, something else that is very important is respecting each other's privacy.

**B:** True, very true. Put a check in the box.

**A:** What about having similar interests?

**B:** Yes, that sounds like a good thing. I mean if you have similar interests, you're alike and maybe can even hang out together. Hey, sis, we're getting a good idea of the sort of person I want for a ...

# Module 3

## Activity A

**A:** OK, do you remember the rules of this game? I describe the words on the card without saying the actual words. You have to guess the words. OK?

**B+C:** OK.

**A:** Here comes the first word... Umm, it's a person who works

for a newspaper, or maybe a magazine. But it's not an editor or a photographer. It's a person who collects information and writes things, but not an author. He writes articles.

**C:** I know. Is it a...?

**A:** Don't say it! Just write it down on the card.

**C:** Oh, OK. Sorry!

**A:** Here's the next word. It's a machine... and you usually have it in the car.

**C:** Do I have one?

**A:** I can't answer questions, Colin. It's kind of like a map, but it's a thing that talks to you and tells you directions. It helps you find the place where you want to go.

**B:** Oh! I know. It's easy.

**A:** OK, but don't tell Colin. Ready for the next one? Here goes. It's something you get when you go shopping.

**C:** Credit card! Sorry!

**A:** It's a piece of paper that has numbers and prices on it. And you get it at the register when you buy something.

**C:** Huh? That doesn't sound like a credit card.

**B:** Shhh!

**A:** Here's the last word. It's a nice place, and people enjoy going there.

**C:** That could be anywhere.

**A:** You can stay there when you go on vacation.

**C:** What kind of vacation, though? Camping? Skiing?

**B:** Will you be quiet?

**A:** It's a building that usually has a swimming pool and a restaurant.

**B:** Ahhhh! I know.

## Activity B

**A:** OK, let me tell you the answers. First word: A reporter is a person who collects and reports news for a newspaper, magazine, the radio or television.

**B:** I got that.

**C:** Me too.

**A:** Number two: A GPS device is a device that gives you directions when you're driving a car.

**B:** That one was easy. Did you get it, Colin?

**C:** I wrote GPS.

**A:** That's OK. The third word: A receipt is a piece of paper that shows that you have paid for something.

**B:** Yes! Correct again!

**C:** Oh, I didn't get that. I got confused.

**A:** And lastly: A hotel is a place where you stay when you're on vacation.

**C:** I got that one.

**B:** Me too.

**1.**

**A:** Oh, this is awesome, isn't it?

**B:** Yes, what's it called?

**A:** It's just called "Horse running" by Cynthia Gray.

**B:** It's just so realistic. I want to touch it.

**A:** Don't! You're not allowed to and we'll get in trouble.

**B:** Don't worry. I'm not a kid. You know, my uncle had a small sculpture of a horse just like that.

**A:** Maybe the artist knew your uncle and used the sculpture to paint this.

**B:** Do you think so?

**A:** No, I was only joking.

**2.**

**A:** Hey, do you want to see John Harwood's latest installation tomorrow?

**B:** OK, why not? I really enjoyed his last one. Do we need to buy tickets?

**A:** No. This time it's outdoors, close to Fable Park.

**B:** What's it about?

**A:** Something to do with the environment, I think.

**B:** OK. Do you want to meet at the park?

**A:** Sure. The installation is on a small street not far from there.

**B:** OK, see you tomorrow.

**3.**

**A:** I'm bored.

**B:** You always say that. You should join an art class or something. My mother goes to a pottery class once a week. She loves it.

**A:** I don't think that's for me. Anyway, I went to a photography class with Gloria a few times, remember?

**B:** Oh yeah. Why did you stop?

**A:** It was boring. We just took pictures of trees for a couple of hours. I'd like to do something a little more useful.

**B:** What, like jewelry making?

**A:** Yeah, that sounds interesting. I could make jewelry and sell it to my friends.

**B:** There you go.

**3d**

**A:** Hi, April.

**B:** Hi, how's it going?

**A:** Fine.

**B:** Did I tell you about my new apartment?

**A:** No, you didn't.

**B:** Well, I moved last week. I live on Corby Avenue now. You know, across from the park.

**A:** Really? What a surprise! Why did you move?

**B:** Well, my old apartment was tiny. My new one is much bigger.

**A:** Yeah, I remember your old apartment. It was pretty small.

**B:** My new apartment is much nicer. There are two bedrooms, a large kitchen and a living room.

**A:** Pretty big. Is there a balcony?

**B:** Yes. There's a balcony with a great view of the park.

**A:** How fantastic! But it sounds like a big place for one person.

**B:** Well, I'm not alone anymore.

**A:** Oh, who do you live with?

**B:** My sister.

**A:** Get out of here!

**B:** Yeah, she moved to the city, too. She found a job here and she needed a place to stay.

**A:** Well, it makes sense for you two to live together, then. I'm really happy for you.

**B:** Thanks.

# Module 4

## 4c

**1.**
Good morning. News is coming in of a huge storm that hit the east coast last night. Experts believe it was a category three hurricane and one of the worst in the last ten years. The strong winds have damaged or completely destroyed several houses as well as important buildings. More than 200 people are without a place to sleep tonight. The Super Stadium is open for people affected by the disaster and volunteers are there to help anyone in need.

**2.**
Good afternoon. Today has been another day of bad weather all over the country. Yesterday authorities closed many of the main roads coming in and out of the city. Many schools didn't open for the third day running. Residents have decided not to stay at home, though, and the streets are full of people enjoying the extreme weather. Experts expect more snow before the week is over, but better conditions and higher temperatures on the weekend.

**3.**
Good afternoon. Here is the main news. Rescue workers are making slow progress at the shoe factory in Northfield, where a fire broke out last night, destroying half of the building. Most of the workers escaped without injuries but part of the building collapsed and some workers didn't make it out. The rescue team is in contact with the workers, two are injured, but the other 18 are healthy and in good spirits. Let's go over to Janice Simpson at the scene...

**4.**
Good evening. Here is the news at 8 o'clock. Strong winds hit the southwest of the country today, causing serious damage in the area. The continuing heavy rain has flooded many areas. Students at Kingsley High School were in danger this afternoon as water levels from the nearby Edison River became dangerously high. Luckily, rescue teams got all the students out and nobody was hurt. In other parts of the country, the storms continue....

## 4d

**A:** Hey, Noreen! You're back! So, how was your vacation in Iceland?

**B:** Awesome. The place was beautiful, but you won't believe what happened on the second day.

**A:** What? Tell me.

**B:** It was pretty unbelievable. I decided to take a bus tour to a volcanic area in the south of the country. We left early in the morning and, after some time, the bus stopped so that all the passengers could take some pictures and relax a little. I was feeling very tired after the long journey and so I decided to go to the bathroom to freshen up. I washed my face, put up my hair and changed my T-shirt and went back to the bus. To my surprise, when I arrived back, everybody, including the driver, was searching for a missing passenger.

**A:** So what did you do?

**B:** Well of course I wanted to help in the search, so I joined one of the search parties. We walked around the nearby area trying to find the missing person.

**A:** Did you?

**B:** No, after about an hour of searching and no luck, we went back to the bus. The driver called the police and soon after, they arrived with a rescue team. They even had a helicopter!

**A:** Wow! And? What happened?

**B:** Well, I was standing close to the driver of the bus. He was giving a description of the missing passenger to the police and rescue team and I suddenly thought "Wait a minute... that kind of sounds like me!"

**A:** Oh, no... You're kidding, right?

**B:** Unfortunately, I'm not! I was shocked! I ran over to the driver and told him that maybe I was the person they were looking for. He looked very surprised and called all the passengers back onto the bus. When he counted us again and called out names, he realized that we were all there. All that time I was looking for someone who was, in fact, me! Embarrassing!

**A:** But hold on a minute. Didn't any of the passengers recognize you when you first got back to the bus?

**B:** No, I think because I changed my T-shirt, I looked different.

**A:** What about your name? Didn't they say your name throughout the search?

**B:** Well, the group I joined didn't remember the name of the missing person, and I didn't ask anyone else. Anyway, in the end we all laughed about it.

**A:** Hmmmm. I bet the police didn't find it very funny...

# Module 5

## 5b

**1.**
This is a final boarding call for passengers on flight R217 to Calgary. Would passengers on this flight please proceed to Gate 14.

**2.**
Your attention, please. Check in for flight 2110 to Paris is closing. Passengers who have not checked in for this flight please proceed to the check-in desk.

**3.**
Ladies and gentlemen, the captain has turned on the Fasten Seat Belt sign. If you haven't already done so, please put your carry-on luggage underneath the seat in front of you or in an overhead compartment. Please take your seat and fasten your seat belt. Also make sure your seat back and folding trays are in their full upright position. Please ask the cabin crew if you need any help. Thank you.

**4.**
This is your captain speaking. I'm sorry to say that we can't land at our destination because there is a heavy snowstorm. We are currently searching for an airport to land at. Again, I'm very sorry for the inconvenience.

**5.**
This is your captain again. Let me be the first to welcome you to Frankfurt. The local time is 9:45 a.m. and the temperature is a cool 59 degrees. I hope you enjoyed your flight and if you are connecting to another flight, please pay attention to the TV monitors in the terminal building for your gate number.

## 5c

**A:** Welcome back. Summer is almost here, and that means it's time for a vacation. But before you go, there's that eternal problem you need to deal with. What to take? What not to take? How much to take? It can be pretty stressful, but don't worry. Carrie is here to give you a few tips.

**B:** Hi, Steve.

**A:** So, what's the first thing to think about?

**B:** Well, let's start with things you shouldn't pack. Airlines lose about 40 million suitcases every year, so you'd better not put valuable things, like expensive jewelry, into luggage you are going to check in.

**A:** Yes, I try to avoid doing that. Anything else we shouldn't take with us?

**B:** Well, most countries don't let you enter with fruit and vegetables, and in fact most uncooked food. But some countries have strange rules about what you can't enter with. For example, in Singapore you're not allowed to bring chewing gum into the country.

**A:** Really? Why's that?

**B:** Well, they're trying to stop people from sticking gum in public places. They like to stay clean in Singapore. But my point is, do some research about the country you're visiting before you leave.

**A:** OK. Now, let's get more practical. Whenever I travel, my main problem is trying to pack light.

**B:** You're not alone, and it's not always an easy thing to do. A good idea is to call the hotel, or friend you're staying with before you leave and ask if they have a hairdryer, towels... Anything that you can leave behind is going to help you travel light.

**A:** That's good advice. I always want to know whether the hotel has an iron or not.

**B:** Also, you'd better have a good idea

of what the weather is like at your destination. That way you can avoid taking clothing you don't need at all. You should try to avoid "just-in-case" clothes, which you're never going to wear. Also, try to wear your heaviest shoes and coat while you're traveling so that you don't need to pack them in your suitcase.

**A:** More good advice. Thanks, Carrie. Now let's talk about...

## 5d

Northern Africa Travel. If you would like information about our day trips to Morocco, press one. For our cruises to Tunisia, press two. For other destinations, press three.

(Beep)

We organize day trips to Tangier, Morocco every week. The trip starts with a drive from the Costa del Sol to the town of Tarifa, at the southern tip of Spain. From there, you travel by high-speed ferry across the Strait of Gibraltar to Morocco. The journey continues on a bus to the beautiful city of Tangier. Our walking tour begins at the main gate entrance into the Medina, the old city. One of the main attractions is the Kasbah. You can also visit a 17th-century palace which today is a museum. There are also souks, or markets, where you can get some souvenirs to take home. Then, we stop for lunch at a traditional Moroccan restaurant where you can taste some delicious dishes and some traditional mint tea. The trip continues with a visit to the impressive Cave of Hercules, about 9 miles outside the city, and to the white sand dunes. Here you have time to explore, take pictures and the more adventurous can even ride a camel. We finally say our goodbyes over dinner and begin our trip home.

Prices start at 60 euros for adults and 40 euros for children and students. For families or groups of five or more, the price is 50 euros for adults and 30 for children and students. To book tickets, please wait on the line for the next available agent...

# Module 6

## 6a

**A:** Hi, Dom. What are you reading?

**B:** It's a quiz with interesting questions about your carbon footprint.

**A:** That's all you hear about nowadays. Everybody knows about it.

**B:** Are you sure? This quiz gives you a better understanding of the problem and I'm sure there are things you have never thought of. Do you want to give it a try?

**A:** Sure. I will get them all right.

**B:** Look at question number 1. A flight from London to Hong Kong is the same as using how many plastic bags?

**A:** Umm... I'd say 300,000.

**B:** Lucky guess. You're right. But isn't it amazing?

**A:** Well, I know traveling by plane is pretty much the worst thing you can do.

**B:** OK, let's continue. Which packaging

helps you reduce your carbon footprint?

**A:** Well, no packaging is the best. But I suppose the answer is "paper".

**B:** That's what I put. But it's actually plastic.

**A:** No way!

**B:** Yeah, producing paper and cardboard creates about ten times more carbon dioxide than plastic bags.

**A:** Really? I use reusable bags, so I'm OK.

**B:** What about the third question? Which of these increases your carbon footprint more?

**A:** Well, I think buying locally produced food is good for the environment. So, I'll say "buying nine pounds of imported bananas".

**B:** Wrong again. Bananas aren't too bad, because they travel by ship, and they have their own packaging. But out-of-season flowers come from hot countries and they travel by plane to stay fresh. So they increase your carbon footprint more.

**A:** I told you about planes. What's the next question? I'll get this one right.

**B:** What produces 2 pounds of carbon dioxide?

**A:** Umm... I don't think it's the plane. The plane produces a lot more. Using a computer for 32 hours? No, I don't think so. But it's definitely not both.

**B:** Come on.

**A:** I don't know. I'll choose "a", the plane.

**B:** Sorry, it's "c". Both "a" and "b".

**A:** Oh, that's not fair. So, using a computer produces so much carbon dioxide?

**B:** Well, yes. It has to get energy from somewhere.

**A:** You're right. This quiz makes you think.

## 6c

**A:** Good afternoon. It's been over 40 years since Neil Armstrong walked on the moon. Since then, people have wanted to know, where next? Well, Mars is top of the list, and here to talk about Martian exploration is Robert Brody, from the University of West Virginia. Welcome, Professor Brody.

**B:** Hello there.

**A:** So, when did it all begin?

**B:** Well, actually, it all started hundreds of years ago with the invention of the telescope. Since then, we have been able to see what Mars is like, and have a better idea of what we might find there.

**A:** When was the first spacecraft sent to Mars?

**B:** Well, space scientists tried to send a few unmanned spacecraft in the early 1970s, but without success. The probe *Viking 1 Lander* landed first, in 1976. It was a successful mission and it sent back information about Mars, including the first photographs from the planet.

**A:** Did it return home?

**B:** No, it's still there. But it sent information to Earth for 2,245 sols.

**A:** Sols?

**B:** I'm sorry, a sol is what we call a day on Mars. It's a little longer than an Earth day. And there are 668 sols, or Martian days if you like, in a Martian year. That's

twice as long as an Earth year.

**A:** I see. Interesting information. So, tell us professor, what is happening at present?

**B:** Well, as we speak, there is a probe on Mars. Scientists at NASA are able to move it around and gather rocks and soil, and analyze them. Basically, they are looking to see if there was any life on Mars in the past.

**A:** Is there any life there now?

**B:** I very much doubt it. Mars is a dry, cold place with very little atmosphere, not the sort of place where life usually exists. But we could change all that with terraforming.

**A:** What's that?

**B:** Terraforming is taking a planet, like Mars, and changing the atmosphere, the temperature and so on, so that it will be possible to live there.

**A:** Is that really possible? I mean, can scientists change a planet's atmosphere?

**B:** We're doing it already, with global warming. Ha, ha. In theory, it could be possible, and many scientists are working on solutions to create an atmosphere on Mars similar to the atmosphere on Earth. But it is an enormous task that would take a long time.

**A:** Still, it gives you something to think about...

## 6d

**Beth**

Young people find it really hard to imagine the world without the Internet, but the way I see it, things were better in the past. When people needed information or an answer to a question, they searched in books or asked around. But most importantly, they tried to think and work out the answer themselves. Nowadays, they immediately go online, even for very simple questions. People have stopped thinking and that is a problem. They depend on the Internet too much.

**Jack**

I can't imagine life without the Internet. I surf the Net or chat every day. I have lots of cyberfriends and it takes time to stay in touch with them. My favorite pastime is playing online video games and I can do that for hours. Then I always watch a movie online, or read the newspapers. I can spend all day in front of the screen, and sometimes I do, which is a problem. I order a lot of junk food because I never have time to cook and, as for exercise, when can I find time for that? To be honest, I think I should start being careful, maybe change my lifestyle a little.

**Julie**

The Internet? Well, it's very useful. You can send e-mail and stay in touch with people all around the world and find information about the strangest topics. And of course, the funny videos you come across are unbelievable! However, there is one thing that worries me: giving out my personal details. For example, I don't feel safe buying things online and giving my credit card number. And as for social media sites, well, my friends want me to join, but I'm not so sure. I mean, anyone can find out all about you, right? And you're helpless. That's a little scary.

**Frank**

I'm not one of those people who use the Internet all day, at work, at home, etc., but I believe it's made our lives easier. For example, it has changed the way we shop and watch movies. I mean, it's very helpful. I remember those Saturdays I used to spend walking around different stores, looking for gifts for people. Now, with a few clicks, I can find whatever I want, and they have great offers. Also, I never have to get in the car and drive to the DVD store again. There are plenty of sites where you can watch movies online, or download them. And they're really cheap, too.

# Module 7

## 7a

**A:** So, Eddie, what are you doing this weekend?

**B:** I might go to the game with the guys on Saturday. Come on United! Do you want to come? Should I count you in?

**A:** I don't know. Have you seen the price of the tickets?

**B:** Yeah, they're $15, I think.

**A:** I'm pretty sure they're $45. Let me check the newspaper. It was in the "Things to do this weekend" section. There you go.

**B:** You're right, Mark. Well, I'm definitely not paying that much.

**A:** Anyway, they said it might rain on Saturday. And United is likely to lose, don't you think?

**B:** You're right. OK, what else can we do?

**A:** There's a bowling tournament. You used to be good at bowling, Eddie.

**B:** Yeah, that was a long time ago, though. How much does it cost to get in?

**A:** It's free.

**B:** Yeah? That's all right, then. We could go for the fun of it.

**A:** True. Look, there's a silent movie festival, too.

**B:** Does your sister know about it?

**A:** Probably. She's crazy about movies, especially old black-and-white ones.

**B:** Maybe we could go with her. It might be interesting.

**A:** I'm not so sure.

**B:** Oh, make up your mind, Mark.

**A:** I'm trying. Hey, what about this photography exhibition?

**B:** Who's Glenn Hunt?

**A:** He's a famous photographer. He published a book last year with some amazing photos.

**B:** Oh, yeah. I remember him.

**A:** So, do you want to go?

**B:** Nah, I don't really feel like going to an exhibition. I'd rather do something else.

**A:** OK, what then? It's up to you. Do you want me to give my sister a call?

**B:** Yeah, we can go to an afternoon showing, and then go out for dinner.

**A:** Sounds great. However, my sister will probably want to see all three showings.

**B:** Yeah, you're probably right.

## 7b

**1.**

**A:** So, what do you say?

**B:** It looks kind of scary, but OK.

**A:** What about your little brother?

**B:** I think he's too short, look.

**A:** Yeah, you're right.

**2.**

**A:** Oh, I can't believe this.

**B:** Stop complaining.

**A:** We need to speak to the manager right away.

**B:** There, look. Press that and someone will come and help us.

**3.**

**A:** No, I don't think it's expensive.

**B:** Yes, it is. You get a good deal online, but then they charge you so much just to bring it to you early. No, I prefer to wait.

## 7d

**Activity B**

**1.**

Hey! It's Hillary here. I tried your cell but you weren't answering. Are you free on Saturday? I'm having a barbecue and I'd love for you to come. I've asked everyone to be here at seven, but I want you to come an hour earlier to help out a little. Is that OK? Also, do you still have that big umbrella for the yard? I don't think it's going to rain, but if it does, we can cook under that, right? Anyway, let me know.

**2.**

It's Ken here. Why aren't you picking up? Anyway, there's been a change of plans. We're not going to have the DVD night on Sunday. We're having it on Saturday instead. But we're still meeting up at Ted's house, OK? The only thing I need you to do is to give Mark a call. I thought I had his number, but I can't find it now. Let him know about the change, OK?

**Activity C**

Hi there. It's Julia here. Everything is OK for Saturday night. The only thing is that I couldn't find a table at the Italian restaurant we usually go to so I made a reservation at a new place a colleague of mine told me about. It's called *The Pasta House*. The address is 239 Bell Street. I hope you don't mind. All the others are coming and we're going to meet there at eight o'clock. See you there. Bye!

# Module 8

## 8a

**Danny**

I've been to so many hockey games but

I think this is the first time I've seen such an exciting game. The Blackhawks weren't playing so well in the first two periods and I was sure they'd lose. What a team! How did they do it? They managed to turn the game around in the third period and win. It was awesome! Benson was awesome! And the fans went wild, of course. I can't describe the atmosphere at the end of the game.

**Robert**

What a game! It wasn't easy, that's for sure, but we're happy we won. I think the fans always make a difference. The atmosphere was beautiful. They were cheering us on even when we were behind. They managed to encourage us to try harder. And we did in the third period. What else can I say? I'm so excited we'll be playing in the finals!

**Craig**

Is this all you can do? What a disappointment you are to all those fans who are cheering you on! Have you seen the score? It's embarrassing! I want to see some goals and I want to see them now. I want all of you to try harder this third period. Are you listening, Benson? You are so slow today that everyone is going to fall asleep. Get that puck and score! Do I have a team or what? Come on, people. Let's make it to the finals. Get your sticks and get out there on the ice. Move it!

**Steve**

... Five more minutes to go till the end and the score is 5-5. The Blackhawks are catching up. It seems they definitely want to make it to the finals, especially Benson who is playing incredibly well in this last period. And as I said earlier, when he decides to play, the whole team plays. And Benson has the puck now. He's heading for the goal. Will he score and put the Blackhawks in the lead? ... and... goal! It's 5-6 to the Blackhawks. What a player! What a goal! Listen to those fans! Three more minutes to go. How exciting! There's Palmer with the puck now and...

## 8d

**1.**

**A:** So, what did you think?

**B:** I'm not sure. With a name like *Total Force*, I was expecting an action thriller with lots of violence.

**A:** Me too, and it certainly wasn't like that. It's a strange name for a historical drama.

**B:** And what about that ending?

**A:** Yes, I wasn't expecting that. It was excellent.

**2.**

**A:** Have you seen *Run to the Hills*?

**B:** Is that the romantic comedy set in Scotland?

**A:** Yes, it is.

**B:** No, I haven't.

**A:** Well, don't. I think it's one of Amy Scott's worst movies.

**B:** Was she starring in it?

**A:** No, she directed it. The leading actors were Cara Ingles and Thomas Balding.

**B:** Oh, I like him.

**A:** Yeah? Well, he was terrible in this movie.

He only got the part because he's married to one of the producers.

**B:** Is he? I didn't know that.

**3.**

**A:** Can we stop it? I want to get something to drink.

**B:** Sure. What do you think of it so far?

**A:** I think it's very interesting. I know it's an old movie, but for its time, the special effects are great.

**B:** That's true. I saw a documentary about it, and they were saying it took ages to make each scene.

**A:** And it's amazing how they imagined sending robots to Mars back then, which is exactly what we are doing now. Hey, do you want anything?

**B:** No, I'm good.

**4.**

**A:** I saw *Hornbury House* on DVD the other day.

**B:** Really? I saw that movie last year. What did you think?

**A:** Well, what's his name? The leading actor was great. In fact, the whole cast was good, but...

**B:** I really liked the music. It was perfect for that time period.

**A:** Yes, you're right. And the plot was very interesting, but there was one thing that bothered me, though.

**B:** What's that?

**A:** Well, they went to all that trouble with that beautiful old house, but the clothes were all wrong, from a different historical period.

**B:** Yes, that was kind of strange.

# Module 9
## 9b

**1.**

**A:** Hey, Ian. How's the new job going?

**B:** Great. I'm really enjoying it.

**A:** So, did you manage to get that company car you were talking about?

**B:** No, my boss said it was too much to ask for, but maybe next year.

**A:** How is your boss, by the way? I hope he isn't as bad as your last one.

**B:** I don't think anyone can be as bad as he was. I know I was earning a lot of money there, but it wasn't worth it. In fact, it's the main reason I changed jobs.

**A:** Well, you're lucky you don't have the same problem in your new job.

**B:** No, he's great. Very helpful and easy to talk to.

**2.**

**A:** Morning, Gary. You look exhausted.

**B:** Well, Mr. Mortimor asked me to work overtime again last night.

**A:** Again?

**B:** Yeah, and I really need to get a second coffee NOW.

**A:** Well, it's almost 11:30. Be patient, it's almost breaktime. So, what time did you leave work?

**B:** Don't ask.

**A:** Was it later than ten o'clock?

**B:** It was about eleven when I finished.

**A:** What? Be careful. You're working too hard. Maybe you should take some time off.

**B:** Actually, I'm thinking of asking for a week off.

**3.**

**A:** Why is it Monday again tomorrow?

**B:** What's up, Dennis? Are you having problems with your colleagues? Are they annoying you?

**A:** No, they're fine. We have a good time at work.

**B:** Then what is it? Did your boss ask you to work more overtime?

**A:** No, he's really nice to me. He even moved me to a bigger office with a great view.

**B:** So, what's the problem?

**A:** I'm just really tired at the moment, because I have to start early these days.

**B:** Can't you go to work a little later?

**A:** Not really. There are lots of things to do before 8 o'clock.

## 9c

**A:** Mike! What a surprise! I haven't seen you for a while.

**B:** Hello, Jenna. I've been studying and stuff.

**A:** What are those books you're holding? Hey, are you learning Chinese?

**B:** Mandarin, to be exact. I've just finished a class.

**A:** Really? So you were serious about learning Mandarin last time we talked. So, how is it? It must be one of the most difficult languages to learn, right?

**B:** I wouldn't say so. It's easier than you think. I thought I wouldn't be able to cope at all, but I'm making some slow progress, at least.

**A:** Really? But it has so many characters! Nothing is similar to English. There aren't even any common words!

**B:** Let me explain. At the moment I'm learning to communicate orally and identify certain written characters. And so far, the grammar, for instance, is not as complicated as English grammar. The pronunciation is pretty difficult, but anyway. You're right about the characters, or pictograms, but that's a different story. I'm not learning to write, for the time being.

**A:** I see. So, you just want to learn to be able to talk to a Chinese person.

**B:** And also read sometime soon, let's say the news online or use different Chinese websites. But it's still too soon. I don't understand anything of what I read on the Internet yet.

**A:** Be patient. How long have you been having classes at the language school?

**B:** Since October. But I've been practicing by myself, too. I've found this great site which is really useful.

**A:** You know what? A friend of mine is learning French, and she's been teaching herself by watching French movies with French subtitles, along with a dictionary, of course. Maybe you

can do the same. It's good listening and reading practice.

**B:** Not a bad idea. There are some great Chinese movies.

**A:** Are you practicing your speaking at all? I mean apart from what you do in class.

**B:** I have this past week and I'm planning on continuing. I recently met this guy from Beijing. He works at the gym I go to, and we've started talking. The basics really, but it's helping me.

**A:** That's great. Keep up the good work, then. You'll be able to accept that job offer in Beijing pretty soon.

**B:** I hope so. Mandarin is spoken by one fifth of the global population. If others can learn it, so can I!

**A:** You maybe, but not me.

## 9d

**A:** Good afternoon.

**B:** Hello, I'm Tim Wilson. I'm here about the graphic designer position.

**A:** Ah yes. My secretary showed me your résumé, but I didn't have a chance to look at it properly. I saw your website, though. Very nice work.

**B:** Thank you.

**A:** Do you have any previous work experience?

**B:** Yes, I worked part time for about a year for another magazine.

**A:** You realize that we're looking for a full-time graphic designer?

**B:** Yes, of course.

**A:** Good. Do you like working as part of a team?

**B:** Well, in my previous job, I was working on my own. But I think working as part of a team would be a nice change.

**A:** What about working hours? We'd like you to be in the office from 9 to 5. But sometimes, not very often, there may be work on weekends, or you may have to stay late in the evenings.

**B:** Well, to be honest, I don't mind working overtime during the week. However, I can't work on weekends because I often go away on trips.

**A:** I see. There's one more thing I'd like to ask you. Do you speak French? We're going to create a French edition and I was wondering whether you'd be able to help in that department, too.

**B:** Well, if you want me to, I can easily learn. I'm good at learning foreign languages. I already speak Italian and a little Arabic.

**A:** That's good to hear. Well, everything seems to be in order. Listen, let me talk with my associates and we'll inform you by the end of the week.

**B:** That's great. Thank you very much.

# Module 10
## 10b

**1.**

**A:** Oh, what's up with this thing?

**B:** What's wrong?

**A:** I'm trying to enter my password but the

screen keeps going blank.

**B:** Is it fully charged?

**A:** No, but I'm charging it now. Look, it's plugged in.

**B:** Before you do anything else, turn it off and on again. That usually solves things.

**A:** OK. Do you think I should unplug it first?

**B:** No, leave it plugged in.

**A:** Let me try.

**2.**

**A:** I'm not sure how to make a smoothie.

**B:** I'll show you. This recipe is so easy to make. First, you cut the banana and put it into the blender.

**A:** OK, I can do that.

**B:** Then we add a teaspoon of vanilla. There you go.

**A:** What next? The milk?

**B:** Yeah.

**A:** We have a pint and a half. Is that enough?

**B:** More than enough. We only need about one cup to make two glasses of this delicious smoothie. Oh, and bring some ice.

**A:** Here you are.

**B:** Great. It's ready!

**3.**

**A:** Whoa! What are you doing?

**B:** I'm cutting this piece of wood, like you said.

**A:** Yeah, but you're cutting it in half. We need three pieces that are each 2 feet long.

**B:** Are you sure? Check the instructions. I think we need two pieces. That's why I'm cutting it in half.

**A:** Let me see. Sorry, you're right. And they're each 3 feet long, right?

**B:** That's right. What do we do next?

## 10c

**A:** Good afternoon. With me today is memory expert... umm... I'm sorry, I've completely forgotten your name. Only joking, it's Dr. Eric Dawkins. Welcome Eric.

**B:** Hello.

**A:** So, you've come in today to give us some tips on how to remember information or facts. I know lots of people, including myself, who have trouble memorizing numbers, like phone numbers or PIN numbers.

**B:** That is a common problem. There are many different methods and techniques that can help, but the best and easiest thing to do is to make associations. That means to connect the new information to already existing information or experiences in your mind, to connect the new information to something real and meaningful. That's what will help you remember it.

**A:** Can you explain what you mean?

**B:** Certainly. Let's take this phone number, for example: 247-365-1879. It's just random numbers in a row and difficult to remember. Let's look at it differently. Let's say the first three numbers are 24 hours in a day and 7 days in a week, the second three numbers are 365 days in a year, and the last four numbers are the year Albert Einstein was born. Then it becomes easier to remember.

**A:** What if I don't know Einstein's date of birth?

**B:** It's better to connect it to something personal to you.

**A:** I see, like 18 is my son's age, and 79 is my mother's age.

**B:** Perfect. Another way to remember things is by "chunking." Say you have a shopping list to remember. A long list of different items isn't easy to remember. But if you chunk them and put them into groups, for example fruit and dairy products, then the whole list seems simpler.

**A:** That's very interesting. What about people? I meet a lot of people and I find it hard to remember their names.

**B:** Here's a trick for that. Look at the person when you say their name, like "Nice to meet you, Tony." Another good trick is to imagine the person holding hands with someone else you know with the same name. Sounds a little stupid and childish, but it works.

## 10d

### Activity B

And we're back. Well, here's your chance to raise some money for charity and have some fun, too. Lincoln College is organizing two all-day charity concerts. It's a chance to spend time outdoors and hear some fantastic local bands. There will also be a surprise guest star towards the end of each event. This will all take place at the main parking lot at Lincoln College, so I guess there won't be anywhere to park. The dates for these concerts are Sunday, July 12th and Sunday, July 26th. Let's hope the weather is nice! The events will begin at 10 o'clock in the morning and end at around midnight. So, you can spend all day there, or just go for a few hours; whatever you like! To attend you'll have to pay $20 but if you can afford to, you can donate a larger amount. Just don't forget, all the money raised will go to the children's hospital, so it's definitely for a good cause. See you down there!

### Activity C

**A:** So, did you go to that charity concert?

**B:** Yes, I did.

**A:** Was it any good? I'm thinking about going to the one next Sunday.

**B:** Yeah, I had a great time.

**A:** Was it free?

**B:** No, there is an entrance fee of 20 dollars, but they ask you to donate a little more if you can, so I gave 30.

**A:** That's generous of you. So, were you there all day, then?

**B:** No, I wasn't. The concert started at ten, but I went there after lunch, so it was about three in the afternoon.

**A:** And did you stay until the end?

**B:** Yeah, I was there until midnight. By then, there were lots of people there.

**A:** So you were there for about nine hours. It must have been worth it.

**B:** That's right. The music was really good. I won't tell you anything more, because you're planning on going. But you will love it!

**A:** So, you think I should go?

**B:** Definitely. But take some snacks with you. The refreshments were pretty awful.

**A:** I'll keep that in mind.

## Module 11
### 11b

**A:** Hey, did you hear about Tony?

**B:** Yeah, he got offered that job in Rio. Is he going to take it?

**A:** Yep. He's leaving next month.

**B:** If I were offered a job abroad, I wouldn't go.

**A:** Why not?

**B:** Well, it's such a big change. You'd have to find somewhere to live, you wouldn't know anyone there...

**A:** I'd go if I found a job abroad. It sounds exciting to me. Just imagine living in Rio.

**B:** Yeah, well, it's OK for you. You can speak the language.

**A:** I suppose that makes a big difference. Well, I'm still jealous of Tony.

**B:** I'm jealous of his salary, that's for sure.

**A:** What do you mean?

**B:** He's going to get paid very well over there.

**A:** I wouldn't go for the money. It's all about experiences. Seeing the world and learning about different cultures.

**B:** Nah, it's not for me.

**A:** But you like traveling abroad. You visit your cousin in Mexico a lot.

**B:** That's different. That's a vacation, and he usually arranges everything for me. Also, I've been there at least five times, and I've never had to speak Spanish. We speak English all the time.

**A:** I wish I knew someone who lived abroad.

**B:** Have you ever been abroad?

**A:** Yeah, I used to go to Costa Rica on vacation every year. But I never really got to experience the culture. I stayed at the hotel the whole time.

**B:** Well, it's never too late to plan a trip.

### 11c

**1.**

**A:** So, you're back from Quebec. How was your trip?

**B:** Amazing. It's a beautiful place, and the winter festival was great.

**A:** Did you go skiing?

**B:** No, but I watched some races. It was pretty exciting.

**A:** What else did you do?

**B:** Well, we went on a ride in a horse-drawn sleigh and we saw Bonhomme.

**A:** Who?

**B:** He's the mascot of the festival. It's a man dressed in a snowman costume. He's pretty funny. And we saw artists who were making snow sculptures.

**A:** Some of those snow sculptures are awesome.

**B:** And they come to life at night because they light them up, but we missed that because we had to leave.

**A:** What a shame!

**2.**

**A:** So, did you find tickets to visit your friend Kim in China?

**B:** Yeah, I'm going next week. I want to be there for the Moon Festival. Kim told me that they make and eat a lot of moon cakes. They are round like the moon, and they are decorated with beautiful designs. But there is another tradition I'm looking forward to.

**A:** Dragon dances and music, right?

**B:** No, I'm not a big fan of dragon dances. But apparently, it's a tradition to go outside and pour some tea in a cup on a stone table. Then you wait until the full moon rises and you see its reflection on the surface of the tea in your cup. It's supposed to be lucky.

**A:** So, not only do you watch the full moon but you also wait to see the moon in your cup? Sounds interesting.

**3.**

**A:** Hey Pablo, do you want to come over on New Year's Eve?

**B:** Sure. Should I bring some grapes?

**A:** If you want. Why grapes, though?

**B:** It's a tradition in Spain. At twelve o'clock, we eat a grape every time the clock strikes. Last year, I only managed to eat ten, but I'll try and eat the whole twelve this year.

**A:** That sounds difficult. I don't think I could eat more than six before the clock struck twelve!

**B:** It's not that hard. It depends on how fast the clock strikes.

**A:** Hello, how can I help you?

**B:** Hi, I was here last week. I booked a business trip to Japan.

**A:** Ah yes, Mr. Gordon, right?

**B:** Yes.

**A:** Is there a problem with your booking? Would you like to make any changes?

**B:** I'd just like to ask a few questions. Maybe you can help me.

**A:** Certainly.

**B:** I'm going to be there for about 8 days, so I was wondering about how I am going to get around. I've never been there before, so I don't know much about the public transportation system. Anyway, I was thinking about renting a car. In other countries I have traveled to, I used my driver's license. Can I do the same in Japan?

**A:** No, I'm afraid not. You need to get an International Driver's License before

your trip.

**B:** Oh, OK. I'll look into that.

**A:** But you know, in general, driving in Japan isn't easy for most visitors.

**B:** Is that because of the traffic?

**A:** No, it's because they drive on the left there.

**B:** Really? I didn't know that. That could be a problem. I've been to the U.K. a few times and driving wasn't easy. In fact, it was a nightmare.

**A:** May I ask, are you planning to travel out into the countryside?

**B:** No, I'll be in the city mostly.

**A:** Well, in my opinion, it's probably better to use public transportation. It's not that easy to get around by car and parking is very expensive.

**B:** I arrive at about 1 a.m. Is there public transportation at that time?

**A:** No, I think everything stops at about one. But you can always take a taxi to your hotel.

**B:** Yes, of course. OK, thank you for your help.

**A:** No problem. If you need anything else, just let me know.

# Module 12

**Emily**

Last month a friend stayed at my house because she had a job interview in the city, near where I live. We both went to bed early, because she wanted to be fresh for the interview, and I had to get up early for work. The next morning I got up and left before my friend woke up. A couple of hours later I was in the middle of a meeting, when I got a phone call from her. She was screaming at me, and rightly so. She told me that I had locked her in my apartment by accident, and she couldn't leave for her interview. Luckily, she arranged another interview.

**George**

I was at the airport and there were lots of people around. Suddenly, I saw a man waving at me. It seemed like he wanted me to go over to him. So, I picked up my bags and went over. When I got close, he said "Can I help you?" I couldn't believe my ears! "Excuse me, you were waving at me," I said. He said he was waving at his friend, and then his friend turned up. I started laughing to make it look like a funny mistake, but I just wanted the ground to open up and swallow me.

**Melanie**

It happened last Monday. I was giving a presentation at the office to some important clients from Japan. It was going pretty well, but I was getting some strange looks from some of the people at the meeting. Anyway, during the break, I went to the restroom and looked in the mirror. And that's when I saw it: a piece of lettuce stuck on one of my front teeth. I couldn't believe my eyes. I looked ridiculous. I went back to continue my presentation, but I

couldn't concentrate, because I knew what they were thinking. Needless to say, the presentation didn't go well and I have a feeling that I made a fool of myself.

## 12d

**Activity B**

| | |
|---|---|
| **Tanya** | Hey, girls. I have a problem and I'd really like some advice. Do you think you can help? |
| **Girls** | Sure, what is it? |
| **Tanya** | You all know that I was accepted to Westhill College, right? Well, I'm very excited because I've heard so many good things about this college. But my cousin Vicky, who also applied, wasn't accepted, unfortunately. She was very disappointed when she found out, and ever since, she's been acting really weird. It's like she's not happy for me, you know? We keep fighting over little things. What am I supposed to do? Not accept? It's not my fault she wasn't accepted, is it? Anyway, the other day we had another big fight and now she's not talking to me. I've tried calling, but she doesn't answer. What should I do? I don't want to lose her because she's not only my cousin, but also a very good friend. |

**Activity C**

| | |
|---|---|
| **Tanya** | So, Maria, what do you think I should do? |
| **Maria** | It's a difficult one. Obviously, she's very jealous and doesn't really know how to react. If I were you, I'd wait for her to calm down first. When she starts talking to you again, I'd sit down and discuss the problem with her. It would be a good idea to make her understand that she isn't useless. It's not the end of the world! Remind her of the things she's good at and her positive qualities. Another thing you can do is help her look for different colleges to apply to. That will show her that you care. |
| **Tanya** | I do care. What do you think, Kelly? |
| **Kelly** | Well, I disagree. It's not your problem to sort out. She shouldn't make you feel down! You were accepted and everyone should be happy for you. OK, she's upset and everything, but she should do something about it so that she starts feeling better for herself. I agree that she probably needs some time to calm down, but I don't think you should be the one to try to get close to her first. Let her come and talk to you in her own time. Meanwhile, don't worry about it too much. I think she just needs some time. |
| **Tanya** | Maybe you're right. What about you, Jill? What do you think? |
| **Jill** | I understand what you're going |

through. You want to be happy, but you can't because you know Vicky is so down. I don't think you should be hard on her, though. It's a very difficult thing to deal with. If I were in your shoes, I'd buy her a present and go over to her house. If she's a real friend, you'll have a nice long talk and everything will be back to normal. Perhaps you could ask her if the situation was the other way around, how she would react. That might make her see things differently.

**Tanya** Thanks. I'm so glad I have you guys to turn to.

## Task: Modules 3&4

### Activity A

**A:** Hello, sir. How are you feeling?

**B:** I'm OK, I suppose.

**A:** Do you mind if I ask you a few questions about the accident?

**B:** Sure, go ahead.

**A:** I understand you were driving the blue car over there?

**B:** No, the green car is mine.

**A:** Oh, OK. And what exactly happened?

**B:** Well, I was waiting at the stop sign on 149th Street over there, and that blue car crashed into me.

**A:** From the side?

**B:** No, he crashed into me from behind, and pushed me across the street and I crashed...

**A:** You mean here on 19th Avenue, right?

**B:** That's correct.

**A:** And the red car was going down 19th Avenue?

**B:** Yes. Luckily, we didn't crash, but, as I was saying, I went all the way across the street and crashed into that tree!

**A:** Yes, I can see that. So, the red car didn't hit you?

**B:** No.

**A:** Well, thank you for your help. Let me talk to a few other people and I may come back and speak with you.

**B:** OK.

### Activity C

#### 1st eyewitness:

I was standing on the corner of 19th Avenue and 149th Street. I saw the blue car coming down the street and I noticed he was going very fast. I'm not surprised he crashed into the green car as he was talking on his cell phone at the same time. I think I heard a motorcycle, too, but when I turned to look there wasn't one there. So, maybe I was wrong.

#### 2nd eyewitness:

Yes, I saw everything. The blue car was speeding down the street when a motorcycle suddenly came out in front of him. The blue car missed him, but unfortunately it crashed into the green car. I don't think he was paying much attention to his driving, that's for sure. The man on the motorcycle just rode away, but I got his license plate. It's 124-545. But, I'm sure it wasn't the motorcyclist's fault.

## Task: Modules 7&8

**A:** So, what are we going to do? Are we going to take up scuba diving or start the astronomy course?

**B:** I'm not sure. I'm really interested in astronomy, but I need to have a look at the days and times because I've also started Spanish.

**A:** Oh, yeah. So, which days of the week are you free?

**B:** Mondays, Wednesdays and Saturdays. What about you?

**A:** Well, I'm free all week except for Fridays. And when I say I'm free, I mean after six, of course.

**B:** OK. Then we don't have a problem with the days because both courses are on Mondays and Wednesdays. Oh, but look at the flyer, the astronomy course starts at 5:30 on Wednesdays.

**A:** That's not convenient for me.

**B:** No.

**A:** And one more thing. If we take up astronomy, we'll need to have our own telescope. It says so here. I can't afford to buy one right now.

**B:** Tell me about it. Maybe we should take up scuba diving instead. We both live close to the beach and the time is convenient for both of us.

**A:** Yeah. But we'll need to buy equipment, like a wet suit, goggles, masks and so on. It's kind of expensive, don't you think?

**B:** No, we won't. Look at what it says here. The club provides all its students with the necessary equipment.

**A:** Really? That's awesome! I wanted to take up something that will help us work out a little too.

**B:** All right then, let's go and sign up!

## Task: Modules 11&12

### Speaker 1

I don't particularly like the idea of traveling alone. When you're with other people, you feel much more confident about exploring new places and trying new things. Lots of places are too risky to visit alone, so it's much better to be part of a group, especially if you're traveling for the first time. What is more, you learn a lot more with organized tours and experienced tour guides who can show you around. Most importantly, it's a lot less stressful. You don't have to plan each day during your trip because someone else has already done the work for you.

### Speaker 2

The way I see it, traveling on your own has more advantages than traveling in a group. First of all, it gives you the opportunity to gain new skills, learn so many things, and it also builds your confidence. You have to research the place you are traveling to before you leave and find your own way around once you get there. In addition, it makes you meet local people and make new friends, instead of just hanging out with the people in the group. It also means you can be alone when you want to be, and you don't have to socialize all the time with people who you might not get along with.

### Speaker 3

I think group trips are a much better option because you can get great deals with travel agents and your vacation ends up being cheaper. When you travel alone, you always have to pay more, for example, to get a private tour guide, but in a group it's easy. What is more, package tours are so much more organized; you don't waste any time looking for places, getting lost or deciding where to eat. In my opinion, it's also much more fun sharing the experience with a group; you make new friends and can help each other out if there's ever a problem.

### Speaker 4

On a group trip, everything is planned ahead by a travel agent so, in my opinion, it's not as adventurous and exciting as it should be. I think it's better to be free to do whatever you want, whenever you want. When traveling independently, you can plan your own schedule and only visit the sights that you are interested in. And if something is expensive, you can choose not to do it. Also, you don't have to worry about losing the group and you can just relax and do your own thing. Furthermore, you are also more likely to experience something out of the ordinary when you are alone. In a group, you always have to stick together and follow the schedule.

## Module 1
**cover**
celebrity
entertainment
gadget
social media
style

**1a**
arrange
at all
at the moment
cancel
catch a movie
chance
come over
discuss
hard
plan (v.)
semester
though
ticket
**Phrases**
Anyway...
Are you doing anything tonight?
Do you have any plans for...?
Don't worry about it
How are you doing?
How's everything?
How's it going?
I can't make it
I don't have any plans
I'd love to
I'm afraid I'm busy
I'm free
Maybe some other time
No problem
Not too bad, thanks
Nothing much
So-so
Sounds awesome
Sure, why not?
Take care
That would be great
What are you up to?
What's up?

**1b**
amount
appear
at the beginning of
available
because of
century
charge (v.) (battery)
common
cost (v.)
environmental issue
flight
fly (v.)
globally
GPS device
graduate (v.)
How long did it take?

imagine
in the 50s...
in the past
incredible
journey
non-stop
normal
nowadays
pay (v.)
perfect (adj.)
produce (v.)
regularly
rich
sell
speed
spend
sports star
talented
user
usual
weigh
wonder (v.)

**1c**
a pair of
a variety of
accessory
ancient
anymore
athletic shoes
bracelet
brand
bright
casual
come out (=appear)
design
develop
formal
harmful
hide
identity
in fashion
indoors
let (=allow)
market
out of fashion
prefer
reach
region
shine
specific
trend
whatever
**Materials**
cotton
denim
leather
plastic
polyester
rubber
silk
wool/woolen

**1d**
collection
comic book

create
especially
gift
in action
in fact
interest
like (prep.)
major in
make sure
on one's own
photography
planet
poem
poetry
review (n.)
train (v.)
**Phrases expressing like/dislike**
be a big fan of
be crazy about
be interested in
be into
can't stand
find sth. horrible/ interesting/etc.
I don't mind it
I particularly like/love
It's nothing special
It's something else!
There's nothing I like more

## Module 2
**cover**
apologize
congratulate
face-to-face

**2a**
above
advise
below
completely
dark (n.)
edit
embarrassed
expect
fix
flash
flat
improve
in the middle of
lately
lens
natural
otherwise
place (v.)
pose (v.)
position
probably
professional
recently
result (n.)
shoot (a photo)
simple
smile (n.)

soft
stand out
subject
surprise (v.)
tip (n.)
turn out
uncomfortable
unusual
upload

**2b**
art gallery
for ages
interview (n.)
recognize
success
unemployed
wish (v.)
**Words/Phrases describing relationships**
acquaintance
buddy
childhood friend
close friend
complete stranger
distant relative
mutual friend
**Phrases**
By the way,...
Do you mind if I (join you)?
Give me a call
Go ahead
Good luck with that
Got to go
How have you been?
How's business?
I didn't catch your name
It could be better
It was nice talking to you
Long time no see!
Tell me about it
We look alike
You (don't) look familiar
**2c**
according to
avoid
be likely to
behave
catch up on
encourage
fear (v.)
frequent
generation
go against
human (being)
if
impossible
last (v.)
less
meaning
method

social skills
statistics
study (=research)
take one's place
There's no doubt
**Words/Phrases related to communication**
be/stay/keep/etc. in contact (with)
be/stay/keep/etc. in touch (with)
communicate
get hold of
have a word with
instant messaging
lose touch/contact
pick up the phone
reach sb.
receive a reply
return a call
Skype
voicemail

**2d**
annoy
annoyed
apart from that
bills
campus
cheer up
consider
extremely
feelings
get along (with)
get on one's nerves
in addition
manage
non-smoker
notice (v.)
privacy
qualities
rely on
respect (v.)
sense of humor
stressed
trust (v.)
upset
worried
**Personality adjectives**
annoying
bossy
cheerful
confident
easygoing
forgetful
moody
optimistic
outgoing
pleasant
quick-tempered
selfish
stubborn
trustworthy
unpleasant

## Module 3

**cover**

acupuncture
exhibition
ice

**3a**

allergic
be worth
bean
book (v.) (a table)
confused
contain
have a look
knowledge
make a reservation
nuts
persuade
reserve (a table)
resist
service
suggest
taste
totally
whipped cream

**Adjectives describing food**

bitter
bland
creamy
crispy
disgusting
fresh
greasy
juicy
mouth-watering
salty
spicy
sweet
tasteless

**Phrases**

Come on
I'll have the...
It's my treat
Just this once
What do you have to lose?
What do you recommend?
What do you say?

**3b**

accept
affect
angry
background
by chance
check out
come across
come from
constantly

couch potato
definition
dictionary entry
enemy
enter (v.)
entertaining
exist
expression (=phrase)
field
keep up with
live (adj.)
look up
post (v.) (on the Net)
presentation
pretend
refer
task
the following
unknown
update (v.)
version

**3c**

at the same time
aware of
cancelation
cause (v.)
ceiling
contemporary
creation
creative
discussion
exhibit (n.)
experience (v.)
experiment (n.)
forever
hearing
humanity
imagination
in general
install
installation art
level
melt
object (n.)
permanent
preparation
prepare
public place
react
reaction
rise (v.)
sculpture
senses
sight (sense)
smell (n.)
sound (n.)
surface
take up
the main point
the poles
tiny
touch (n.)
turn into
various
warning

wet
work of art

**Hobbies**

jewelry making
knitting
origami
pottery

**3d**

absolutely
details
exhausted
instructor
martial art
opponent
progress (v.)
realize
technique
try sth. out
violent

**Phrases**

Anyway, enough about me
Are you serious?
Congratulations!
Get out of here!
Good for you
Guess what!
How awesome!
How lucky!
I can't believe it!
I'm looking forward to hearing from you
Lucky you!
Sorry I didn't reply sooner
Sorry I haven't written for so long
Unbelievable!
Waiting for your reply
Well, here's the latest
What a surprise!
What have you been up to?
What wonderful news!
You're kidding!

## Module 4

**cover**

get caught (in a storm)
get lost
get stuck (in an elevator)
run out of gas

**4a**

ankle
blackout
cafeteria
come on (lights)
finger
go out (lights)
knee
Look out
scream
sore throat
suddenly

wrist

**Verbs related to accidents**

bump into
drop (v.)
knock over
slip
spill
step on
trip over

**Words/Phrases related to injuries**

bandage
Band-Aid
bleed
bruise
bump
burn
cast
graze
grazed (adj.)
hit
injured
lose one's balance
scratch
sprain
sprained (adj.)
stitches

**4b**

break the law
cross (v.)
dead (phone/battery)
illegal
lose control
pay a fine

**Words/Phrases related to cars**

break down
crash into
engine
flat tire
go/run through a red light
headlights
honk a horn
license plate
park (v.)
parking space
passenger seat
pick sb. up
pull over
reverse (v.)
seat belt
slam on the brakes
spare tire
speed (v.)
steering wheel
take one's license away
ticket
trunk
windshield

**Phrases**

How unlucky!
Is everything all right?
Is there anything I can do to help?

It's my (own) fault
Oh you poor thing!
Watch where you're going
What do you think you're doing?
What were you thinking?
What's the matter?
You should know better than that

**4c**

authorities
break out
chaos
cloud
collapse
damage (n.)
death
destroy
double
enormous
entire
eyewitness
homeless
lose one's life
major
missing
news bulletin
occur
put out
report
rescue
resident
several
shake
smoke (n.)
survive
terrified
trapped
wave (n.)

**Natural disasters**

aftershock
earthquake / quake
flood
hurricane
tsunami
wildfire

**4d**

alive
all of a sudden
amazingly
at once
be on strike
catch (a flight/bus)
continue
description
disappear
fall asleep
fortunately
get rid of
helicopter
immediately
land (v.)
luckily

manager
miss (=not hit/reach)
panic
pass by (a place)
relieved
search
search party
shout
stain (n.)
to one's surprise
truck
unfortunately
unluckily

**Adjectives: -ed/-ing**
amazed / amazing
disappointed /
  disappointing
embarrassed /
  embarrassing
exhausted / exhausting
frightened / frightening
shocked / shocking
surprised / surprising

## Module 5
**cover**
destination
landmark

**5a**
bury
catch up (with sb.)
challenge (n.)
consist of
continent
crowd
discover
expedition
experienced
explore
explorer
gather
government
heat (n.)
in charge
leader
load (v.)
necessary
order (v.) (=give
  instructions)
particular
progress (n.)
pull
purpose
reward (n.)
set off
shortly after
succeed
successful
supplies
vehicle
weak
wheel

**5b**
brochure

car rental
clerk
collect
delay (n.)
Here / There you go
inform
insurance
offer (v.)
official document
on time
permission
rent (v.)
request (v.)
welcome (v.)

**Words/Phrases
related to traveling
by plane**
aisle seat
arrival
board (v.)
boarding pass
cabin crew
carry-on
check in
check-in agent
conveyor belt
departure
fasten
flight attendant
gate
land (v.)
luggage
monitor (n.)
overhead compartment
take off
terminal
window seat

**5c**
airline
awake
caffeine
deal with
dizzy
empty
enjoyable
focus
have difficulty
iron (n.)
jet lag
mess up
motion sickness
pack (v.)
plenty of
point (n.)
prevent
reduce
resort
ruin (v.)
schedule (n.)
serve
set (the time)
side effects
sleepy
solution
solve

suffer from
symptom
time zone
tour guide
towel
travel agency
truth

**5d**
ancient ruins
attract
attraction
bargain (n.)
birdwatching
elderly
ferry
local (n.)
location
nickname
once in a lifetime
port
sand
suitable
wonder (n.)

**Adjectives
describing places**
breathtaking
fascinating
historic
hospitable
ideal
impessive
peaceful
unforgettable
unique
well-known

**Phrases**
Personally, I believe…
You have a point

## Module 6
**cover**
robot
solar power
touchscreen

**6a**
air
alternative energy
approximately
as a result
as well as
breathe
carbon footprint
certain
climate
decrease
disease
e-waste
fossil fuel
garbage
global
increase
low
natural resources
packaging

pessimistic
polluted
predict
prediction
product
quantity
source
such as
take place
view (=opinion)
way of life
weather conditions
wind power

**6b**
adjust
advertisement
allow
borrow
brightness
cash
delivery
discount
excursion
Go for it
guarantee (v.)
lend
owe
promise (v.)
regret (v.)
satisfied
simply

**Expressions
with "make"**
make a decision
make a difference
make a mistake
make a prediction
make a promise
make money
make plans
make sense

**6c**
ability
afford
along with
astronaut
atmosphere (air)
bottom
dream (n.)
eager
exploration
float (v.)
gravity
individual (n.)
interview (v.)
lower (v.)
majority
medical check-up
millionaire
opportunity
ordinary
possibility
require
risk (n.)
rock (n.)

space
spacecraft
spectacular
telescope
the public
tourism
training
wealthy

**Prepositional
phrases: "at"**
at first
at last
at least
at present
at the end (of)
at the latest

**6d**
advantage
be addicted
careless
connect
convenient
danger (n.)
disadvantage
distract
fail (=not work)
false
get informed
hacker
hardly ever
harm
harmless
have access to
helpless
inappropriate
involve
outdated
own (v.)
pay attention
practical
reliable
route
skillful
so that
socialize
steal
useless
valuable
virus
worthless

**Phrases**
First of all,…
Firstly,…
Secondly,…
The way I see it,…
There's not much
  point in…
To begin with,…
What is more,…

## Module 7
**cover**
choice

whether...or...

**7c**
achieve
anchorman
approve
argue
career
complicated
cope with
delay (v.)
disapprove
dissatisfied
energetic
expected (adj.)
gossip (n.)
lead (v.)
lifestyle
make a change
make an
  announcement
miss sth.
on air
pause (v.)
producer
publish
put sth. off
quality
quit
stressful
studio
unable
uncertain
unexpected
unfriendly
unnatural
unnecessary
unsuitable

**7d**
arrangement
by one's side
corn
eggplant
get-together
grill (v.)
honeymoon
pepper
put sb. up
raw
refuse
sort out
suggestion
**Phrases**
As for...
Get back to me
Sounds like a plan

**Module 8**
**8a**
admire
be over
cheer on
coach
enthusiastic about
just in time

let sb. down
lift (v.)
miss out (on)
play a role
referee
sports commentator
tennis match
trophy
turn out (=be present)
**Phrases**
What a
  disappointment!
What a nightmare!
What a shame!
You can say that again!

**8b**
a good night's sleep
aircraft
automatically
complete (v.)
contact (v.)
hesitate
in shape
inexperienced
make the most of sth.
physical condition
priority
provide
skydiving
thrill
video record (v.)
**Sports equipment**
bat
board
goal
goggles
helmet
knee pads
net
parachute
racket
stick
wetsuit

**8c**
across the globe
basket
be related to
cricket
describe
except (for)
goalkeeper
have in common
hold (an event)
international
mostly
origin
points
round (adj.)
rugby
rules
whichever
**Verbs related to
  sports**
bounce

catch
dribble
hit
kick
pass
shoot
throw

**8d**
action-packed
assistant
be based on
be set in
blockbuster
cast
costume
direct (v.)
director
financial problems
from start to finish
hilarious
leading actor
main character
manage (=run)
movie review
original
plot
realistic
role
scene
society
soundtrack
special effects
star (v.)
unrealistic
**Types of movies**
action
adventure
animated
biopic
crime drama
documentary
historical drama
horror
romantic comedy
sci-fi
thriller
war
**Phrases**
It's nothing special
Overall, I found...

**Module 9**
**cover**
do volunteer work
learn a trade
obtain a higher
  education
take a gap year

**9a**
degree
earn (a living)
firm (n.)
full-time job
get a loan

industry
job prospects
part-time job
studies (n.)
**Academic subjects**
Accounting
Business and finance
Economics
Graphic design
Law
Media
Medicine
Philosophy
Social and political
  sciences
Software engineering
**Jobs**
accountant
bank teller
graphic designer
lawyer
paramedic
pilot
plumber
politician
receptionist
surgeon
**Phrases**
Are you employed at
  the moment?
Have you decided on a
  career?
I work for/in/at/with/
  as...
I'm a... major.
Time flies when you're
  having fun
What do you do for a
  living?
What kind of work do
  you do?

**9b**
airbag
be/get fired
benefit (n.)
bonus
break (n.)
cartoon
colleague
crash (computer)
employee
employer
excuse (n.)
facility
figure out
hire
introduce
overtime
pay (n.)
raise (n.)
rent (n.)
retire
salary
staff
therefore
time off

**7a**
atmosphere (mood)
car racing
change one's mind
clumsy
contest
count sb. in
cup final
drop by
dry (adj.)
feel like doing sth.
festival
flyer
for sure
free entry
from the comfort
  of one's home
give sth. a try
ice skating
make up one's mind
rink
skate (v.)
track
**Phrases**
Do as you please
I doubt it
I give up
I'd prefer...
I'd rather...
I'm not so sure
I'm positive
It's up to you
There's a good
  chance...

**7b**
admission
adopt
anonymous
bell
comment (n.)
complain
complaint
deal (n.)
depend on
donation
express (adj.)
feed
fill out
form (n.)
in case of
minimum
remain
ride (n.)
ring (v.)
single ticket
standard
support (n.)
valid
whale

workplace

**9c**

a great deal of
behavior
benefit (v.)
come to grips with
drop out
enroll
get used to
hold a conversation
imitate
intensive
interest (v.)
just for the fun of it
nearly
obstacle
participate
pick up (words)
proud
speak a word of
speech
subject (=topic)
subtitles
suit (v.)

**9d**

applicant
apply (for)
be computer literate
be fluent in
cover letter
first-aid
flexible
hard-working
in person
lifeguard
plus
previous
qualifications
responsible
résumé
sales
uniform
university
**Phrases**
As you can see from
   my résumé...
I am currently
   working...
I am writing to apply
   for the position of...
I believe these qualities
   make me suitable for
   the job
I strongly hope you
   consider my résumé
Yours sincerely
Yours truly

**Module 10**
**cover**

facts and figures

**10a**

ATM
be broke
be short of cash
bill (n.)
break (money)
change (n.)
charge (a service)
check (n.)
commission (at bank)
currency
currency exchange
   office
debit card
directly
exactly
exchange rate
free of charge
ID
incorrectly
interest rate
It's no use
make a deposit
online banking
open a savings
   account
payphone
PIN
receipt
repair (n.)
spaghetti
swallow
waste (money)
withdraw

**10b**

apply
brush (n.)
cardboard
cover (v.)
diagram
distance
draw
dye
electric mixer
fill
hole
ingredients
keep out of reach
medication
on an empty stomach
packet
pot
pour
powdered sugar
seed
shampoo (v.)
shape
soil
spices
stir
tablespoon (tbsp.)
thick
unplug
use (n.)

vanilla
wide
**Units of
measurement**
centimeter
fluid ounce
foot
gallon
gram
inch
kilogram
kilometer
liter
meter
mile
milliliter
ounce
pint
pound
quart
ton
yard

**10c**

annual
bits
brain
break a record
by heart
challenge (v.)
composer
crossword
digit
fill up
limit
memorize
memory
mind (n.)
prime minister
process
puzzle
repeat
room (=space)
shampoo (n.)
store (v.)
throughout
toothpaste
winner

**10d**

band
be packed
charity
entrance fee
google (v.)
mug (n.)
raise money
refreshments
venue

**Module 11**
**cover**

culture
custom
tradition

**11a**

anniversary
bend (n.)
corner
crosswalk
mention
misunderstand
nearby
per month
phrasebook
sidewalk
**British English**
chips
cinema
crisps
CV
flat
holiday
jumper
lift
mobile phone
pavement
petrol
queue
rubbish
shop
trainers
trousers
underground
zebra crossing
**Phrases**
I can tell by your
   accent
I didn't get that
I'm not following you
I'm not sure I get what
   you mean
Never mind
What do you mean by
   that?

**11b**

a sense of direction
actions
adventurous
celebrate
consequence
curious
embassy
exotic
home country
ignore
in the first place
independently
live life to the fullest
organized
out of the ordinary
package tour
photocopy (n.)
plan ahead
risky
scare
to the last detail
unfamiliar
well-prepared

**11c**

artist (=performer)
carnival
celebration
come to life
community
decorate
demonstrate
dressed in
drums
express (v.)
float (n.)
grapes
homesick
multi-ethnic
musician
outdoors
parade
remind
set up
sound system
stage
stall
typical

**11d**

accommodations
citizen
exact
have a hard time
in a hurry
in advance
in mind
in particular
public holiday
travel agent
visa
**Phrases**
Enjoy your stay
Furthermore,...
I am writing to request
   information about...
I would like to thank
   you in advance
Thank you for your
   time and assistance

**Module 12**
**cover**

bug
That's life

**12a**

allergy
be booked up
be in pain
be supposed to
bee
chew
come down with
come out
cream
examine
fever
filling

fluids
get over
go away
illness
itchy
pain reliever
patient (n.)
pharmacist
pill
prescribe
prescription
put up with
rash
relieve
runny nose
skin
sting
stomach bug
the flu

vitamin
**Phrases**
Nothing to worry about
What exactly are your symptoms?

**12b**
approach
be going on (=happening)
be pregnant
by accident
eventually
furious
in the opposite direction
lady
on purpose
peace and quiet
ridiculous
shoulder
smash into sth.
the other day
thief

wave (v.)
**Idioms**
drive sb. up the wall
fall flat on your face
go red as a beet
make a fool of yourself
nearly jump out of your skin
not believe your eyes/ears
want the ground to open up and swallow you

**12c**
courage
elbow
fear (n.)
filthy
hope (n.)
hunger
nudge
orphan
poor
push

rags
raise sth.
rush
signal (n.)
silent
skinny
special occasion
speechless
stare
starving
torn
whisper
wink

**12d**
addiction
build one's confidence
chores
come up with
concentrate
count on sb.
fight (v.)
get into an argument
insecure
insist

jealous
lie around
make the first move
note down
share (n.)
split in half
stand by sb.
support (v.)
take it easy
trouble (v.)
turn to
unfair
**Phrases**
I understand what you're going through
If I were in your shoes, I'd...
It would be a good idea to...
I've been having problems with...
There's no need to panic
What would you do if you were me?

---

Pioneer Pre-Intermediate
American edition
Student's Book

H. Q. Mitchell - Marileni Malkogianni

Published by:   **MM Publications**
www.mmpublications.com
info@mmpublications.com

**Offices**
UK  China  Cyprus  Greece  Korea  Poland  Turkey  USA
Associated companies and representatives throughout the world.

Produced in the EU

ISBN978-4-7647-4159-1

C2304006034-20665